A Story Is a Promise
&
The Spirit of Storytelling

Bill Johnson

(7th Edition)

A Story Is a Promise & The Spirit of Storytelling. Copyright ©
2011 and Copyright © 2013 and Copyright © 2014
Copyright © 2019 by Bill Johnson. All rights reserved.

Published by
Blue Haven Publishing
Portland, Oregon 97219

Revised 12/2019

Book Design: Bill Johnson
Cover Design and Photograph: Nancy Hill
http://www.nancyhillphotography.com/

Seventh Edition
10 9 8 7 6 5 4 3 2 1

ISBN 978-0-9673932-2-3

Johnson, Bill
    A Story Is a Promise & The Spirit of Storytelling by
       Bill Johnson — 7th
       ed. p.cm.
       Includes bibliographical references and
       index. ISBN 978-0-9673932-2-3
       1. How-to 2. Story Writing
       I. Title

Dedication

This book is dedicated to

    Elizabeth Lyon, a true friend

    and

    Monty Metawa, who understands much

This book is designed to guide writers toward a new understanding of the process of creating and writing dramatic stories.

Section One explores...
>How a story functions like a promise
>How to fulfill a story's promise to its audience

Section Two explores how a story's elements are designed, including...
>Techniques to create a story premise
>Developing dynamic characters
>Creating a plot
>Understanding what's at stake in your story
>The role of ideas in stories
>The role of conflict in storytelling

Section Three offers essays that explore how to outline a story, including...
>Story Director™, a unique process of outlining a story
>How a complex story can have a simple plot

Section Four explores principles of storytelling through reviews of popular novels, screenplays, and plays.

Deep Characterization

This new section explores the difference between characters created to act out a story for an audience and characters created to act out a writer's internal dramas. A story written for an audience is a promise to take that audience on a story journey; a story written for the writer's needs is a promise to transport him or her to the fulfillment of personal needs.

This work is meant to help writers who have been 'stuck' at a certain level of storytelling without understanding why.

The Spirit of Storytelling

This new edition explores how writers can give their story characters fully realized, internal lives that do not revolve around an author's needs and dramas. The goal is to help authors bring their character to life.

Foreword

Twenty-eight years making short films had convinced me I was well prepared to write a screenplay or a novel. I'd written, produced, and directed almost a hundred films for theatrical release, television, corporate presentations, documentaries, and education, receiving forty-four awards and a grant from the American Film Institute. Yet, as I struggled to write my first novel, I soon floundered and found myself lost in a maze without a map. What I hadn't grasped was how great the leap from a short film to a novel or feature length script.

I began to read everything I could find on writing novels and screenplays, nearly eighty books altogether. Each focused on pieces of the larger picture, not the whole. All were filtered through the author's own unique perspective, each different enough from the others to create confusion. They wrote as though the essential principals of dramatic writing were too vast for anyone to cover in a single book. However, a handful did come close enough to convince me it was possible. I also had this nagging feeling there was a higher level to storytelling that none of them were discussing, and I sensed that if I didn't understand that, I wasn't going anywhere.

One night in March, 1995, while searching the Writer's Forum on AOL, I came across a series of postings that got my attention. They began, "I would like to open a discussion into story movement, what it is, and how to create it." I read them all, then read them again. Nothing I'd come across before had so clearly cut to the very essence of how to tell a story. Here was someone who understood that higher level for which I aspired and who knew how to teach it.

Though I'd never met him, I offered my help as an editor. Perhaps I could be a sounding board for his ideas, someone to raise questions. I was pleasantly surprised when he responded to my email by accepting my offer. It was the start of a lasting friendship that began my own journey into the heart of storytelling. It would change my writing life forever.

I'd read many a story but never fully understood what was behind "paint on the walls." It was clear that stories worked, but why did the writer choose a particular plot, or set of characters, or locale, or the individual words on the page for that matter? The beauty of what Bill does is contained in the series of steps he led me through, each building on the previous one, until I could see those principals in action in a story I was writing. He even taught me how to go about
choosing the right dramatic words—no small feat. For the first time, things began to make sense and my writing began to steadily improve.

As time went by, Bill's personalized style of teaching was an inspiration. I was struck by the fact that this book was written in the same conversational style, one on one, as though Bill were talking to me, anticipating my questions, even raising issues that stimulated my thinking about the story I was writing, or one that I planned to write. It was clear that from his years of teaching experience that he could anticipate the kinds of questions I might ask, and even anticipate why I asked them. I came to realize that Bill has a unique understanding of what a writer needs to know to become a storyteller and all of that is reflected in this book.

Now, whenever I'm in the midst of writing a story and am uncertain about where it's going or how to get there, this is the book I return to time and again for answers and inspiration.

Lawrence Booth

Founder, Half Moon Bay Film School

Acknowledgements

This book owes a debt to...

Lawrence Booth, founder of the Half Moon Bay Film School. His editorial assistance, probing questions, and friendship helped bring this book into being.

Tom Shaw, of Tom Shaw Productions, a filmmaker who generously helped others. Tom gave me a place to stay in his studio for a year to support the creation of the essays in this book. He was a true friend.

David Morgan, who introduced me to story analysis. David is a friend and mentor, and the country's finest story analyst.

Bill Snowden, whose friendship and support helped give me direction.

Elizabeth Lyon, a wonderful friend who introduced the ideas in this book to many people and has been a long-time sounding board.

Nancy Hill, for her lovely book covers and friendship.

section one

A Story is A Promise

Contents

Dedication..v
Introduction..vi
Foreword..vii
Acknowledgments..ix

SECTION ONE:

A Story Is a Promise

    Understanding the Human Need for Stories.............2
    A Story Is a Promise..5
    Naming Your Promise..8
    Sustaining a Story's Promise.......................................14
    How to Make a Down Payment on Your Promise.....20
    Writing Dramatic Moments..23
    Suggesting a Dramatic Truth.....................................27

SECTION TWO:

Designing the Elements of Your Stories

    Premise—Understanding Your Story Foundation..36
    Techniques of Creating a Story Premise..................45
    Characters, Story, and Premise..............................50
    What Is a Plot?..54
    Creating a Dramatic Plot...58
    What's at Stake in Your Story?...............................62
    What Is Conflict?...68
    Escalating Your Story's Conflict..............................72

The Relationship Between Stories and Ideas.........76
Thrust and Counter-Thrust...................82
Writing Dramatic Dialogue.........................86

SECTION THREE:

Outlining Your Story

Using Story Director (TM) to Outline Your Story..95
Complex Story, Simple Question..........................115
Writing Down a Story's Spine................128

SECTION FOUR:

Reviews of Popular Stories

Using the Reviews..134
Using Families in Storytelling..........................137
Developing and Sustaining Suspense...............141
The Power and Passion of Love & Hate...........148
The Art of Creating Drama..............................166
Story as Physical Journey................................172
The Artist as Storyteller..................................178

THIRD EDITION:

DEEP CHARACTERIZATION

Deep Characterization..186
Character Types..190
Listening to Your Characters.............................216
Writing Fear..221
Understanding Emotional Triggers....................225
What Lies Beneath..227

Writing About a Stuck Main Character............231
Writing About a Wounded Psyche....................234
Storytelling, the Unconscious, and Subconscious Minds...239
Transformation..243
Science and Characterization.......... 249

SEVENTH EDITION

THE SPIRIT OF STORYTELLING

The Spirit of Storytelling..................................255
Storytelling and the Superconscious Mind..257
Forestalling the Conceptual Mind....................262
Meditation and Creativity................................264
Intuitive Storytelling..267
The Musicality of Writing Fiction.....................270
Writing as Exploration......................................273
Writing in the Spirit of Storytelling..................276
Telling a Story in the Spirit of Storytelling.......280

A Letter to My Readers......................................282

APPENDIX

Resources..283
End Notes...286
Index...290
Contact Information..294

section one

A Story is A Promise

Understanding the Human Need for Stories

Since prehistoric times, when our ancestors gathered around fires in caves, storytellers have been aware of how arranging events in a story-like fashion engages and satisfies audiences. This chapter explores how a well-told story satisfies an audience.

In the Beginning Is the Story

Coming into this world, we have needs for food and shelter. When those immediate needs are met, others come to the surface.

One is a need for acknowledgement. Yet, from the time we are born, how we are acknowledged shapes our expectations of what we can expect from life. From our families, we might take in the idea that we have worth. Or that we don't. That we're destined to be a success in life. That we're destined to fail.

While we're digesting these ideas, we're also interpreting our experiences in life and developing our own sense of who we are. A sense of the meaning and purpose. A sense of how we fit in and what we deserve from life. A sense of how we matter to ourselves and to others.[1]

While we integrate our sense of who we are, our cultures suggest something about our place in the world, even as stereotypes. For example, if we're American, we love freedom. If we're French, we're romantic. If we're Italian, we're hot-blooded. If we're German, we're cold and unemotional. If we're blonde, we have more fun and are more desirable. We might enjoy having a particular kind of "mattering" bestowed on us by our culture. Or, we might enjoy rebelling against an external definition of who we are.

All of these cultural definitions are stories. To the degree with which we accept them or are forced to deal with others who believe them, these stories have an impact on our lives and our sense of place in the world. Take away a person's sense of place in the world and you'll have an unhappy person.

Unfortunately, life doesn't revolve around ensuring that we feel we matter. That we fit in. That our lives have a meaning and purpose that is desirable to us. Even worse, life is often unpredictable. Events happen, but to no clear purpose. We get things from life—relationships, jobs, recognition—but not always what we want. Or, what we want goes to someone else. How do we deal with this?

Because people are inventive and creative, we make do. One way we make do is to tell ourselves stories that fulfill our needs. For example, regardless of the outward appearances and realities of our lives, we are heroic. We have honor. We are brave. Or we're fearful—but we have good reason to be. And God loves us. Or hates us and has cursed us, if that's our story need.

Because life can operate to remind us we *aren't* heroic or courageous, or whatever need we desire to have validated, stories provide the shortest path for accomplishing this.

If we feel life is unjust, we can experience in stories a place where justice prevails. A place where redemption can be dramatically won, if our lives lack hope of redemption (or worse, if our redemption is out of our control). A place in which we can imagine ourselves courageously exploring new worlds, even if we're too shy to say "hello" to our neighbors. Where our senses can be enlivened through thrilling experiences, albeit from a safe distance. Where true love conquers all. Where difficult issues can be examined in ways we find stimulating. Where mysteries are resolved. Where good defeats evil. Where evil defeats good, and we get to set a book down or leave a movie theatre having survived the experience.

That's why issues such as courage, redemption, renewal, love, and honor are most often at the heart of stories. A well-told story is an arrangement of words and images that re-creates life-like characters, issues, ideas, and events in a way that promises dramatic fulfillment of human needs, and then delivers on that promise.

A story, then, is a promise.

A story that clearly communicates its promise draws in an audience. When stories fail to suggest their promise readers struggle to feel engaged because all people gravitate toward stories that promise to meet their particular needs.

A well-designed story, then, is a vehicle that transports its audience to a resolution of human needs that is satisfying and fulfilling. When we find a particular story journey to be dramatically potent and pleasing, we desire to re-experience the same story journey again and again. A successful story journey promises to move us through desirable states of feelings, perceptions, or thoughts in a way that is more "true" than life (or life as we wish it to be).

Knowing what needs a story promises to fulfill for its audience creates the beginning of a foundation for understanding the craft of storytelling. Learning that craft is at the very heart of the art of storytelling.[2]

Which raises the question: how do you set out a story's promise?

That's answered in the next chapter.

Chapter Questions

> What needs do stories fulfill in your life?
> How are the stories you tell yourself about who you are different from your experiences in life?
> What needs do the stories you create promise to fulfill for others?
> What kind of stories about who you are as a person have been assigned to you by your cultural background? Your income level? Your level of education? Your family background?
> Do the stories you most enjoy validate your choices in life? Or, do they help you to believe that under different circumstances, you would be a different person?

A Story Is a Promise

Perceiving that a story is a promise is a cornerstone of the foundation for understanding the art of storytelling. This chapter takes a closer look at how a story functions as a promise.

A writer sets out a story's promise by offering details of lifelike characters, issues, events, and circumstances, then editing and arranging those details to move an audience toward a desirable experience of resolution. For example, when a story created around the issue of courage fulfills its promise, the audience experiences a fulfilling state of courage. The audience experiences the truth of the story's promise.

Popular stories are often designed to revolve around a promise of some human need that is acted out to dramatic fulfillment. The film *Rocky*[3], written by Sylvester Stallone (who also stars as Rocky), promises to be a story about self-respect. *The Wizard of Oz*[4], by L. Frank Baum, promises to be about Dorothy's dramatic journey to a new sense of who she is and her need to belong. *Romeo and Juliet*, by William Shakespeare, promises to be a story about tragic love. The Harry Potter novels revolve around the issue of Harry fitting in. In *The Lovely Bones*[5], a family deals with grief.

This focus on shaping the events and details of a story to a particular purpose makes a well-told story fundamentally unlike the vagaries of real life. The "true" facts of life generally don't arrange themselves to promise a story-like resolution and fulfillment. If they did, a factual account of the suicides of two teenagers distraught that their parents kept them apart would create the effect of the story *Romeo and Juliet*. The two versions are clearly not the same in mood, tone, or dramatic purpose.[6] The fact that two teens committed suicide simply offers information. It's an account of an event. The truth of a story like *Romeo and Juliet* leads us to deeply feel the nature of powerful love.

Often, a story's promise is set through the introduction of characters designed to act to resolution some clearly established issue of human need. As the characters act to fulfill a story's promise, a story's audience comes to feel that the characters ring true and are "life-like." Characters in well-told stories should, more correctly, be called story-like, because it is through their actions revolving around a discernible dramatic purpose that a story's audience chooses to identify with the characters. By internalizing a story's journey to fulfillment of a particular promise, via the actions of its characters, an audience can resolve powerful unresolved feelings and beliefs.

By editing away all the details not "true" to this journey, a storyteller creates a story that becomes all the more "real" to an audience. Characters in stories about courage often perform impossible feats, not because it's humanly possible, but because the audience demands that the actions of the story be story-like. That's why characters not created around a clearly defined dramatic purpose can appear to be lifeless, cardboard cutouts. It doesn't matter how carefully they are described or how true the details of their description. A carefully described character who acts to no discernible dramatic purpose can appear to be a lie, which leads an audience to turn away, just as we in real life turn away from those who lie to us about their promises.

A story, then, is not created by assembling details that are realistic or true to life; it is created by assembling details that have a dramatic purpose that resonates with an audience. Details that are story-like in their design and intent and that evoke the world of a story in a dramatically engaging way.

The same logic applies to what details of a story's environment the storyteller should set out, based on an understanding of a character's role in fulfilling a story's promise. Only those details that revolve around setting out a story's promise in a way that makes a story's world ring true should be included. Others have no purpose.

When writers create characters, events, and descriptive details that dramatically act out to fulfillment a story's promise, such writing is innately satisfying. The romantic can read novels that fulfill a need for romance. The lover of action, the need for heroic quests. The lover of literary fiction, stories that explore the human condition.

That's why there's a story for every need, even needs we didn't know we had until a storyteller draws us in to experience a particular story's world. As long as people desire to have their curiosity satisfied, their questions about life and existence explained and answered, their issues of human need validated, there will be a desire for stories.

That's why a story must promise something to its audience. For the writer to promise nothing is to violate the unwritten contract of a storyteller with his or her audience: that the story transport its audience to a satisfying, fulfilling resolution.

How a storyteller suggests a story's promise is set out in the following chapter.

Chapter Questions

What does your story promise its audience?
How do you introduce your story's promise?
What events fulfill your story's promise?
What is the promise of your life story?
How does that impact the kinds of stories you enjoy?
What details evoke the drama of your story's promise?

Naming Your Promise

A story's opening scenes are vital. If they don't suggest a story's promise, that story risks either not fully engaging or losing its audience. How does one set out a story's promise? It's done by a process I call *naming*.

For example, *Rocky* is a story about self-respect. When the storyteller arranges for Rocky to be called a "bum" and thrown out of the gym where he trains, the story acts out Rocky's self-respect being actively undermined. That cues in the audience that the story is about self-respect. It *names* the story's promise.

By raising the issue as a question—can Rocky gain self-respect?—the story begins in an active voice. When an audience hears questions arising out of issues of human need, it naturally feels engaged over a story's course and outcome. The opening scenes of *Rocky*—or any well-told story—revolve around more than the introduction of a story's characters or plot, or an account of a character's life and situation. They operate around *naming* a story's promise in a dramatic way, i.e., in a way an audience is made to care how a story will turn out. When a story's promise is clearly named, the narrative tension over a story's course and outcome can be transferred from a story's characters to its audience. When this narrative tension is internalized by a story's audience, that audience is compelled to experience how a story resolves the issues of its characters and its events for the relief of that tension.

One can see this process in the film *The Usual Suspects*[7], written by Christopher McQuarrie. The character Verbal refers to the men in a lineup—the usual suspects—as being men who would not be broken. That names the issue at the heart of the story: the power of will. It also presents the issue as a dramatic question. Could these men be broken? The dramatic answer is yes—by someone with a more powerful will. Getting to the answer of who that is draws viewers to the end of the film.

The events that begin *The Usual Suspects* also operate to suggest the story's promise. One man interrupts another man's attempt to set a fire that will destroy a ship. When the second man, Keyser, is through with Keaton, the man who was trying to set the fire, he takes Keaton's life. These events *name* the story—by introducing two men engaged in a contest of wills—while raising questions, what happened on this ship and who are these men? In answering these questions, the story's audience is drawn into the story's world and the resolution of its promise.

To better understand this process of *naming*, imagine someone showing you a childhood photograph. The physical frame around the photograph encloses the world of the photograph in much the same way a storyteller sets the dimensions of a story in the frame of a novel, play, or film. Now you're told that one of the children in the school photo just inherited a million dollars and wants to donate the money to charity, but needs help making decisions. That suggests a particular plot. It only *suggests* a plot because it implies some events might happen, but that in itself is not a story. It is not a story because there is no promise to resolve some issue of human need. Writing about the inheritance would just be an account of a particular situation.

Now you're told another child in the photo is the secret son of Osama bin Laden. That suggests another plot. A far-fetched one, but it serves my purpose of making a point. This character only suggests a plot because there's no indication of any kind of story revolving around that character or any sequence of actions, just a question of what will happen next.

Your friend tells you that he or she found true love with someone in the photo. That *names* the story. We now know it's going to be a story about true love. Such a story could conceivably have Osama's son and the new millionaire as characters, as long as they have clearly identified dramatic purposes and then act to resolve issues arising from the story's promise.

What often leads storytellers down the path of failing to *name* their stories is their focus on presenting what is visual and apparent, using details to describe the characters, actions, and environments. Unless the storyteller *names* the dramatic purpose that underlies these events and suggests a need for resolution of the deeper issue at play in them, all that other work is dramatically inert; it is an account that simply makes statements about static things. It's true that some accounts, a history of a civil war battle, for example, will satisfy a particular audience. An account of that battle is not the same as a story about the characters involved, and how the experience affects or changes them.

For example, to say that "John is five foot eight, one hundred thirty-eight pounds, blond, blue-eyed" might be true, but it fails to *name* a story issue around John. To say, however, that "John thought he knew what loneliness was, until he met Mary," *names* a story that John will act out, one about loneliness.

The above example is obvious, but that's better than being obscure to the point of suggesting no dramatic purpose at all. Once writers learn how to clearly suggest a dramatic purpose, they can then learn how to make it more suggestive and less obvious.

Often writers understand their story's promise but they overlay it with so many static descriptions of characters and events they obscure it. In a story's opening scenes, any character action, scene description, plot event, or character dialogue not arising from a story's promise and suggesting a need for its dramatic advance toward resolution, risks having no clear meaning. When a storyteller communicates his or her story's promise and dramatic purpose, he or she can naturally reveal the motivations of their characters as they react to resolving the story's issues and events. The details then serve a purpose. To offer details that serve no purpose is comparable to trying to study facts for a test without knowing the subject of the test. It's a situation that quickly becomes frustrating for a reader.

The quicker the storyteller communicates the role of characters and a story's events in fulfilling a story's promise, the more quickly an audience will desire to enter a story's world to experience its promise played out to resolution and fulfillment.

To be able to set a story's promise in an active voice, the storyteller needs to make a distinction between a story, its plot, characters, environment, and ideas.

(Continued on page 12)

Being Dramatically Suggestive In a Sentence

To help writers make a distinction between being dramatically obvious, obscure, or suggestive, I ask that they consider a scale that runs from zero to ten (see diagram page 12). Zero represents obscure, five, obvious, ten, suggestive. Starting with what is dramatically obvious about a character can be a starting point toward being dramatically suggestive, and moving away from being obscure. To avoid being obvious, most struggling writers move toward being obscure, which often reduces a story to an account of what characters are doing.

"My name is Rocky" is obscure, a zero. "My name is Rocky and I'm a nobody and I want to be a somebody," is obvious, a five. Rocky winning the bloody fight that opens the movie and his 'winnings' not being enough to buy a post-fight hamburger, and his reaction to that, is suggestive of his desire to be somebody.

To help writers create suggestive, dramatic sentences, I ask that writers start with an obvious statement about what's at stake for a character in a story. I then ask that the writer create an obscure sentence that suggests nothing about what's 'true' for a character, then a sentence that is dramatically suggestive.

(See diagram next page)

Obscure	Obvious	Suggestive
0	5	10
'My name is Tom Wingo' is obscure. It suggests no dramatic truth about Tom, no beginning to a story.	'My name is Tom Wingo and I want to tell you about my dysfunctional family and how I survived my childhood' is obvious.	'My wound is geography. It is also my anchorage, my port of call,' is dramatically suggestive about a wounded character seeking healing.

(Continued from page 11)

A story's core dramatic issue might revolve around courage, for example. In such a story, the plot is the actions that make the story dramatic. The characters will have issues of courage to resolve. The story's environment would be the places that would also potentially act as obstacles. For example, in a story set on a mountain, the mountain itself could test the courage of the story's characters. In this story, the storyteller might explore ideas about courage, such as whether it's better to fight a losing battle with courage or to avoid the battle and stay alive.

Each of these story elements needs to be named—whether directly, indirectly, as a metaphor, etc.—in a way that makes its dramatic purpose clear, without being obscure, or too obvious. If a scene merely highlights the actions of a story's characters but the dramatic purpose of those actions is unclear, it inherently risks failing to resonate with the story's audience.

In *Prince of Tides*, the details that describe where Tom Wingo grew up evoke what made that place an anchorage for his life and a wound. The details have a context.

In *Avatar*, a wounded marine dreams of flying, then wakes to the reality of having crippled legs and the thought, you always have to wake up. But this story takes place in an environment where that is not always true, and the question of whether he can continue to be awake in a world where he can fly becomes a compelling question.

I once had an exchange with someone who didn't understand that a
film called *The Bourne Identity* had anything to do with identity. She saw herself as a purely intuitive writer, but her writing reflected her lack of understanding.

When a storyteller understands that opening scenes revolve around setting out a story's promise, he or she has a guide to how to write such scenes.

The next chapter of the book offers examples of how to set out a story's promise.

Chapter Questions

What kind of events or actions or dialogue names your story's promise in its opening scenes?

What did you do to create drama around the introduction of your story's promise?

How do the actions of your main characters revolve around resolving your story's promise?

How do the events of your story highlight your story's promise?

Sustaining a Story's Promise

You now understand what needs your story promises to fulfill for your intended audience. You understand how to *name* your promise in a clear, discernible way. This chapter offers an overview of how to sustains a story's promise.

The process of sustaining a story's promise begins with understanding the meaning of drama.

> Drama is the anticipation of an outcome for an unresolved dramatic issue, character concern, story event, or idea.

You create an anticipation of a story's promise by suggesting that something around an issue such as courage, redemption, or renewal needs resolution. If you haven't set out that an issue, event, character goal, idea, etc, is in need of resolution, *there can be no drama over an outcome around it.* This holds true whether the issue is the outcome of a story's promise, the complications of a story's plot, the outcome of character actions, or the outcome of the issues and ideas a story raises. By interweaving the introduction of characters with issues to resolve that arise from a story's promise, a storyteller creates an anticipation of such characters moving the story toward the fulfillment of its promise.

For example, placing a character whose issue is gaining self-respect in an environment that denies him self-respect is the introduction to Rocky. What makes the story dramatic is that the only way Rocky comes to feel he can gain self respect is to box Apollo Creed and remain standing at the end of the fight. I call that—Rocky's need to prove that he's a somebody—a dramatic truth. When characters both embody an issue of human need and are compelled to resolve that issue for internal or external reasons, they have a dramatic truth to resolve. Characters who don't embody a dramatic truth are dramatically inert; they have nothing to resolve, no reason to act to shape events. They just react to them.

An audience wants to feel a story's dramatic purpose is generating, scene by scene, experiences of resolution and fulfillment more potent and true than real life. More true because the edited arrangement of a story's elements is designed specifically to dramatically transport the audience toward a resolution of a story's promise. This is what makes stories so magical in their ability to transport audiences.

To understand this process, consider *Romeo and Juliet*. It is a *story* about great love. Romeo's heartfelt, poetic longing for Rosalind introduces the issue of love. From the core dramatic issue of the story, the storyteller creates a *story line* composed of the events, dialogue, and actions that *name* what the story is about as it moves from its introduction to its fulfillment.

It is this quality of a story moving along its story line that makes a story satisfying to an audience. To not *name* and highlight a story's advance along its story line is to risk that a story fails to offer a compelling, dramatic journey. Worse, this lack of a story line suggests the storyteller is confusing an account of events with how to tell an engaging story.

That's why the members of an audience who are confused about a story's dramatic purpose generally aren't emotionally or thoughtfully engaged by the actions of its characters or plot. In effect, the storyteller races his or her characters and plot events about to create the effect of a story moving toward a dramatic destination. But, in reality, the audience realizes they aren't going anywhere, and boredom sets in, or a story becomes work because all the details have to be memorized until something happens that gives the details a context. A good story is visceral in its ability to transport an audience. People feel moved or they don't. They feel caught up in a story or not. They feel like a story is worth the effort they are extending to follow the action or not.

The most common mistake of inexperienced writers is not clearly establishing and sustaining their story's advance along its story line. This is ruthlessly damning. It creates a story that is a collection of meaningless details that suggest no promise or dramatic purpose, just as a collection of railroad cars sitting isolated on sections of broken or disconnected tracks fails to suggest the possibility of a journey toward a destination. Offering more detailed descriptions of the railroad cars doesn't change that they sit motionless on disconnected tracks.

Just as a typical railroad train travels on two rails that compose a track, for a story to advance toward its resolution and fulfillment of its promise there needs to be a second rail to accompany the story line. That second rail is the *plot line*. When a story's characters act to overcome obstacles generated by a story's plot, their actions compose a story's plot line.

In *Romeo and Juliet*, for example, the *story* is about great love. Its plot is about what makes this love great. This story advances from its introduction along both a *story line* and a *plot line*. Together, they create the mechanism that allows for the story's audience to experience a discernible dramatic progression toward a story's resolution and fulfillment. Storytellers, in fact, create the plot obstacles their characters must overcome for the very purpose of making a story's progression along its story line dramatic. The catch is that those plot obstacles must arise from a story's dramatic purpose and promise in the same way the issues that compose and name its story line arise.

The issues characters bring to stories to resolve must also impact a story's events in a way that can be assigned meaning. How characters respond to a story's plot events enable an audience to judge how far a story has advanced along its story line. The closer Romeo and Juliet come to proving their love, the closer the story is to its fulfillment, even if that fulfillment revolves around their deaths.

Many writers struggle with the issue of creating a story line that parallels their plot line because a story line only exists to the degree that the storyteller evokes it through the response of a story's characters to a story's events, or the reaction of an audience to these events. Many struggling writers assume that characters + conflict + plot + resolution = story. Only, however, when a writer's story and plot elements interweave to create the effect of a dramatic progression toward fulfillment and resolution of issues of human need, or offer potent illuminations and revelations about life, does a story fully engage the attention of an audience. Without that arrangement, character actions and plot events become merely a sequence of events that suggest no dramatic significance.

Some writers so seamlessly weave together their plot and story lines that they appear joined. This could be compared to a magnetic train that runs on a single rail. The inexperienced writer trying to duplicate this process, however, must be careful that he or she is not simply overlaying personal feelings about a story's promise onto plot events. If a storyteller's plot events fail to inspire or evoke feelings of fulfillment for an audience, such a story has failed to transport its audience. That's why stories that are merely sequences of action—this happened, then that happened—can fail to emotionally or thoughtfully engage an audience. Such stories lack a discernible story line composed of events with resolutions that evoke desirable perceptions, feelings, or epiphanies for an audience.

Some plot events can be designed to be so creative, shocking, nerve wracking, titillating, exciting, intriguing, oddly humorous, or imbued with a grand sense of spectacle that they engage and reward the attention of an audience on those merits alone. When the events on a plot line become divorced from a story and its promise, they become life-like and inconsequential. They have a beginning, middle, and end, but no frame of reference as to what it is that they're a dramatic beginning, middle, and end of.

The craft required to create multiple plot threads or time lines that evoke a story advancing along a single story line leads to the difficulties some inexperienced storytellers encounter when they try to create complex stories. If there's no unity of purpose at the heart of a story and its events, there's no common story line or plot line along which a story as an entity advances. The different story threads split apart into disconnected fragments of plot lines that don't move in a common direction. The audience senses that the different story elements aren't creating the purposeful, organized effect of a well-designed story.

Often, struggling storytellers compound this mistake by introducing more plot threads and characters to maintain some hold on the audience. Unfortunately, it only proves that the authors are unaware of why their stories aren't engaging. Well-told film stories with multiple time lines include *The Limey, Toto le Hero, Eternal Sunshine of the Spotless Mind, The English Patient,* and *Inception.*

The Glass Castle: A Memoir[9] by Jeannette Walls opens with a frame, also called a book-end. A Park Avenue socialite is being driven through New York in a taxi when she sees her mother dumpster diving on the sidewalk. How this socialite was raised by a dumpster-diving mother requires going back in time. It creates quite a compelling plot question. The memoir ends in the present, answering the question raised in that opening scene or frame about how this woman survived being raised by a mentally ill mother and an alcoholic father.

In Good Grief[10], by Lolly Winston, a young woman is overcome with grief after the death of her husband. Many of her daily experiences trigger intense memories of her life with her husband, both good and bad. Dealing with her grief involves dealing with her past and present.

In Steigg Larrson's *The Girl with the Green Tattoo*[11], a young woman with special talents must deal with a court-appointed overseer who sexually abuses her. During the course of the novel, this abused girl takes a step toward feeling love for a man. This is a small but heart-felt step for her.

Keep in mind that a simple story line for *Romeo and Juliet* could read: The beginning of the story line introduces a story about great love. The middle of the story line sets out the complications around this great love proving itself. The end of this story line is the fulfillment offered by this great love proving itself. There is a beginning, middle, and end.

A simple plot line for *Romeo and Juliet*: The beginning of the plot line sets out events that introduce a story about great love. The middle of the plot line consists of events that escalate the drama around the outcome of whether this great love can prove itself. The end of this plot line is the resolution of the story that proves that great love can overcome all obstacles, even death. Again, a beginning, middle, and end.

If understanding the distinction between a story line and plot line is still difficult, think of a story as heat and a plot as flame. Heat is the tangible presence of flame, while flame is a concrete manifestation of heat. A story that generates no quality of heat also struggles to generate a visible manifestation of flame. It risks being a flame that generates no sensation of heat for its audience. An audience that comes to a story for the emotional, sensory, and intellectual heat it generates will turn away from a cold and lifeless story/flame.

If you understand the difference between an account of an event and a story inspired by events, you're on the right path.

The ability to set out and sustain a story's promise in a way that dramatically transports an audience is an important part of a foundation for understanding how to write dramatic stories.

In the next chapter, I'll explore how one demonstrates the ability to fulfill a story's promise.

Chapter Questions

Can you describe a story line for your story in simple terms and in three sentences?
Can you describe your plot line using three sentences?
Was your first attempt to write a story line and plot line obvious and clumsy? Good! If it's visible to you, it should be visible to your audience.

How to Make a Down Payment on Your Promise

If a story is a promise, how does the storyteller demonstrate to an audience his or her ability to fulfill a story's promise? By making a down payment on it. That communicates an ability to *pay off* on the story's larger promise, just as someone making a payment on a debt suggests an ability to pay off the whole debt.

How does one make this down payment?

The Usual Suspects opens on Keaton, a survivor of great carnage on a ship. Keaton is ready to destroy himself in a fiery explosion. This makes clear that Keaton has a powerful will. But will he succeed? The dramatic answer is that a man of even stronger will interrupts and won't let Keaton die. This man speaks to Keaton, and Keaton gives the other man a name, Keyser. They speak briefly, then Keyser kills Keaton and walks away. He reignites the flame Keaton began and makes a narrow escape from the explosion that consumes the ship. A dramatic entrance and exit, indeed.

This scene suggests the story will be about the power of will by showing this life and death contest of wills. That's how the story makes a *down payment* on its promise. It sets up a question within the initial scene revolving around the power of will, and dramatically answers the question. At the same time it sets up larger questions that will draw the audience through the story. Who is Keyser? What happened on the ship?

In the opening chapter of *The Hunt for Red October*, by Tom Clancy, Clancy sets up the question: will Ramius, the commander of the *Red October*, be able to implement his plan to escape the oppression of Soviet communism? The dramatic answer is yes. While that provides a down payment on the story's promise, the "how" and "where to" of Ramius's intent to escape are left for future chapters.

In *Rocky*, an early question is: will Rocky find a way to convince a young girl that by hanging out on the street she's picking up the wrong kind of reputation? The dramatic answer is no. The girl recognizes Rocky is everything he's telling her not to be, a nobody hanging out on the streets. That sets up an even more powerful question: will Rocky be able to gain the self-respect he obviously thinks is valuable? Getting the answer to that question requires sharing the dramatic journey to the end of the story.

Romeo and Juliet opens with a lethal brawl that raises the question, is Romeo safe? When Benvolio is sent to check on Romeo, he discovers that Romeo is lovesick for Rosalind. He advises Romeo to go someplace he can see other beauties, advice which Romeo rejects because of the depth of his feelings for Rosalind, but wanting to see Rosalind leads him to Juliet.

The Wizard of Oz opens with Dorothy trying to keep Toto safe from a neighbor. Trying to make sure Toto has a place where he belongs leads to Dorothy's adventure in Oz.

To test whether you're making a down payment on your promise, use the zero-five-ten scale to write out how you're making that down payment in a way that is obvious, then obscure, then suggestive. Let yourself be obvious, then obscure, then move into being suggestive. If you want to start with being suggestive and work back toward obvious and obscure, that's fine as well. The important point is to understand the difference.

Demonstrating an ability to make a down payment on a story's promise is another important aspect of creating a well-told story. How to sustain that promise throughout the course of a story is the focus of the next chapter.

Chapter Questions

How are you making a down payment on your promise in your opening scenes?

How does your initial down payment draw your audience deeper into your story?

How are you setting up a story question in your opening scenes so that it will draw your audience to the end of your story?

Writing Dramatic Moments

Just as a story engages the interest of an audience by introducing its promise in a dramatic way, the moments within a story's scenes can also suggest a smaller kind of dramatic promise. To that end, moments in scenes can be designed to be emotionally or thoughtfully engaging, or illuminating of ideas that add depth to a story, or designed to offer fresh, vivid perceptions of a story's events.

To understand this process of writing dramatic moments, keep in mind that anticipation is the key to creating drama. To create anticipation, something must either be set into motion as a scene opens, or something must be presented as ripe with a sense of impending movement. To show this process in action, consider again *The Usual Suspects*. The opening scene introduces Keaton, a wounded man. Dead bodies close by suggest a recent battle. Keaton lights a cigarette, then ignites a line of fuel that leads toward some fuel tanks. We anticipate that the explosion and fire will kill him.

That's the introduction to this moment. Note how it's tied to the central issue of the story's promise—the power of will. Keaton is presented as a man of strong will, ready to take his own life. If the moment continued and the ship had blown up, the audience would have been left with simple questions. What happened on the ship? Who was the man who set the fire?

Before the line of flame sets off an explosion, however, someone urinates on the flame from above, extinguishing it. This develops more drama around the outcome of the initial moment. It takes the moment in a direction not expected. Because the scene was taken in an unexpected direction, the audience is given an answer to one question: will the line of flame set off an explosion? The answer is no. Which sets up a larger question: who is the man who put out the flame? Note how the dramatic shape and details of the moments of this scene draw us into desiring answers to this larger question.

With the attention of the audience drawn to the question of the identity of the second man, he joins the first man and asks, "How you doing, Keaton?" This answers the question: who is the first man? At the same time, the sequence of action sets up other, larger questions. What was Keaton doing there? Was he trying to set off an explosion that would kill himself as well as the second man? Who is the second man? What starts out as a simple moment—will the line of fire set off an explosion?—continues to deepen. There is a process here of both setting up a moment with a potential outcome and then shaping the moment to have an unexpected twist that heightens its dramatic impact.

In that vein, the process of setting up questions and providing answers continues. Keaton gives an identity to the second man, the name Keyser. This gives a partial answer to the question, who is he? Note, however, that we don't see Keyser's face, and that sets up other questions. What does he look like? Why is his identity being withheld? To get those answers, we have to journey forward. That's the purpose of these moments, to draw the story's audience deeper into the story in an engaging way.

This same process can be applied to any moment in any scene. By each moment in a story having a dramatic question that sets up a desire for an answer, the storyteller creates moments that draw an audience through scenes.

This does not mean that every moment in the story must have a dramatic shape with a beginning, middle, and end. As *Suspects* continues, Verbal, the narrator, testifies before a grand jury and says, "It all started..." This is a promise to give us the answers to what happened on the ship. Once that purpose is met, the scene is over. The scene is only as long as it needs to be to fulfill its dramatic purpose.

What follows the opening scenes of *The Usual Suspects* are the quick introductions to several characters. Each introduction is given a dramatic shape around the outcome to a question; hence, each introduction continues to draw the story's audience forward. Each scene also comments on the underlying story issue of the power of will.

Todd Hockney works in a garage. As armed police rush into the garage and toward him with guns drawn, he calmly reaches for something. Will he be shot? Will he shoot someone? This moment demonstrates the power of his will. The other character introductions follow. Each introduction gives each character a distinctive personality while also suggesting how tough each man is. As an audience, we've been set up to expect something to come out of the powerful willfulness of these men.

The dramatic moments in *The Usual Suspects* generally revolve around action. Another storyteller telling a story about the power of will might create scenes that revolve around a process of illumination of ideas about the power of will. For example, Fellini's *8 1/2* dramatically presents a film director who is adrift in a sea of choices with no ability—no will—to make up his mind. It's a story that covers some of the same terrain but with an entirely different artistic purpose and outcome from *The Usual Suspects*. The storytelling process—how to set into motion a story via scenes that advance the story along its story and plot lines—is the same.

Struggling storytellers often damage their stories by simply presenting information about characters without creating dramatic moments that suggest anticipation of some outcome around their actions. To give us details about what Verbal and the others look like is not the same as setting a story into motion via their actions. Filling scenes with details about the environment of a story risks creating scenes that collectively have no dramatic tension, no conflict over an outcome, no sense of dramatic purpose. Such moments are inert. A collection of non-dramatic moments creates a non-dramatic story.

Beginning a screenplay with an action that raises questions is also called an inciting incident, or a hook. Some novels open with prologues that raise powerful questions; getting to the answers requires reading to the end of the book.

A moment in a scene has a beginning, middle, and end. Its outcome can be made dramatic, unexpected to both the characters and the story's audience. That is what makes some stories so stimulating. Both the audience and the characters can never quite know, moment to moment, how things are going to turn out. Both the audience and the characters have to keep going deeper into the story to find out.

A storyteller who gives an audience no choice about having to find out what will happen next understands a vital aspect of the craft of storytelling.

Chapter Questions

Can you describe the beginning, middle, and end of a dramatic moment from the opening scene of your story?

What did you do to make the outcome of that opening moment dramatic?

What information did you offer in that moment that names your story's promise?

How does your opening moment set your plot into motion?

Suggesting a Dramatic Truth

Characters in a story ring true because they have a role to play in fulfilling a story's promise. When a story's characters embody dramatic truths, those characters feel compelled to resolve issues of human need. Drama is an anticipation of an outcome. A character who embodies a dramatic truth suggests to a story's audience a character's purpose. A character who fails to embody a dramatic truth risks coming across as a collection of details; worse, purposeless. Let me demonstrate.

"John was five foot eight, with blond hair, a senior in college, an avid chess player."

This collection of words makes a statement about John. It creates no sense of anticipation about John as a character, nor does it suggest an issue of human need that John feels compelled to resolve. A collection of similar statements in sequence would risk simply assembling details about John for an audience to try and understand. This quickly becomes frustrating for readers because there's nothing to assign meaning to all the details.

If I write, "John was lonely," that's still a statement about John, but in a story about loneliness, it serves to *name* the story. Still, it fails to create a sense of anticipation about what might arise from John's loneliness, or what might compel John to act to resolve his loneliness.

Writing, "A sense of loneliness radiated from John," makes John's state of emotion more vivid, but not more dramatic. It still creates no sense of drama over an outcome to what we know about John. But if I write, "John thought he understood the true depths and pain of loneliness until he met Mary," that creates a sense of anticipation, and that anticipation revolves around the issue of loneliness. Now a description of John's loneliness ties into John's dramatic truth. It is part of the beginning of a story about loneliness with characters named John and Mary, and it suggests that something about Mary has made John's loneliness untenable. It's an obvious beginning, but a beginning that could be revised to be more subtle or suggestive, artful or elusive.

To avoid being obvious, many writers offer details about characters that are obscure, that do not suggest a dramatic truth. I advise writers be obvious about a character's dramatic truth as a way station toward writing about a character that is dramatically suggestive.

Just as characters can embody a dramatic truth, a story's environment embodies a dramatic truth when it impacts a story's characters in a purposeful manner. For example, a lonely character might be put into a warm, loving environment that increases his or her loneliness. A character struggling to control his or her temper could be placed into an environment that is aggravating, sunlight too bright, noises too loud, etc. The movie *Insomnia* places a character who can't sleep into an environment where the sun never sets.

Environments that fail to embody dramatic truths risk being passive details that fail to ring true because they lack a context within a story's truth.

Words that lack an active sense of purpose that revolves around a dramatic truth are passive. They are literal truths that simply describe. This holds true even if a writer is describing characters in actions or events that are explosive, if no underlying story movement around resolution of a dramatic truth is created.

When words revolve around a discernible dramatic purpose that advances a story, they can create a vivid, palpable sense of movement toward a story-like destination. Note the quality of purposeful drama suggested by these words from the opening of *Moby-Dick*[13], by Herman Melville:

Call me Ishmael. Some years ago—never mind how long precisely—having little or no money in my purse, and nothing particular to interest me on shore, I thought I would sail about a little and see the watery part of the world. It is a way I have of driving off the spleen and regulating the circulation. Whenever I find myself growing grim about the mouth; when it is a damp, drizzly November in my soul; whenever I find myself involuntarily pausing before coffin warehouses, and bringing up the rear of every funeral I meet; and especially whenever my hypos get such an upper hand on me that it requires a strong moral principle to prevent me from deliberately stepping into the street, and methodically knocking people's hats off—then, I account it high time to get to the sea as soon as I can.

By introducing a man obsessed with this "November in my soul," a story issue about obsession is named. The storyteller also sets out how Ishmael's obsession has grown and threatens to take over his life. He is a ripe dramatic character, both physically and emotionally, because he is compelled to deal with his obsession.

The story deepens with the introduction of Ahab and his obsession that, unlike Ishmael's, will lead to the deaths of a number of others. The issue of obsession in this story evolves into a thoughtful story question. When does an obsession for a good cause become evil? That is one of the more compelling questions of modern times, with the many millions who have died as a result of others' obsessions. It is one reason *Moby-Dick* is acknowledged as a classic. Melville took a dramatic truth that spoke to future generations and wrote a compelling story that fulfilled its promise via rich, poetic language.

Great writers can perceive how to communicate great states of emotion and a need to act in a few words. For example, in *Prince of Tides*[14], by Pat Conroy, the opening line is:

My wound is geography.

Note how Pat Conroy creates a sense of who the story's narrator is through taking a literal fact—that Tom Wingo is from Colleton, South Carolina—and overlaying it with a truth about Tom, that he is wounded.

The story question of *Prince of Tides* is:

Can Tom Wingo be healed?

Phrased another way:

Can Tom Wingo move toward healing?

That is the dramatic purpose of this story. In just one sentence, this brilliant writer captures not only a beginning of a portrait of a complex character, but he also sets out the novel's story question and begins the process of creating drama over the question of Tom's ability to find healing and resolve his dramatic truth.

On a deeper level, the storyteller is asking if *any* of us can find healing for our wounds. That is why the story, with its answer to this question, is so emotionally and thoughtfully moving to its audience.

Catherine Ryan Hyde's *Funerals for Horses*[15] opens with this subtitle:

The God of Growing Up

This suggests a story about growing up. It also raises questions: Who is the god of growing up in this story? What led someone in the story to need such a god?

The opening lines of the novel:

My brother Simon was forty-two years old. I pray he still is.

This suggests a story about loss, and raises an immediate question, what happened to Simon? Continuing:

> I shame and cajole his family into believing with me, but their wicks have burned down, their flames left to flicker, like the light they pretend to leave on in the windows for Simon, like their own dwindling lives.

In a few graceful, beautifully written lines, Hyde suggests the dramatic truth of this family, that they aren't as concerned about Simon's disappearance as the narrator. The descriptive details about the family that come later ring true because they have a context.

This following opening is from *A Confederacy of Dunces*[16], by John Kennedy O'Toole.

> A green hunting cap squeezed the top of the fleshly balloon of a head.

This sentence introduces the story's odd main character. The description speaks a truth about him.

> The green earflaps, full of large ears and uncut hair and the fine bristles that grew in the ears themselves, stuck out on either side like turn signals indicating two directions at once.

Again, this is both description, but description that informs the audience in a comic tone about the nature of this character.

> Full, pursed lips protruded beneath the bushy black moustache and, at their corners, sank into the little folds filled with disapproval and potato chip crumbs.

This suggests this character's outlook on the world, and, in return, suggests what the world would think of this character.

Christy Yorke's novel *The Secret Lives of the Sushi Club*[17] begins:

> In her dream, of course, he lived.

This immediately raises the question, who lived? What

happened?

> They fell overboard together into a cauldron of foam. The river's brutality was more shocking than the cold; Zach was upended and slugged, Jina dragged along jagged boulders and gravel beds, but they came up laughing. They found their footing in the rapids, and Zach held out his arms.
>
> He presented her with an oyster overflowing with pearls, the star-shaped logo of an electronics company stamped on its shell.
>
> It was the triviality of the vision that woke her–the print design that had eluded her for weeks, one more ultimately unimportant piece of her other life, her unchosen life.

This line about an unchosen life helps name the promise for this story, that the main character is caught up in a life she didn't choose.

> She reached out to slap away the oyster and touched only bed sheets. It shouldn't take death or pain to create something beautiful, but later, when the design won accolades, she'd remember that the way things ought to be is often a far cry from the way things actually are.

This wonderful opening is about a woman still haunted by the death of her husband, who died in a rafting accident. She wakes up to an empty life in an empty bed because her unexciting boyfriend who doesn't compare to Zach has already left for work.

While there is no one right word for a story, there is a process that underlies how strongly some words suggest a story's dramatic truths. Storytellers like Jane Austen and William Faulkner are revered in part because of the masterful sense of command and artistic craft they bring to creating characters and story environments that fully embody dramatic truths. Their fiction is never less than deeply realized truths.

The zero-five-ten scale (obscure, obvious, suggestive) is meant to help writers create dramatic sentences and state in an obvious way the purpose of a sentence. Obscure: "John talked about the weather." Obvious: "John is angry about his failures in life." Dramatically suggestive: "Life kept a half-step ahead of John, even in his dreams."

When a storyteller uses words to convey a character's dramatic truth, and the tension a character feels around resolving that truth, compounded by the storyteller creating plot events to heighten that character's narrative tension, such words become entry points for an audience into a story's world and into the life of a character. It creates a journey of feelings that an audience can share and is a significant part of the story experience. Characters who don't embody a dramatic truth are dead. The longer you take to set out a character's dramatic truth, the longer you'll be dragging a corpse through your story. Generally getting a whiff of dead characters in a story's opening pages is enough for most readers.

It's critical for memoir writers to be sure the deeper truths of their characters is conveyed to an audience; the risk is the creation of characters who are symbolic and meaningful to the author, but the details evoke nothing for a reader.

Play with creating dramatic, engaging sentences that suggest your character's dramatic truths and draw your audience forward to read a second sentence, to find out more about a character or situation. Don't be concerned with right or wrong, good or bad; just think about the dramatic truths you want to express, then think of a way to be suggestive about that truth while avoiding being obscure. If you can create one vibrant, suggestive sentence, you're on your way to creating a story.

Chapter Questions

Can you write a sentence that makes a statement about a dramatic truth, and then rewrite it as a sentence that creates an anticipation of a potential outcome for that truth?

Can you write a sentence that vividly expresses the promise of your story?

Can you write a sentence about a character that sets up an anticipation of an outcome for an issue such as courage, self-respect, or gaining understanding?

What is the dramatic truth for your life?

section two

Designing the elements of Your Stories

Premise— Understanding The Foundation of Your Story

Beginning a story in an active voice—a voice that suggests the beginning of a journey—is a crucial aspect of storytelling. It suggests the ability of the storyteller to transport an audience to a dramatic destination. Creating a premise can be a great help toward understanding how to set a story journey in motion, and how to sustain it dramatically.

A premise does three things. It sets out a story's core dramatic issue, it offers a description of the movement of that issue toward resolution, and it describes the fulfillment that resolution offers a story's characters and its audience.

Dramatic Issues

Dramatic story-issues revolve around issues of human need. The need to be loved. To have control of one's fate. To feel a sense of purpose. To be able to overcome obstacles. To be able to grow and heal from life's wounds. To understand and make sense of the events of life.

It is important that you are able to *name*, in your own words, the dramatic issue at the heart of your story. The opening scenes of your story should clearly suggest it is the beginning of a journey, and that you understand how to create this journey.

If perceiving your story's main dramatic issue is difficult for you, think about the issues in your life that you enjoy seeing acted out as stories. Then put a "name" on those issues. Do they revolve around finding love? Gaining knowledge? Good defeating evil?

If you can't name the issue at the heart of your story, it risks being unclear to your audience. Once you understand that issue, you can go back and edit your opening scenes to a clear dramatic purpose.

If you need to write a story to discover the issue at its heart, that's fine.

Movement

The second part of a premise identifies the movement of a story. I believe that the idea of movement is a fundamental key to understanding the craft of storytelling. This concept has three interweaving facets.

First, by setting a story in motion toward a destination, a storyteller demonstrates an ability to transport an audience.

To understand the general movement of a story—fear to courage, hate to love, ignorance to understanding—enables a storyteller to better understand what types of characters, events, and environments serve the dramatic purpose of a particular story. A story might express movement toward an illumination of an idea, or a journey of emotions, of beliefs, or a physical journey toward a new understanding of life.

That is the first meaning I assign to movement. It is a demonstration of a storyteller's ability to introduce a story issue and give it a sense of direction and movement toward a goal.

The second meaning of movement revolves around how an audience experiences a story. In a well-told story about a character moving from being fearful to courageous, a story's audience is led to internalize and experience this character's progression. The audience feels *moved* from a state of fear to courage; from one state of perception about the meaning of fear and courage to a new understanding or affirmation of beliefs.

When a story journey is experienced in a potent, vivid way, an audience feels an inner quality of being purposefully moved through different states of feelings, thoughts, and perceptions. Since life does not operate to move people to experience these deeper states of clarity, people readily perceive when a story moves them in an emotional or thoughtful way. Or, conversely, when a story leaves them feeling unmoved. It's why badly constructed stories so quickly put off an audience. The effect of being unmoved is immediate and visceral.

A story is dramatically inert—lacking movement—when no issue of human need or an idea about the human condition is introduced in a way that engages the attention and emotions of an audience. When a storyteller compounds that with a failure to advance toward some state of potent resolution and fulfillment, a story is, as Shakespeare put it, "All sound and fury, signifying nothing."

The third and last issue of story movement I want to define revolves around what I call narrative tension. As a character in a story about courage (or any other expression of movement around an issue of human need) overcomes issues of fear, it is the job of the storyteller to transfer the tension from the characters to its audience. Once the audience has fully internalized a need for a story's characters, events, or ideas to have a particular resolution and fulfillment, that audience desires to experience a story's resolution, which offers an audience a potent release of feelings, and a potent experience of heightened perceptions.

Once the members of an audience are fully engaged in a story's dramatic movement, they desire, need, to experience a story's resolution and fulfillment for the relief it offers.

To understand its movement, then, is to see into the heart of a story, and what kind of journey it promises its audience, and why an audience desires one over another. Understanding story movement—or its lack on any of these three levels—can lead to an understanding of why audiences turn away so quickly from stories that fail to generate this internal quality of narrative tension that the storyteller both creates and relieves. People crave this release of narrative tension because most people live in a stew of unresolved conflicts. Stories are a prime source of relief from this tension.

To sum up this idea of movement as it relates to a story's promise and its premise...

> A story's promise speaks directly to the issue of human need that a story explores. It offers a reason for an audience to enter into a story's world.

A story premise speaks to the mechanics of how that issue of human need will be introduced, the path it takes toward resolution and fulfillment, and what will make concrete a story's fulfillment of its premise for both its characters and audience.

A story must operate to transport characters toward a heightened state of resolution and fulfillment, while at the same time resolving issues and story concepts in a way that emotionally or thoughtfully moves an audience to an intense experience of dramatic relief. These requirements make the concept of movement in storytelling both simple and difficult to understand. Gaining that understanding is a path toward learning to be a gifted storyteller.

I know my conception of story movement is difficult to explain and to understand. Some of my students have needed years to fully understand the concept. I also know from working with writers that some facet of weak movement is the benchmark of a struggling storyteller's efforts. But, once a storyteller understands fully this concept of story movement, every well-told story and every badly told story offers a lesson because the "why" of the story's strengths and weaknesses is fully apparent.

To complete my definition of premise, I'll now discuss the third aspect of a premise—fulfillment.

Fulfillment

A story's fulfillment is what a story's characters gain or achieve from the resolution of a story's promise...

and...

...the heightened feelings, thoughts, perceptions, and affirmations of beliefs a story's resolution offers the audience.

I offer this dual definition of fulfillment because a storyteller both writes *toward* a physical destination (a character finding his way home, for example), and *about* that destination with an understanding of the feelings, thoughts, and perceptions that reaching this place generates for an audience. To not write with this dual understanding is to risk having an ending that resolves the action of a story in a way that satisfies the storyteller, but leaves the storyteller's audience unmoved, unfulfilled, or unsatisfied.

Because so many events of life leave people feeling unfulfilled, a story that offers a powerful fulfillment can create tremendous inner feelings of relief, a cessation of conflicted and unresolved feelings and ideas. When the hero saves the world, we share that ability and experience. When the underdog rises up to defeat an oppressor, we experience that we can defeat that which oppresses us. When the unloved finds true love, we share that experience of love, and we are able to feel we could have the same experience. In those moments, the inner voices that whisper to us that our lives lack meaning, that we will never escape that which oppresses us, or that we don't deserve to be loved, are silenced.

This makes a good story something that people hunger for. Good stories meet needs buried deep in the human mind and heart. Or, for some people, good stories offer salve for emotional wounds that are raw and aching and in need of constant story medication.

To understand fulfillment, consider what your favorite stories led you to feel or think. What feelings about life did you have renewed, affirmed, enlivened? What epiphanies about life did you experience? That is each story's fulfillment.

What I often find in stories that lack a strong quality of fulfillment is that storytellers are overlaying personal feelings about story characters and ideas onto a story. They do this without realizing their writing isn't generating a satisfying fulfillment for an audience. That is why I teach premise. To help storytellers see into the heart of a story and to understand both why it affects them, and how it can be told in a way that it affects—transports—an audience.

I call writing intended to be story like that fails to create the effect of a story journaling. This kind of writing is meant for the writer to explore his or her own feelings and experience a relief from their personal narrative tension around life issues through the actions of their characters. Such writers are the audience for their stories. These kind of stories can work, but often I see struggling storytellers creating novels around characters who are "stuck" because that's the basic life situation/feeling for the author. These novels often end with the main character finally free to act, which would be the beginning of a story. But, at that point the authors have found relief of their own feelings, so they have no need to continue, and they often are bewildered why others find their journals/stories dramatically unsatisfying. It's an evening spent looking at slides of someone else's great vacation getaway.

A premise can help writers avoid this situation by understanding the fulfillment a story offers an audience.

To visualize a premise, think of it as a house foundation. Just like a foundation supports a well-constructed house, a premise supports a well-constructed story. Like a house foundation, it is not meant to be artistic or original so much as clear and direct in setting out a story's main dramatic issue, and what action dramatically advances a story toward its fulfillment.

To visualize this, consider a community of expensive homes. Every home would likely be different, unique, expressive. Now think of that community burned to the ground. After the fire, when all that's left are bare foundations, and all the foundations have a similar quality. They look alike.

A premise is like that. It's not meant to be different, artistic, or unique. It's meant to set a foundation that supports the more visible aspects of a story, the characters and events, just as a house's foundation supports the more visible aspects of a house, its walls, roof, windows, etc. Just like a house foundation, a story's foundation is not meant to be visible to an audience.

It's meant to serve the purpose of the storyteller, the builder of the story.

Different storytellers could start with the premise of *Romeo and Juliet* and write entirely different stories. Each storyteller would bring a different writing style, word choices, characters, plot events, ideas, and concepts to the same premise.

Lajos Egri in *The Art of Dramatic Writing*[18] explores the concept of premise. His premise for *Romeo and Juliet* is "Great love defies even death." (page 15)

The dramatic issue in this story is love. Because readers desire to experience love in a fulfilling way, love as a dramatic issue is at the heart of many stories. It is an issue many people will choose to become emotionally invested in.

The dramatic movement of *Romeo and Juliet* is about love overcoming obstacles that escalate to include death. By defying even death, the story fulfills its premise. It is a story about great love. The word "defying" describes the movement of the story. The characters must defy everything that stands in the way of their love. Shakespeare's job was to keep making those obstacles larger and larger, rising to include death, normally an obstacle that cannot be overcome.

Note, also, that to defy something suggests drama. What will this defiance lead to, gain, lose, cost? From the opening scenes of a story, it should be clear the storyteller understands how to set a story into motion through the introduction of a dramatic situation.

Because every premise expresses an active quality of a story's movement, it can serve as a guide to what constitutes a dramatic beginning. A story about identity might begin with a character being stripped of her identity. Such a character must act to regain that which she has lost. Knowing what a story is about, a storyteller can embed the core dramatic issue of a story in action, dialogue, events, and descriptions of an environment or character.

To manifest a story's movement toward resolution and fulfillment, a story is populated with characters who feel compelled to act to resolve that issue. *Rocky*, for example, is about someone who feels compelled to prove he's somebody by overcoming insurmountable odds.

In *Romeo and Juliet*, the love the title characters feel for each other is threatened by characters who love to hate. The result is conflict between characters who must love and characters designed to block the expression of that love. The unwillingness of both sets of characters to be blocked advances the story dramatically.

In *The Accidental Tourist*[19], an emotionally numb man who writes guide books instructing business people how they can travel around the world in a self-created cocoon finds his personal cocoon destroyed when his son is killed in a senseless murder. When his wife leaves him because of his inability to display his grief, he's forced onto a path of learning how to feel.

Characters who simply have goals opposed by others do not create the effect of a story. It is because characters act to advance a dramatic issue toward the resolution and fulfillment of a story's promise that their actions transport an audience in a thoughtfully or emotionally satisfying way.

A subtle point must be made. *Romeo and Juliet* is a story about great—if tragic—love. Its plot operates to make the story's fulfillment dramatic and deeply felt. Its characters create for the audience this experience of great love. But, a storyteller can think about the deeper story issue here, this concept of great love and how it affects an audience, without talking about specific characters or plot events. This is sometimes necessary to help create characters who are fully engaged and committed to gaining a goal that arises from a story's promise.

Don't worry, then, if your premise seems too simple. It's meant to help you understand your story in a clear, direct way. Once you understand how to create a dynamic story premise, it will help you with every other element of storytelling, such as what kinds of characters might populate your story, how to create plot events that serve to make your story's movement dramatic, and which characters' actions and story events best manifest your story's fulfillment.

Or, you might write your story first, then explore it to see the premise that lies at its heart.

The ability to create a premise offers writers an opportunity to understand the foundation of a story *before* they begin to write it. Such an understanding can help writers avoid multiple rewrites in an attempt to "find" their story.

Whatever form for creating a premise works for you—one sentence, three, a full page of notes, or an entire novel, screenplay, or play—do what works best for you. A premise is a tool meant to help you. And, if you can write well-told stories without creating or understanding how to create a premise, good for you. But, if you struggle to tell stories—if your stories lack a strong beginning, middle and end, dynamic characters, a plot that creates rising tension, endings that are fulfilling, or a lack of narrative tension—I suggest you keep on trying to learn and understand how to create and use a story premise.

If you can learn to use a premise to understand how to promise an engaging story journey to an audience, and how to fulfill that promise, your writing will improve.

In the following chapter, I offer techniques for creating a story premise.

Chapter Questions

What dramatic issue in stories most appeals to you?

How do the stories you enjoy most move their plot questions toward resolution?

Are you giving your characters the freedom to act out their own story issues, or using them to act out your issues in life?

Can you create premises for some of your favorite movies?

Techniques of Creating a Story Premise

To create a premise, start by writing three sentences. The first should lay out the dramatic issue that arises from your story's promise. The second, your story's movement toward the resolution of your promise. The third, your fulfillment of that promise.

To begin, write a sentence that starts:

My story is about...

Using the movie *Rocky* as an example, the dramatic issue at the heart of the premise is about self-respect. A simple way to state that:

Rocky is a story about gaining self-respect.

Gaining self-respect, a sense of mattering, is the dramatic issue at the heart of many stories.

When you write your sentence, write about the dramatic issue or idea at the heart of your story, not character goals or plot devices. Love, hate, redemption, rebirth, the desire for revenge, courage: these are the kinds of dramatic issues and ideas found at the heart of stories.

Second, write a sentence that begins:

The movement of my story toward the resolution of

its promise can be described as...

Does your story's advance center around overcoming, defeating, understanding, or avenging something? Is the action of your story leading to something, such as rebirth, or redemption, or renewal? A sentence that describes the movement of *Rocky* could read:

> *Rocky is a story about someone discovering within himself the courage to overcome insurmountable obstacles.*

Again, be clear that you're writing about the movement of your story toward its dramatic destination, not just describing the actions of your main character to attain a personal goal. You must make this distinction because the action of every character in your story should contribute to your story's overall movement toward its resolution and fulfillment.

Third, write a sentence that begins:

> *The fulfillment of my story is...*

The fulfillment of *Rocky* is that Rocky's courage to overcome the odds proves he is somebody to himself and the world. He achieves a self-respect he lacked. Because there's a need in our world to believe that if we just had enough courage we could prove to the world that we are somebody, this story drew audiences to experience its powerful fulfillment. Through Rocky's character, others experienced how courage and belief in oneself could be transforming.

The premise of *Rocky* can be reduced to one sentence:

> *The courage to persevere in the face of overwhelming obstacles leads to self-respect.*

Now, I want you to look over your three sentences and reduce them to a single sentence. Begin by writing:

> *The premise of my story is...*

Was it a struggle for you to think of your story in terms of a single sentence? If it was, look over what you've written. Return to my analogy of a premise as a house's foundation. Are you trying to actually build a house when you write your premise? A premise is a simple, solid statement, in the same way that a house foundation is a solid, simple structure. When I work with people struggling with writing a premise, it is usually because they're trying to use a premise to tell a story—the characters went here and did this, this is the plot, etc.

The premise of *Romeo and Juliet* would never begin:

Romeo is a young man who falls in love with Juliet, and to be with her, he must…

Again, that leads writers to mistake character goals for what's at the heart of their stories.

Examples of other faulty premises include:

History creates change.

This premise is too general. It is not specific about what kinds of events create history. It doesn't set out how this history acts on some group of people in a way that a story would offer resolution or fulfillment of particular issues.

The premise could be recast as:

War leads to senseless destruction.

This premise is still general, but it is more specific about what war can lead to. The active verb, "leads," suggests this story is moving toward a destination. The specific fulfillment identified by the premise, "destruction," describes the outcome of the story. This is a premise one could use to answer the question: What kind of characters and events bring this story to life?

What's at stake in this story is whether the destruction of war can be avoided. For this particular story premise, the answer would be no. In this story, the destruction of war would ruin both victor and defeated. That defeat might be material, moral, or physical; that is a choice of the storyteller.

A more uplifting premise about war could be:

The destruction of war leads to rebirth.

While this story would have the same background as the premise above, it would move toward a different fulfillment. The fulfillment of this story might be that out of the aftermath of war and its destruction, life begins anew. This could be shown through a character's renewal, or the renewal of a country.

Another false premise is:

Love is its own reward.

This premise is not specific. What kind of love does this story talk about? What kind of reward? Keep in mind that a moral is not a premise. While a moral might give insight into some state of human need or state of affairs, it is not a premise because it does not suggest a state of dramatic advance toward a specific destination.

To make the above a premise, it could be rewritten as:

Going through the pain of young love leads to growth.

Such a premise would be a natural in a coming-of-age novel. Now the premise refers to a specific kind of dramatic issue with a specific movement and a clear fulfillment. In a possible story based on this premise, two teens might meet, have a rocky relationship, break up, and date others. But, through those events, they come to a deeper, richer understanding of love. Because most people have their own painful memories or experiences of young love, a story that offers a dramatic, deeply felt, positive outcome to such a dramatic issue is pleasurable.

One more false premise:

Hate destroys itself.

This has a focus on a dramatic issue and movement, but it needs to be more specific about its fulfillment. Recast it as:

Hate destroys those who wield it as a weapon.

See how that premise suggests the characters who would populate that particular story world? How its movement suggests the way in which the story progresses? And its fulfillment?

If you're still having trouble writing a premise, consider your main character and answer the following questions. What goal motivates your main character? Rocky, for example, desires to prove that he is somebody.

What verb would you use to describe your main character's actions—what he must do—to attain what he seeks? In *The Hunt for Red October*, Ramius battles the communist system of oppression that denies him his freedom.

Lastly, what makes concrete the fulfillment of your character attaining some goal? Rocky's fulfillment is that he feels he is somebody and that the rest of the world knows it.

Ramius gains his freedom.

Scrooge is renewed.

Dorothy learns valuable lessons about herself and what's important in life.

Once you understand how to create a dynamic story premise, it will help you understand the kinds of characters who populate your story's world; how to create plots that serve to make your story's movement dramatic; how to understand what character actions and story events best manifest your story's fulfillment; or how to explore your story to find the premise that lies at its heart and use that to guide rewrites.

A well-designed premise is a foundation for a well-told story.

Chapter Questions

> How does your premise set out your story's promise in an active voice?
>
> How does the goal that your main character seeks to resolve move your story toward its fulfillment?
>
> How does your premise describe your story's fulfillment?

Characters, Story, and Premise

Because a story's characters promise to take the story's audience on a rewarding journey, dynamic, active characters are a vital element.

Because characters resolve issues of human need—resolve dramatic truths—they engage the attention of an audience. When introducing a story's characters, then, writers need to suggest in some way that their characters are "ripe." For example, if love is the main issue in a story's premise, the storyteller can give a character an issue of love to resolve in a story's opening scenes. Romeo and Juliet are designed to be strong-willed characters in love with the idea of love. They are separated by characters who love to hate. But Romeo and Juliet love even unto death, refusing to let it be an obstacle to their love. By their actions, they bring this story about love to life in a way readers have enjoyed for centuries. Because their actions arise from and act out the story's premise, they manifest the story's movement to fulfillment.

Introducing characters with issues that resonate with a particular audience also draws an audience into a story. For example, a story aimed at teenage boys might call for a protagonist who's a young man. A story aimed at an audience of middle-aged women would have a different protagonist. This is not to make a value judgment about either story; rather, it is to say that the storyteller must design his characters for the particular fulfillment he wants to create for the intended audience.

To give your audience a reason to identify with your

characters, have your characters react with strong feelings and actions to a story's events. In a story about redemption, characters could confront feelings about redemption. How they react both names the story and gives voice to the character's feelings. By resolving a character's conflict around the feelings aroused by the events of a story, it has meaning to those in the audience with similar feelings and issues.

No matter how compelling a dramatic issue, a story needs characters clearly compelled to resolve its issues. One way to introduce such characters is in situations where they are actively attempting to achieve goals. And if their goals arise from a particular premise, their actions will advance the story itself.

Indiana Jones, in *Raiders of the Lost Ark*[21], is introduced as an adventurous character who must deal with immediate and pressing issues of trust and morality. In *L.A. Confidential*[22], three men are stripped of their identities and have to struggle to regain and re-establish a sense of who they are. In *The Sixth Sense*[23], a psychologist who misdiagnosed a boy, leading to fatal consequences, gets a second chance to help another boy with similar problems. In the novel *Twilight*[24], a young girl decides to leave her home so her mother can spend time with a new boyfriend. She travels to live with her father in a small town she dislikes. While the novel became hugely successful, the movie turns the girl, Bella, into a passive character who only reacts to what others want.

You can also introduce characters in odd, unusual, or active environments. James Bond films often open with dramatic action scenes meant to be thrilling and unique, but that also *names* a story issue. *Speed*[25] took an old idea and made it fresh by having the action revolve around a bus that would blow up if it slowed to less than fifty miles per hour. *The Limey*[26], a wonderful film directed by Steven Soderberg, opens on a black screen with a man's voice urgently asking, "Tell me, tell me about Jenny."

In *Dallas Buyers Club*[27], a homophobic Texas cowboy hustler learns to accept and appreciate others when he comes down with AIDS and must work with gays and transgender individuals to save himself.

In *Avatar*[28], a crippled marine gains the use of a healthy body when he becomes an avatar, a human experiencing life in the body of an alien.

In the film *Inception*[29], a man must journey through his own subconscious to resolve being wracked with guilt over his wife's death.

In *The Hunger Games*[30], a young girl will not be fenced in. She becomes the champion for a society that lives behind fences.

In *Joker*, Joaquin Phoenix brilliantly plays the character as a troubled soul slipping into madness and becoming an icon for those who feel dispossessed.

In *Peanut Butter Falcon*, a young man fleeing the scene of arson, comes across a young man with a disability who wants to be a pro wrestler.

If there's nothing interesting about the environment you're using to introduce a character, why did you choose it? Can you make a better choice? Are you describing your environment in a way that clearly impacts your audience? Think of your environment as a character in your story, rising up to act, to block, to help, to frustrate, your main character.

If characters have nothing to do in a scene, edit them out, create a purpose for them, or introduce them later when they do have something to do. A storyteller who begins a story in a static voice with static characters risks an audience turning away. Describing a static character in detail creates details that ring false.

By carefully choosing how and when to introduce characters in active situations, and describing those situations with details that evoke the purpose of a scene, a storyteller greatly expands the appeal of characters to an audience.

Active characters by their very introduction promise something to an audience.

I've found that some writers struggle to create dynamic characters because they project their feelings onto them. For example, I worked with one writer who created a main character who was in a "happy" marriage, but nothing the character did or said suggested he was happy about being married; to the contrary, his complete lack of feeling for his wife suggested otherwise. In this case, the writer projected his own feelings about marriage onto his character.

When all the characters in a story are a projection of the storyteller, the risk is that all the characters have one voice, the storyteller's, and all have one unresolved dramatic truth, the author's. In extreme cases, characters come across as soulless, lifeless automatons in the service of their creators.

Creating and understanding a premise for a story and its character is one method to ensure that a character goes into motion to resolve and fulfill clearly defined issues.

Chapter Questions

Who are some of your favorite story characters? Why? What issues did they resolve?

How are some of your characters similar to your favorite story characters?

What are your favorite story characters able to accomplish that you struggle with in life?

Did being such a character help you deal with your feelings?

Are you allowing your story characters to be larger than life, to resolve issues that you struggle with, to accomplish goals that are beyond you, or different than your goals?

What *Is* a Plot?

Understanding what a plot is creates a foundation for the ability to create one. Unfortunately, most writers are consumed with the idea of creating the effect of what a plot does without first understanding what a plot is.

What a plot does: It raises dramatic questions that a reader or viewer will want answers for.

What a plot is: It is the process of generating questions and drama around the advance toward a story's resolution and the fulfillment of a story's promise.

What a plot does: By blocking a character from gaining what he or she seeks, a plot increases the narrative tension a character experiences. And, by making that tension accessible, helps transfers it to a story's audience.

A good plot heightens a story's narrative tension and relieves it in a powerful way. This is the catharsis mentioned in Aristotle's *Poetics*. The catch is that it only happens when an audience feels invested or caught up in the action of a story (based on its promise and the dramatic truths of its characters). No investment or involvement, no catharsis.

In any story, as characters act to achieve goals and resolve their dramatic truths, their actions should advance the story toward its resolution and fulfillment. Because other characters are driven to shape a story to their own design, characters in opposition are naturally in conflict. As different characters act and block each other, they generate new obstacles to each other's progress. This escalates the drama around a story's outcome.

The purpose of a plot is to make a story's progression toward resolution and fulfillment dramatic. But it's only when events are in motion toward a destination that there is any movement to block. Further, without any dramatic tension around this movement, a story appears to be a collection of incidents. Such incidents may be dramatic in their own right, but collectively they fail to engage the interest of an audience. They fail because they lack a discernible purpose.

The key here is to understand that to describe a story about love is not to describe its plot. A story is about an issue of human need; a plot is a way of heightening the tension over that issue being acted out.

Romeo and Juliet is an example of a well-crafted plot that heightens the dramatic effect of a simple story. By loving each other in spite of the mutual hatred of their families, Romeo and Juliet set the story in motion. But it is the plot that makes the story's movement dramatic. By generating obstacles that block the young lovers from being together, Shakespeare creates a plot that makes the lover's plight more dramatic. Even knowing the outcome, the action of its plot—moment by moment—generates for the audience a dramatic experience of undeniable love.

To illustrate how a plot grows from a premise, consider the novel *The Hunt for Red October*. On the surface it appears to be a plot-driven thriller about a commander of a Russian nuclear submarine attempting to flee to America and freedom. The core story issue here revolves around a battle between freedom and authoritarianism. The issue of human need is a man's desire to be free of oppression. This is laid out in the premise: The courage to battle oppression leads to freedom.

Because readers desire to experience the values of freedom winning over oppression, they readily internalize this story's movement and the goal of its main character. Because the story in its every action proved its premise, it rewarded its readers. Its highly praised plot succeeded because it made the conflict of the freedom battling oppression clear, dramatic, and accessible.

Tom Clancy succeeded in creating a great plot because he understood how to manifest the movement of his story toward a specific resolution and fulfillment. Every character, situation, and action grew out of his premise and existed in the world it created. To the extent readers feel emotionally or thoughtfully enmeshed in whether or not Ramius gains his freedom, they must find out how the story ends. That ending offers readers a share of Ramius' victory, and relief from the narrative tension over whether he would gain that victory.

When someone is compelled to finish your story to see how it turns out, your plot has fulfilled its purpose.

The writer who doesn't see the connection between a story, its characters, and plot risks introducing characters or plot devices that have no real bearing on a story's course or ultimate destination. Setting up a situation common to action or horror films, "Who's going to get out of here alive," is plot-like. Lacking a deeper issue, however, such films struggle to engage a wide audience. Simply tacking on an issue to an action plot is not the answer. A strong issue must be woven through all the elements of a story if it is to powerfully affect an audience. *Event Horizon*[31], for example, has an interesting plot and a weak story. The plot is concrete, what happened to the crew of a ship that took the first jump into hyper-space? The story is about characters haunted by their pasts.

This principle also applies to art films. In *The Winslow Boy*[32], a play by Terence Rattigan adapted for film by David Mamet, the plot revolves around whether or not a young boy wrongly accused of a crime can find justice. The deeper truth is the price this justice costs, and whether the characters are willing to pay it, particularly the stern father and the moral adult daughter. As the price of truth escalates, the plot strikes at the characters, compelling them to reveal the truth of their feelings about what price they will pay for justice. Again and again, the plot strikes at these characters, compelling deeper and deeper revelations. A plot must operate to propel characters to experience these potent revelations of truth. Without such plot-fueled revelations, the description of the actions of characters remains cold and lifeless.

In *Eternal Sunshine of the Spotless Mind*[33] a man who can't experience intimacy because he lives in his head (always caught up in his thoughts) arranges to have his memories of a failed relationship erased. As his memories are being erased, he rediscovers why he fell in love and fights to retain a single memory of the relationship so he can find his lover again.

In *Take Shelter*, a man dreams of the sky raining oil, then has terrible visions of a storm destroying his family. Is he seeing a portent of something real, or is he slipping into mental illness as his mother did at the same age? The plot witholds the answer until the final moments of the film.

In the wonderful film *Arrival* (based on a short story by Ted Chiang), a woman scientist has what appear to be flashbacks about the birth and death of a daughter. In this story that explores language and how it relates to an understanding of time, what appear to be flashbacks are really flashforwards. She's been seeing her future.

To create a great plot, start with your premise. Understand how what's at stake over your story's outcome raises questions to which your audience is led to desire answers. Understand that your plot should make the journey to get those answers potent and dramatic.

When you start to write, be clear about the obstacles that block the movement of your story. That forces your characters to act with ever-greater determination if they would shape the story's outcome.

When your audience is fully invested in the outcome of your story, that's when you'll be told, "Wow! Loved your plot!"

Chapter Questions

> How does your plot escalate the drama around your story's course and outcome?
>
> How do the events of your plot name your story?
>
> How does your plot operate to give your characters a clear dramatic purpose?
>
> How does your plot make your story's fulfillment dramatic?

Creating a Dramatic Plot

What is the main dramatic issue of your story? Hate? Desire? Courage? Rebirth? Redemption? Revenge? When George Lucas was asked what *Star Wars*[34] was about, he had a one-word answer: Redemption.

Perceiving your story's central dramatic issue should help you identify what's at stake in your story. If you've identified your dramatic issue of your story, finish this sentence:

> *The central issue at stake over the outcome of my story is...*

You should be able to answer this question without mentioning your characters. It is the job of your characters to manifest the answer, but the answer is separate from them. Once you're able to verbalize your core dramatic issue, you must perceive how your plot operates to make its movement toward resolution dramatic.

To do that, finish the following sentence:

> *My plot serves to escalate the drama over my story's outcome by placing the following obstacles before my character(s)...*

Be clear that the actions of your characters advance your story toward its outcome. To win his freedom, Ramius must escape to America in the *Red October* by outwitting the combined forces of the Soviet and American navies. Ramius manifests the premise of the story, that the values of freedom can defeat oppression. His dramatic truth is that he will not be denied his freedom. A weak or indecisive character would not propel the action.

One of the issues that can make a plot seem so compelling is that it raises a dramatic story question. In *The Hunt for Red October* that question is:

> *Will Ramius make it to America and gain his freedom?*

To get the answer, one has to read—is compelled to read—to the end of the story.

For your story, complete the following:

> *Readers will care about the outcome of my story because they care about the following character's dramatic truth...*

This is where the ability to create characters who have dramatic truths to resolve comes into play. First, you must have an ability to create characters driven to resolve the issue at your story's heart because of their emotional makeup, beliefs, goals in life, and their determination to gain what they want. Second, you must understand how your plot serves to make their actions compelling and dramatic.

Finish the following:

> *My plot raises the following story question...*

That a story can have a story question and a plot question can mask which is which. Together, they operate to draw an audience forward. Unfortunately, that is one reason inexperienced writers confuse plot with story. The story question for *The Hunt for Red October* is whether or not Ramius will gain his freedom. The plot question is whether or not he'll manage to escape to America in the *Red October*.

Tom Clancy succeeded in creating a great plot because he understood how to create a plot that manifested the movement of his story toward resolution. His story question revolved around whether Ramius would be able to gain his freedom. His plot question revolved around what actions would gain him his freedom.

To confuse these two issues is to risk creating a series of questions that have no dramatic impact on a story's characters or its audience. In a weak story, there's no underlying sense of why characters or audience should care about the outcome of events, hence no narrative tension. Recognizing the distinction between a story and plot question can help writers avoid that trap.

Some writers succumb to the danger of introducing characters and then creating false plot elements to generate dramatic tension. No matter how dramatic such plot devices appear in isolation, if they do not heighten the effect of a story's advance toward its resolution, they fail to meet the expectations they raise. Therefore, any issues injected into *The Hunt for Red October* not tied to its premise would not serve the story because they would not affect its outcome.

Some writers need to write a novel, play or screenplay to discover the deeper layer of meaning and connections of their plot. If that's your path, just be sure to return to your beginning and shape your story to the design you discovered.

To create a great plot, start with your premise. Understand how what's at stake in your story raises questions for which your audience desires answers. Understand that your plot should make the journey to get those answers potent and dramatic. When you start to write, be clear about the obstacles that block the movement of your story. That forces your characters to act with ever greater determination if they would shape your story's outcome.

Chapter Questions

How do the events of your plot operate to block the movement of your story?

How does your plot operate to escalate the drama over the course of your story?

How does your plot operate to escalate the drama over the outcome of your story's promise?

If you look at your life as a story, what is the central issue that you've strived to accomplish in life in spite of obstacles? Are you creating characters who act with the same passion and commitment?

What's at Stake in Your Story?

Why do a story's characters persevere to the end of a story? The storyteller provides a clear indication at the outset that something of consequence is at stake that characters feel compelled to resolve.

Why do readers read to the end of a story? Because they have become emotionally or thoughtfully invested in how characters will resolve and fulfill what's at stake in a story.

A writer trying to see clearly what's at stake in a particular story should look to his or her premise and its core dramatic issue. Is it about love? Fear of death? Rebirth? Redemption? What must be overcome or changed by the telling of the story for this issue to be resolved? That's what's at stake.

While characters shape a story's course and outcome, it's only when what's at stake is visible are those in an audience led to feel invested in the outcome of those actions. Writers struggle when they keep what's at stake obscure for dramatic effect or a revelation.

In *Romeo and Juliet*, it's clearly set out that Romeo is in love with the idea of love. It's only then that his obsession focuses on Juliet. Also established very early on are the consequences of what will happen if he openly professes his love for her, and she for him. The drama grows from whether or not Romeo and Juliet can find a way to be together. By finding a way to be together, in defiance of every obstacle, they prove the premise of the story. What's at stake is whether their love can defy all obstacles, and, by extension, offer the audience an experience of great love.

The pitfall for inexperienced writers? That they confuse what's at stake for individual characters with what's at stake in their stories. Thus, they fail to make what's at stake visible and concrete. Consequently, the actions of their characters do not move their stories toward a dramatic resolution. If the consequences of a character's actions are unclear, a story's drama comes across as weak or diffuse. Such stories appear to be of no particular consequence, populated by characters working to achieve goals that have no unity of purpose.

To demonstrate how what's at stake can be made concrete, consider the movie *Die Hard*[35]. The premise for the story is:

Courage in the face of adversity leads to renewal.

On the surface, this is about a lone New York detective, John McClane, trapped in a building taken over by terrorists. What's visible on the screen is the fighting among McClane, the L.A. police, the FBI, and the terrorists. But what's really at stake is whether McClane can get back together with his wife. By reuniting with her, he proves the premise, that having the courage to overcome adversity leads to the renewal of their love.

All the action of *Die Hard* serves as obstacles to McClane shaping the story's outcome in a way desirable to him. The fiery, explosive spectacle makes visible the obstacles he must overcome and the lengths he will go to overcome them.

What's at stake in *Die Hard* draws in viewers to emotionally invest in the outcome. By proving its premise, the story lets its audience experience the fulfillment when McClane and his wife reunite. In the second *Die Hard* film there's still a strong connection between McClane and his wife; in the third, and weakest film, none at all. With the fourth film McClane fights to rescue his daughter, making the action more personal and resonant.

A story like *Die Hard* is more than the sum of its visible action: a lone cop battling terrorists. It's a story that raises an emotional issue that viewers are led to feel invested in. Thus, the film promises a story-like experience of the power of renewal, and fulfills that promise. Its fiery explosions and spectacle are built on a strong foundation. Spectacle without that foundation generally doesn't attract a wide audience, for example, in *Die Hard III*.

In *Spiderwick Chronicles*[36], the children of a family going through a divorce move with their mother into a decrepit mansion. The family is splintering and unhappy; the oldest son has tremendous issues with anger and impulse control. He wants to abandon his mother and sibling to live with his father. When he discovers a book that opens his eyes to a world of fairies, trolls, ogres, and other hidden creatures, he puts his family at grave risk. As they must work together to survive, the family re-bonds.

The premise is:

Overcoming a shared catastrophe leads to renewal.

What's at stake is whether these families can overcome this catastrophe, which sets the stage for this story. The plot revolves around how, and if, this re-bonding will happen, or what might prevent it. The action of the plot—the difficulties the children and their parents face—escalates the drama over how what's at stake will be resolved. The consequence of these families not overcoming this catastrophe is death. Because this story has a happy ending, these children and families prove the premise, and what's at stake is fulfilled in an uplifting way.

If what's at stake over your promise reaching fulfillment is something an audience wants and needs to believe, the story is emotionally engaging.

In *Batman Forever*[37], what's at stake is that Bruce Wayne (Batman) finds a way to integrate the two sides of his personality. This gives direction to what kind of characters populate the story. The Riddler and Two-Face make visible his inner conflict. Robin as well as Bruce Wayne's therapist also forces him to confront his need to integrate his personality.

The action builds to a climax when The Riddler and Two Face confront Batman with making a choice to save either Robin, his new companion, or Kidman, Bruce Wayne's potential lover. The action here makes visible what's at stake. Can Wayne-Batman integrate as one personality in time to save both his psychiatrist and his sidekick? Because Wayne-Batman succeeds in integrating his personality, he is able to save Robin and Kidman.

In *The Accidental Tourist*[38], Macon struggles to deal with his grief over his son's death. In *Lethal Weapon*[39], what's at stake for detective Martin Riggs is resolving his grief over his wife's death. The end of the film shows him at her graveside, finally able to let go of his grief and live again. *Good Grief*, by Lolly Winston, is also about a character overcoming her grief, but the "action" revolves around shifts in feelings and foreplay with a new boyfriend, not crazy stunts and gun-play.

Within the main question of what's at stake might be dozens of individual issues and conflicts that are raised and resolved as a story progresses. The resolution of these events advances the story toward its fulfillment. If this is not true, they should be eliminated. Just as characters can have something at stake, a scene can also present something at stake. In *Batman Forever*, Bruce Wayne goes to a party where Enigma demonstrates a device that will reveal Bruce Wayne's identity. Just as Bruce Wayne enters, Two Face crashes the party. In this scene, several things are at stake for several of the characters: for Two Face, it's finding and killing Batman; for Enigma, it's unmasking Bruce Wayne; for Wayne-Batman, it's keeping his identity masked; for Robin, it's his desire to confront Two Face; for the therapist accompanying Bruce Wayne, it's resolving her feelings for both Bruce Wayne and Batman.

All of these issues play out in the scene. All push the story forward to resolve what's ultimately at stake: Wayne-Batman integrating his dual nature. In any story, individual scenes have a specific focus and purpose, with a discernible outcome that acts to shape a story's course and outcome. In totality, the scenes of a story advance it toward its fulfillment across a range of levels, plot, promise, and character goals. Understanding what's at stake and how to make it visible offers you another tool to ensure your story resonates with an audience. How can you do this?

Put your characters into a situation where they react with

strong feelings. Feelings that compel them to take action.

As your plot heightens the impact of what's at stake for your characters, the reactions of your characters should change. Revelations about what drives your characters should become deeper. Actions compelled by these revelations are more forceful, more desperate. Feelings should become deeper and more potent.

Many stories have a character whom the main character can talk to about feelings or plans that shape events, like Sam in *Lord of the Rings*[40], or the patrolman John McClane speaks to over a walkie-talkie in *Die Hard*. In Hollywood films, that's often the purpose of a main character having a friend or confidant. It's a way to let audiences know what characters feel.

Create characters who act out their feelings when they've resolved what's at stake in your story.

If you want to see an example of what happens when what's at stake is introduced at the end of a story, watch *The Mothman Prophecies*. In that film, what's at stake for the main character—that he find a way to escape his life revolving around investigating supernatural oddities—is revealed at the end of the film. Most of what precedes that moment is artificial drama, the movement of a digital clock shot at a strange angle to suggest something momentous is about to happen, but all that happens is time passes uneventfully. There are multiple POV shots that suggests a supernatural creature is flying through the sky, ob- serving events below...but nothing comes of this.

I once broke down a film that was used in the Mystery Science 3000 series (with characters mocking bad movies). After every scene, I paused the film and asked the class, what's at stake here? What's the point of this movie? No one could ever answer the question.

When the movie **Snow Falling on Cedars** came out to weak reviews, I took the film to my screenwriting class and paused after every scene in the first twenty five minutes and asked, 'What is this story about? What's at stake for these characters?" No one knew.

In the documentary *The September Issue*, what drives the

main character, the senior editor at Vogue, only comes out at the end of the film. What drives her assistant—who fights to get the photo shoots she values into the issue—are immediate and passionate. She registers in a way the central character in the documentary never does. What's at stake for her is always accessible and apparent.

Big-budget Hollywood films that fail to satisfy an audience are often object lessons in what goes wrong when what's at stake in a story is weak or diffuse, or off-stage for most of a film to create a dramatic revelation.

In your stories, ask yourself, how do you make visible what's at stake in your opening scenes?

How do you make visible how your characters feel about what's at stake in your story?

When you can clearly communicate that something is at stake in your opening scenes, you let your audience know you understand how to tell a dramatic story.

If you fail, you're letting your audience know you don't understand the craft of storytelling.

Creating characters who act to resolve what's at stake over clearly presented dramatic issues arising from a story's promise is a sure path to writing dynamic stories.

Chapter Questions

What's at stake in your story?

What's at stake for the main character in your story?

What's at stake for the character who opposes your main character?

How do you resolve what's at stake in your story?

What events make it clear what's at stake for your main character?

What events make it clear what's at stake for the character who opposes your main character?

What *Is* Conflict?

On the surface, conflict appears to be characters in opposition, events in collision, ideas in a battle for supremacy. Just as with trying to understand a plot based on what it appears to be rather than what it is, trying to understand what conflict is by describing what it looks like leads to a faulty understanding of conflict.

Conflict in a story is a manifestation of a story's movement. When a storyteller creates movement toward resolving some compelling idea, issue, character goal, or event, and then blocks that movement, the result is conflict. By creating conflict around an issue that resonates with both characters and audience, the storyteller heightens the dramatic effect of a story.

The catch is, if characters aren't collectively moving toward something—a personal goal, an outcome for events—they cannot block each other or otherwise have a discernible reason to come into contact and conflict. Such characters are simply in the service of a plot, but not acting on their own dramatic truths.

Just as character details that serve no discernible dramatic purpose weaken a story, conflict that serves no purpose is ultimately dramatically inert. Random, purposeless conflict fails to fuel the advance of a story toward resolution and fulfillment. It's sitting in a car that isn't moving, even if the car is on fire and the people inside are fighting to get out.

When a character is designed to feel compelled to overcome the obstacles that block him or her, the result is escalating conflict. Elements that create that blocking effect serve to escalate the drama over whether and how a story will advance. Stories that lack events that block their advance lack conflict. Thus, the actions of characters that do not operate around advancing or blocking movement fail to create a discernible quality of story-like conflict (conflict that heightens drama) for an audience.

Conflict only rings true when it serves a dramatic purpose. Otherwise, it's a flame that doesn't burn, an explosion with no force, heated dialogue spoken with no volume.

The conflict around a story's advance is not necessarily physical. It can involve ideas or feelings, or it can revolve around a struggle for understanding or even around a set of beliefs being tested or explored. Conflict can also be generated by focusing on what blocks characters from gaining the insights that enable them to overcome the obstacles that block their path.

The issue here is that the storyteller comprehend the movement toward resolution and fulfillment and how and why it is carried out by its characters and events. In that sense, conflict and movement are a separate if interwoven issue from the goals and conflict that drive particular characters. It is because characters and their goals do entwine with what's at stake that their actions generate a quality of story-like conflict with a discernible purpose. Because the actions of Romeo and Juliet prove their love for each other in spite of any obstacles, the conflict highlights the fulfillment of the story's premise in a dramatic way.

Only when characters are willing to engage in conflict do their actions communicate that what's at stake has value to them. Therefore, conflict is the pulse, the life force, of a healthy story. One that lacks that pulse is dead because no one cares enough about its promise or its outcome to act.

Conflict, then, is not simply two characters with opposing goals. A manuscript filled with such characters often fails to create the effect of story-like conflict. Only when the conflict at the heart of a story serves a dramatic purpose (generating resolution and fulfillment for an audience, and a heightened release of narrative tension) does it create the effect of a story.

To understand the conflict at the heart of your story, you must understand what fuels the advance of your story and what blocks that advance. Then, you should populate your story with characters who will not be blocked. Who will not be denied. Who will not be resisted. Who will not be put down as they try and shape the outcome of your story's promise.

Characters who have opposing dramatic truths are naturally in conflict. For example, a character who wants to be rooted in a particular time or place will be in conflict with a character who insists they move. A character determined to avoid being in love will be in conflict with a character who demands love. A character who wants freedom will be in conflict with someone who seeks to oppress him or her.

In the Harry Potter novels, the narrative tension revolves around Harry being a wizard and having a place to fit into that world, and the Dursley's hatred of magic and their desire to block Harry from that world. Harry Potter novels, no matter that they are aimed at a young audience, are chronicles of relentless narrative tension and powerful conflict.

In *Blade Runner*[41], artificial humans have developed a stronger will to live than the humans trying to destroy them. Their great desire to live radiates from the screen. The Blade Runner hunting them becomes conflicted when he discovers just how human-like the replicants are; and that he must kill a female replicant he's fallen in love with.

In *Avatar*, the main character must choose between his loyalty to his military commander and humanity over the aliens he has come to identify with.

In Allen Esken's novel *The Life We Bury,* a young man with a bi-polar mother and severely autistic brother goes to college to try and create a better life for himself. The novel opens with his mother who self-medicates with alcohol arrested and demanding his college money for bail.

In life, we avoid conflict and the tension it unleashes. In stories, characters often initiate conflict at every turn. That conflict heightens both a story's narrative tension and the power of the release of that tension offers an audience. If you want a large audience, learn how to put your characters into conflict that involves and consumes them.

If you give your characters the freedom and will to engage in deeply felt conflict, you give your audience a powerful gift.

Chapter Questions

- Why are your characters willing to engage in conflict to shape the outcome of your story?
- What events block your characters from achieving their goals?
- What conflicts do you avoid in life, and how does that impact the kind of conflict you enjoy experiencing in stories?
- What kinds of conflict do you enjoy in life? Find arousing? Stimulating?
- Describe the conflict around your characters shaping the outcome of your story's promise.

Escalating Your Story's Conflict

Because characters feel the pull of what's at stake in a story and over resolving their dramatic truths, they act to shape a story's outcome. As the storyteller deliberately increases the obstacles they must overcome, the characters must act with greater determination. The result is dramatic action in the form of escalating conflict.

To explore the relationship between character goals, premise, and conflict, consider *Romeo and Juliet* once more. The conflict arises from the fact that Romeo and Juliet are *deliberately* separated by those who hate. Because Romeo and Juliet believe in love but belong to families who are in love with hate, there can be no compromise. These characters have opposing dramatic truths.

If Romeo and Juliet can find a way to be together, love is able to defy all the obstacles that hate puts in its path. Conversely, if Romeo and Juliet cannot find a way to fulfill their love, the story would prove that hate is stronger than love. A story's audience generally desires a fulfilling outcome—that love overcomes hate—even if it means the death of Romeo and Juliet. Their deaths in the cause of love heighten the story's dramatic impact exactly because they *are* willing to die to prove their love.

For Romeo and Juliet, what's at stake is not so much the love between them, as the idea of proving the power of their love to themselves. To prove the power of their love, Romeo and Juliet must find a way to be together, no matter the cost. Their conflict is internal as well as external. They are in conflict around living up to their own perceptions of what love should be.

Introducing Romeo and Juliet during a family feud is what is meant by *in medias res*, i.e. in the middle of things. From the opening moments, Shakespeare generates a sense of conflict around the outcome of Romeo's actions. That Romeo is in conflict in his world is not something that must be established so much as managed.

To intensify and heighten the story's conflict, the Capulets and Montagues are bound together not just by hatred but by physical proximity. Any action on one character's part compels a reaction by another character. The reaction always serves to escalate the conflict by creating further obstacles that Romeo and Juliet must overcome.

A story with unripe characters has characters who stand inert and unmoving, no matter how much the storyteller dashes around flinging adjectives and adverbs. This kind of effort at description routinely fails to create the effect of real conflict. Unripe characters are dramatically inert because their actions do not advance the story. Their superficially conflict-fueled actions offer an audience no reason to internalize their goals because they do not revolve around a discernible dramatic purpose.

Because a character's actions tie into a premise, blocking the movement of characters causes an escalating level of conflict. This makes a story's drama visible and concrete. That is the purpose of a plot. The escalation in dramatic tension it generates for a story's resolution creates a more deeply felt state of fulfillment for its audience.

As characters act with greater determination, they reveal the feelings and needs that drive them. Because an audience can more easily invest in emotionally accessible characters, conflict-driven characters are desirable to an audience. Through identifying with characters presented in deeply felt states of emotion, the audience also shares their heightened state of feelings. A story that lacks conflict often fails to set up those states of charged emotions or intense thoughts and sensory experiences and risks denying an audience a prime reason for entering a story's world.

Storytellers *design* the environments their characters operate to block a characters ability to advance toward a goal. Storytellers deliberately design a story's environment with as much purpose as they describe other elements of a story—to make more potent and dramatic its effect on a story's audience. Harry Potter, for example, goes to school at Hogwarts, a magical place where inanimate objects often come to life.

Scrooge is taken into an environment—spiritual realms—where he is powerless to avoid confronting his past, present, and future. Dorothy in *The Wizard of Oz* must overcome obstacles in an environment shaped by her private fears. Cinderella struggles to exist in a world where her beauty is a threat and an affront to her stepsisters and mother.

The main character in *Ironman* is an irresponsible wastrel, but when he's held against his will and forced to build a weapon for terrorists, he develops a new respect for being responsible. It's a muscular action film. It's sequel demonstrates what happens when a story's central conflict is weakened through the introduction of a buffoonish character, another arms dealer who opposes the main character.

Lisbeth, the main character in the Steig Larrson trilogy, must fight to survive the men who abuse her, starting with an abusive father and then an abusive, male-oriented system for dealing with juvenile offenders. But when she is aroused to combat, she fights with every fiber of her being.

A story fueled by escalating conflict compels characters to achieve goals and break through to a new sense of who they are. This epiphany makes the fulfillment of a story both potent and dramatic. Rocky's courage to fight Apollo Creed and remain on his feet at the end of the fight gives him a new sense of self-respect. Dorothy, by confronting her fears, comes to appreciate who she is, and to appreciate her parents and friends. Harry Potter, by fighting for what he believes, finds a place in life he can fit in, at least until the next sequel.

In *The Kite Runner*[42], the main character finds himself in hand-to-hand combat with the bully who raped his step brother as a young boy. By saving the son of the step brother, he can begin to heal.

In *The Glass Castle*, the narrator is angry at her mother for giving in to her alcoholic husband's demands for drinking money while his children go hungry. When her mother goes off for a few months, she discovers what it's like to deal with the father's pleadings and threats for money. She gives in just like the mother even though this sours her life-long feelings of love for him.

These characters take audiences on story journeys fraught with dramatic conflict. In turn, that conflict makes each character's journey all the more dramatically fulfilling.

Chapter Questions

> What conflict is inherent in fulfilling your story's promise?
> How do you introduce the conflict at the heart of your story?
> How does the goal of your main character put him or her into conflict with either the other characters in your story or with himself or herself?
> Can you describe the conflict at the heart of your favorite story?
> Can you describe the conflict at the heart of your life?
> Can you see how your conflicts in life affect what kinds of stories are more emotionally or thoughtfully engaging for you?

The Relationship Between Stories and Ideas

The relationship between a story and the ideas embedded in it is both subtle and profound. My objective is to help writers perceive the relationship between a story and the ideas that bring it to life. When writers confuse this issue, they come to believe that if they create a story with the required number of ideas, or base a story on ideas that are original or unique, they will create the effect of a dramatic story. That is not true. A storyteller creates the effect of a story by understanding the process of how to arrange its elements—its ideas, characters, events—to create a discernible, dramatic progression toward resolution and fulfillment.

A thoughtful storyteller can be taught to see that the elements of a story can also represent ideas. Consider Romeo and Juliet. Romeo and Juliet convince us that great love can defy even death. Romeo does this by wooing Juliet, gaining her love, and dying to prove his love for her. Juliet, finding Romeo dead, joins him in death, so proving her love for him. The characters in this story take concrete actions that prove the premise of the story, and consequently the story's audience is led to experience the power of great love.

A central issue in this story, however, is also the idea of love.

What does it mean to love someone the way Romeo loves Juliet? Is it right that his feelings should lead him to act in a way that brings tragedy to his family? What does Romeo owe his family? His clan? Should his allegiance be to them or to Juliet? What does Juliet owe her clan? Her father?

These are some of the ideas the story explores. By raising and exploring ideas that arise from what's at stake, it becomes clear that these ideas are rooted in—arise from acting out—the story's premise. Because this story's ideas are rooted in and arise from its premise, how they are presented serves to create a quality of discernible advance toward resolution and illumination. Every idea must operate to make a story's advance visible and concrete. Ideas that don't serve that purpose are superfluous and dramatically inert, no matter how they might appear in isolation.

As part of this process of making a distinction between story and idea, consider that the premise of *Romeo and Juliet* can also be seen as an idea, an idea about love that has within it still other ideas. By how these ideas are presented, they become part of the process of the story dramatically offering illumination around the idea of love. Because a story like *Romeo and Juliet* represents ideas as well as characters and events, directors and actors can choose to emphasize a particular idea or ideas. One version of the play could emphasize the idea of whether Romeo should have been more subservient to his clan instead of to his feelings. Another could emphasize Juliet's rebelling against her parent's arrangement of her marriage, thus showing that the issue of a woman having control of her fate is not just a current one. The idea that young people should have some right to choose a mate would be in the service of the story. In a culture where it was unthinkable for a young couple to have any say about whom they marry, the "idea" of *Romeo and Juliet* might fail to carry dramatic weight, might risk not affecting its audience on an emotional level, or might not generate any interest over the story's outcome. Or, the ideas of the play might seem so threatening—young couples disobeying their parents—the play would be met by a host of negative reactions, or disbelief.

A director of the play could even change the ideas of *Romeo and Juliet* so they have an outcome and effect entirely different than what it appears Shakespeare intended. Juliet could be played as another young man, or a woman of another race. Similarly, a skilled actor might interpret a character in a way that brings out ideas not necessarily apparent in the text. This isn't so much changing a story as bringing to life ideas latent in its text. Hamlet and Richard the III are other Shakespeare plays that have been transported to different times and cultures.

Conversely, when actors fail to understand the ideas of a story—and the dramatic truths of its characters—they can act—or be directed to act—in a way that brings characters to life, but not in a way that relates to the ideas that other characters represent, or that arise from the story's premise. There's no strong sense of a collective purpose, hence, no strong sense of conflict or drama. The end result is a play or movie that feels muddled or confused about its intentions.

The writer, director, or actor who injects ideas into a story that serve no purpose weakens it, no matter how insightful the ideas.

The storyteller designing story elements must perceive the quality of movement that those ideas generate. When blocking that movement, the storyteller must choose the ideas that best serve as obstacles to a story's movement. Characters who represent ideas about the power of love in *Romeo and Juliet* are blocked by characters who represent ideas about the power of hate.

In *The Plague*[43] by Camus, the story is about how middle-class people deal with the certainty of impending death when their city is quarantined after an outbreak of the plague. Camus' *The Stranger*[44] is about alienation. A young man shoots an Arab for reasons that aren't clear to those who investigate the crime.

Dorothy, in *The Wizard of Oz*, is aided by characters who represent ideas about intelligence, courage, and love. The yellow brick road is symbolic of the idea that life is a journey, and that it is only by making that journey that we discover who we really are. The tornado embodies Dorothy's conflicted feelings.

A simple story might operate with a few ideas plainly on its surface, i.e., good in conflict with evil. A thoughtful story might have characters, events, and actions that represent layers of ideas about life, good, and evil.

The writer who prefers to create a story that operates more purely as a work of ideas must learn to see a story's characters, events, and environment as embodying ideas. Ideas that, because of how they are arranged, create a quality of movement toward an illumination of their dramatic purpose.

A story told through ideas creates characters and events that represent those particular ideas. Through their actions, such characters prove the main dramatic idea at the heart of a story's premise. *Animal Farm*[45] is an example of a story of ideas where characters represent not just themselves, but also ideas about the larger society. A premise for *Animal Farm*:

> *The misuse of power leads to misery and destruction.*

Note how the story's dramatic idea revolves around power. Its movement deals with what the misuse of power leads to, and its fulfillment is reflected in the resulting misery and destruction. As the animals' actions shape the outcome of the its ideas, readers are engaged both emotionally and thoughtfully by the story's fulfillment of its core idea.

The film *Splice* revolves around the idea of what can happen when scientists play god. In this film, a young husband and wife who are scientists create a new life form and can't bring themselves to destroy it when they lose their research funding. The new life form grows up to be an odd, girl-like being that is not quite human. When the creature decides it's time to mate with the husband, tragedy ensues.

While science fiction is identified with space opera stories like Star Wars, there has always been a vein of science fiction that thoughtfully explores what it means to be human in new and different worlds. Another vein of stories are alternative histories like Steve Barnes' *Lion's Blood*, where America is settled by an

Islamic Africa that has an advanced technology, while slaves are imported from Ireland and Europe, which is backwards and rural. William Gibson became associated with a style of writing called cyber-punk, set in a future world where humans and computers were joined. A more fanciful vein is Steampunk, set in a Victorian time but with advances in technology. Mary Rosenblum writes about what life will be like having thousands of people living in cramped quarters with no privacy on a space station in her novel *Horizons*.

When I was young, books like *Brave New World*, about a genetically designed human race, and *1984*, about a world of tyranny, were required reading.

Great artists like Joyce, Woolf, Faulkner, and Austen write stories on this dual level of ideas and emotions progressing toward a fulfilling resolution. On the most accessible level, their stories revolve around human needs such as love, hate, the need to matter, redemption, and rebirth. On a deeper level, each artist's unwavering perceptions of life comments on our world and the ideas that underlie the why of our beliefs about love, hate, the need to matter, and so on. Great artists who explore this deeper level through stories have great powers of insight, but their ideas must also revolve around a story premise. Otherwise, their ideas, no matter how brilliant, would fail to create the effect of a story's dramatic movement toward the resolution, fulfillment, and illumination of some facet of the human condition.

What happens when writers confuse ideas with the effect of a story is that they assemble characters who represent ideas. These characters act in clearly symbolic ways. But the actions of the characters don't create the effect of a story because they are not arranged to create movement toward illumination.

That fundamental issue of what a story is and how its elements must be arranged to create the effect of a story must be identified and respected. Even when the storyteller's only aim is to create a contest between good and evil in an action film, the ideas must be at the service of the story.

I'm often approached by people who have an idea for a screenplay or novel with the offer that if I turn their idea into a best-selling novel or hugely successful movie we'll split the profits, as if one idea is equal to a year of my creative life and labor. I always pass on such projects. Many people don't realize their great story idea is a half-remembered plot from an episode of Barnaby Jones, or that their idea has been done over and over on television, or their unique science fiction concept was considered overdone and played out in the 1940s.

What comes first, the story or the idea? My answer is the story. An understanding of storytelling allows storytellers to turn ideas into stories. The storyteller who perceives the relationship of a story's elements to its deepest dramatic issue understands how to blend and arrange his or her story's ideas, character, environment, and events in a satisfactory mix. Every idea can then be used in its rightful place in a story.

Chapter Questions

What do you consider to be the central idea of your story?
How do you introduce the central idea of your story in a dramatic way?
How do the characters of your story embody its ideas?
What would you say is the central idea that embodies your life? Your needs in life?
How does that central idea or those needs impact the types of story ideas you find engaging?
What story ideas affirm your ideas about life?
What ideas challenge your ideas about life?

Thrust and Counter-Thrust

When a story begins with events in conflict, characters in collision, ideas challenging each other—it begins a process I call thrust and counter-thrust. *Romeo and Juliet* is an example of this.

The play opens with two kinsmen of the house of Capulet on a street talking about their hatred of the Montagues. Within moments, men of the Montague clan happen by. An insult is hurled, a brawl erupts, members of both clans join in the fray.

This is the first active thrust of the story. It quickly introduces the hatred and feuding between the families. It doesn't *tell* us about their feuding; it acts out the ferocity of the generations-long feud.

Dramatically, this opening thrust leads to the appearance of the Prince of Verona who declares that the next person to break the peace risks death. This is the counter-thrust.

Another aftermath is that someone asks where Romeo is. His family is concerned for his physical safety. It is revealed that he has been seen alone and obviously unhappy. A clansman is sent to find out why. He finds Romeo, and, after some quick probing, discovers he is lovesick over Rosalind. So we have an answer to the question, what's bothering Romeo? That small thrust of the story is resolved.

The clansman and Romeo come across an unlettered servant who asks Romeo to read an invitation list to a masked ball. Rosalind's name is on the list of the ball being hosted by the Capulets. Romeo, lovesick, ignores the danger and immediately goes to the ball. There he meets Juliet, a Capulet, and falls in love.

That thrust carries the action of the story through to the counter-thrust, the complications that ensue from their illicit love.

One sees this process of thrust and counter-thrust in the openings of many well-designed stories. For example, *The Wizard of Oz* has Dorothy taking action to save Toto. That thrust takes her into Oz. *Rocky* opens with Rocky being booed in a fight for beating a man after he's down. After the fight, someone yells into his face that Rocky's a bum. That first thrust of the story takes us to a counter-thrust, where Rocky is being paid for winning the fight, but most of the money is deducted for various expenses. Rocky's victory is empty.

Lethal Weapon opens with a woman appearing to commit suicide, then moves on to a suicidal detective, Martin Riggs, with a gun in his mouth. One thrust—the woman falling or jumping out the window—pulls us into the story's plot; the other thrust pulls us into the story about why Riggs wants to die.

The Exorcist[46], by William Peter Blatty, opens with a quick thrust: a Jesuit priest realizing that an ancient evil is manifesting itself in the world and that he will be drawn into battling it. It's not a battle that will happen later; it's a battle that is beginning as the story opens. That thrust leads us to the house where the battle will take place.

Funerals For Horses, by Catherine Ryan Hyde, opens with a young woman making a decision to find her missing brother.

The Accidental Tourist, by Anne Tyler, opens with Macon and Sarah driving onto a divided highway as they return early from a vacation meant to rekindle their marriage also heading down a divided highway. The first chapter ends with Sarah asking for a divorce.

The Bad Beginning[47], by Lemony Snicket, opens with the deaths of the parents of the story's three children, Violet, Klaus, and Sunny Baudelaire. Then the situation for the children gets infinitely (which in this context means as much as you can imagine and then some) worse.

The first Harry Potter novel, *Harry Potter and the Sorcerer's Stone*[48], opens by setting out the dramatic truth of the Dursley's, that they want above all else to be considered normal, but they have a terrible secret: Mrs. Dursley's sister is a witch. They loathe witchcraft and how it threatens their sense of mattering. Then, Harry Potter, the son who mysteriously survives the death of his parents at the hands of a powerful wizard, is dropped off at the Dursley's house to be raised in a world of muggles.

In Kristy Yorke's *The Secret Lives of the Sushi Club*, a novelist with a fading career turns the lives and secrets of her best friends into a best-selling novel. The public revelation of their inner lives becomes a goad for the characters to examine themselves and change.

In the movie *Safety Not Guaranteed*, an intern who isn't sure what to do with her life goes on an assignment to assist a reporter running down a story about a mysterious ad that suggests the possibility of time travel. She finds herself caught up in a quest that gives her life meaning.

In *Her*, a man who writes letters for strangers accepts an A.I. (artificial intelligence) operating system that will function as his girlfriend. He quickly finds himself falling in love and pushed to discover deeper truths about himself, all while not noticing his A.I. girlfriend is evolving to a point she will no longer be involved with him.

Each of these storytellers, in describing so clearly the movement of the characters as they act out the story's promise, drew audiences into their worlds.

Writers need to consider if the opening of their stories thrusts it forward in a way that is engaging to an audience. Conversely, if a story doesn't open with some kind of thrust, there's nothing for the characters to respond to. By giving characters something to respond to, they reveal who they are and what drives them.

A story doesn't have to open with a physical thrust. It might open with the thrust of an intriguing idea, or the thrust of some state of emotion that calls for explanation and resolution, or the thrust of a time and place so unique that an audience wants to know more.

Keep in mind that if by the time you've written your third sentence you aren't three steps into your story, you've given your audience three reasons to set your manuscript aside. That's why publishers, producers, and agents can generally read the first few pages of a manuscript and know if it's something they're going to reject or not. A writer who can't create scenes that dramatically thrust a story forward isn't going to miraculously display that talent on page ten or one hundred. Yes, by the time most screenplays have gotten to page twenty-five, most novels to page one hundred, and plays to the climax of their first act, the writer's plot devices generally have kicked in and begun supplying momentum to the story. It's just getting past that first twenty-five, forty, or one hundred pages that's an ordeal.

Understanding how to put a story's elements into play with a dramatic thrust on page one is one more tool in the storyteller's tool kit.

Chapter Questions

How does the action of the opening scenes serve to thrust your story forward?

What counter-thrust blocks your story's initial forward advance?

Why do your characters persevere when they are blocked?

Writing Dramatic Dialogue

If you want to write tight, spare, evocative dialogue, be clear about what your story is truly about, and what dramatic truths your character's embody. That way you can be sure each character's dialogue acts out your promise.

In the beginning of *The Accidental Tourist* the main character's sparring about driving in a storm becomes a request for a divorce. What they say speaks to how each is emotionally numb and bereft over the death of a son, and sets out the main issue of an emotionally numb character regaining the ability to feel. Thus, their dialogue moves the story forward.

This is important because readers or viewers first entering a story wants something that orients them. Dialogue that makes clear what's at stake provides this orientation. This is not to suggest characters turn to the audience and say, "This is what this story's about, this is why I'm here." That's too obvious. Instead, the writer must decide how best to dramatically introduce a story by what characters say and do; that is a part of the writer's craft. To accomplish that engaging beginning, a writer can have characters speak to the point of the dramatic purpose in a scene, not away from it.

To understand that process of writing to a dramatic point, consider that you're in a room attending a workshop on writing. A bomb goes off outside the room. Do you continue talking calmly about writing and what brought you to this workshop, or do react in a way that reveals your inner nature?

When characters react to what's at stake in a story as it exerts pressure on them, their actions naturally reveal who they are and how they view their situations. What's at stake in your story might not be as immediate as a bomb blast. It might be a quiet pressure on your characters. But it should still exert some kind of pressure on what your characters say.

Reservoir Dogs,[49] by Quentin Tarantino, opens with several armed robbers at a diner making small talk, but the viewers don't know they're armed robbers. In subtle, hip ways, however, the dialogue suggests what's at stake for these ambitious, ruthless men and their sparring to establish dominance in their pack. When we listen to these men talk, we hear a bomb ticking, even if we don't see it.

For those listening to the opening dialogue of *Reservoir Dogs*, it could be compared to being in a roller-coaster car climbing up that first steep hill. Those in the car—the viewers of that opening scene—don't necessarily know what's in store for them. When, at the conclusion of that scene we see that one of these men carries a gun, that roller-coaster car we're in hits the last stop before it takes those in the car on a screaming, thrilling ride.

Tarantino, or any storyteller, is the builder of that roller-coaster ride. Dialogue that doesn't ring true or that doesn't suggest something is at stake over the outcome of an exchange offers no reason to pay attention; it's the idle chatter of people sitting in a roller-coaster car on flat ground, not moving. That kind of experience we can get from life; it's not what people want from a story.

Keep in mind the following to create well-written dialogue:

Consider how people talk when they find themselves in a dramatic, emotional situation. Their dialogue is often short and focused, to the point. Are the people riding on the roller coaster having relaxed discussions about life when instead they should be screaming or taunting each other or fighting to establish the superiority of their ideas? Or should they be laughing, crying, and holding on to each other for dear life as your story picks up speed and hits a blind turn? Characters' reactions to their environment should be reflected in their dialogue.

When characters are in a dramatic situation, they respond to each other; they are intensely aware of each other's presence.

To create dialogue with "voice," dialogue that feels unique and expressive of each character, avoid packed dialogue. Packed dialogue is dialogue that, to the reader, seems to ask for a response, but none is allowed. An example of packed dialogue:

> BIG MOUTH: "A bomb just went off…I have to call my wife…tomorrow's my birthday and I'll be 41…and this is my first roller-coaster ride!"

Note that any one line here calls for a response—if the writer actually was intending there be a conversation. The true purpose of the above dialogue is for the writer to use this character as a mouthpiece to get out information the writer feels is necessary to impart. Such dialogue is flat. It's flat because the only way a character can provide information to the audience is by no longer responding to the situation around him or her. In so doing, the character has detached from the story to do the bidding of the writer. The movement of the story at that moment comes to a stop. And if a reader is engaged by your movement, you've found a way, only part way through this roller-coaster ride, of bringing your roller-coaster car to a dead stop.

Dialogue should advance the story. That means if you have witty, forceful dialogue that doesn't serve some purpose in your story, you're in trouble. In *Last Action Hero*[50], from the time the character Danny is introduced to the moment he enters the movie world of Jack Slater, the dialogue is funny, sharp, witty, clean, and terse. But when Danny enters the movie within the movie, the dialogue stops revolving around the point of the story; consequently, it doesn't add anything. Much later in the film, the characters again act and react to the pressures of what's at stake in the story, and all that funny, tight, clean dialogue amounts to something. It advances the story and takes the film into that higher sphere it tried to find by being clever. In order that the stalled roller coaster pick up speed and provide the thrills it initially offered, you should edit out even clever dialogue when it serves no purpose.

In *The History Boys*[51], a teacher who has taught his students to think finds himself forced to collaborate with an instructor brought in to teach the boys how to be glib when they apply to attend a prestigious college.

Have characters say only what needs to be said. Don't automatically start a scene with characters making introductions unless that serves a dramatic purpose. Don't have characters address each other by name more than once unless you have a reason; repeating of names to no dramatic purpose gets old fast. Also, avoid dialogue that carries a scene to a weak ending. Audiences are very familiar with what needs to be said to move a scene forward. Many writers inadvertently let a scene dribble on with an extra line or two or three. Trust your readers to get the point.

The *Silence of the Lambs*[52] is a movie where the writer paid careful attention to what the actors could communicate with body language. When Clarice Starling enters an elevator with several hulking men, we don't need the writer to tell us about the world she's in and what kind of expectations her character must deal with.

Written English is fundamentally different from spoken English. Oxford dons speak very correct, formal English, but few others speak that way. I once critiqued a play by an Ethiopian writer and director who had worked as a cab driver in New York. The dialogue of the cab driver characters was strong, barbed, observant, and witty. But the writer had his main characters speak a more formal English that robbed them of vitality. I encouraged him to have his main characters speak with the same passion and feeling as his minor characters. Root out written English from your dialogue. It's almost always unnatural and stilted, unless your characters really are Oxford dons meeting in formal debate. I would suggest, however, that if a bomb went off in the middle of such a debate, it would affect how those Oxford dons spoke.

All characters should have a personal rhythm for speaking that is a reflection of their dramatic truth. This does not mean a writer should load up a character's dialogue with mannerisms as a way to suggest individuality. Too many insincere mannerisms often creates oddly artificial characters. But a dramatic truth should be animating your characters, giving them purpose. That dramatic purpose should be reflected in how characters voice thoughts and feelings.

Avoid having characters be too elusive in their speech. Unless it's well done, it can come across as dramatically flat, or worse, mystifying. Imagine in real life trying to carry on a conversation with someone who never quite gets around to making some clear point. Unless you have a compelling reason to do otherwise, let characters speak forcefully and directly about what's on their minds, or about what they want the other characters to think is on their minds. Once they've said what's on their minds, have other characters respond in a direct fashion.

The play *Betrayal*[53], by Pinter, starts with a relationship ending, then goes back in time one scene at a time to the beginning of the relationship. The conceit of the play adds great dramatic power to the dialogue that would have seemed more ordinary in a straightforward telling of the story.

In my award-winning play *The Baggage Handler*, two characters in the afterlife discover they can leave behind some of the baggage they are supposed to take into their next lives together. They scheme to outwit a baggage handler until they learn the real cost of their deception.

Trust your actors. In a film or play script, actors are trained to express feelings and moods with body language. Many beginning writers load their scripts and plays with reams of unnecessary dialogue to convey information that could be acted out.

If your characters don't have strong feelings that compel them to speak out about what's happening around them, why are they in your story? Unless they care about something or have something at stake that compels them to speak out, edit them out.

Finally, individual characters should have different tones of voice during the events of a story. An angry man will talk one way to his boss, another to his wife, another to his son, and still another to his daughter. A character with a sad voice might be elevated to a triumphant voice at the climax of your story. To have a character with only a single note "voice," no matter the circumstances, is most often to have created a plot device for the use of the writer. When all your characters have the same voice, they are extensions of you and probably lack their own dramatic truths.

A plot that heightens and makes visible what's at stake in a story, and that sets out dramatically which characters are achieving goals and which are losing out, allows characters to travel through various states of emotion—from anger to pain to ecstasy to grief to jubilation. The climax comes when the characters develop a different sense of themselves, a new voice.

Keep in mind when you write dialogue that actors love roles that give them a chance to play strong, dramatic characters. They want to feel pride in their work, be recognized for their craft. Even if you're writing a low-budget action-adventure movie, you should understand what your story is about. Write tight, clean dialogue that gives your actors a chance to show what they can do. They'll appreciate you.

If you're struggling with writing strong dialogue, remember the axiom about the three things that sell real estate: location, location, location. If you're struggling to write powerful dialogue, keep in mind the three main principles of writing powerful dialogue: reactions, reactions, reactions. Let your characters react to each other. Let loose with what they think and feel in a direct, forceful way that compels a response.

If you're writing scripts for a particular genre, action-adventure or romantic comedy for example, watch a movie in that genre. Pay close attention to how many exchanges of dialogue happen in individual scenes. Watch how the actors use body language to communicate information. Turn the sound off if that's what you need to do to see what's happening on the screen. Learn to see the story as it's told via visual images; don't get lulled into being a passive viewer who creates passive characters who tell each other the meaning of everything. As a writer, it's your job to dramatically shape the material that others will view.

Study movies, watch plays, take an acting class, even write a one-act play and direct it yourself as a staged reading for the public. Actors love to work with fresh material. Finding actors, even in small communities, is usually never more than a few phone calls away. Directing your own one-act play can teach you volumes about dialogue. Are you overlaying your feelings on a scene? Direct it for the twentieth time: you'll start to hear if the dialogue is alive and fresh. Well-written dialogue holds up over time. Weak dialogue quickly grates on the ears.

Do your actors stumble over the same lines again and again? Rewrite them. Listen to your actors when they tell you a line doesn't ring true or is difficult to say. If you can't find actors, ask a friend to help you read the dialogue from your script out loud. If you don't have a friend to help, do it yourself and record it, then play it back and listen to it. You're competing against people who will take the time to make their dialogue tight and clean.

If you want to write an action novel, read a popular action novel and see how the author handles dialogue.

Well-written dialogue invites readers and viewers into your story by promising them that what they'll hear has dramatic meaning and purpose.

Chapter Exercises

Write a scene with two characters who say something concrete about their dramatic truths in five words or less.

Write five exchanges of dialogue, with each character saying something to the other about his or her dramatic truth that provokes a response.

Write a scene with two characters who express anger. Write five exchanges. Keep each expression under ten words.

Write a scene with the same two characters sharing their true feelings toward each other for the first time. Again, keep the exchanges brief, under ten words.

Create characters who have opposing dramatic truths and put them into a room in a situation where both characters want something, but only one person can leave that room with what they both desire.

Write a scene with five exchanges of dialogue. Have two characters interrupt each other and not allow the other to finish a thought because each is so excited about what they are talking about.

section three

Outlining Your Story

(A outline diagram is posted on my website at http://www.storyispromise.com/storydiagrams.pdf. It is more detailed than the diagram in the book.)

Using Story Director^(TM) to Outline Your Story

(paragraphs double spaced in this section)

The ability to understand the dramatic purpose of every story element is an important tool. With such a tool, a writer has a method to check whether every event, character action, and plot device serves to dramatically advance a story toward the resolution and fulfillment of its promise.

For some writers, an outline is a beginning. For others, it is a tool for revision. For writers new to the craft of storytelling, outlining a popular story can be a method to internalize an understanding of how to tell a story.

This chapter includes a story diagram that outlines the dramatic elements of *The Lovely Bones*, by Alice Sebold. This is a deeply felt novel with a complex plot and wonderful story mechanics. The novel has a number of significant characters, each with his or her own dramatic truth and narrative tension. The story is advanced along a story and plot line by the collective actions of these characters, unlike some stories that revolve around one main character.

The objective of setting out the steps for outlining a story is:

1) It helps writers identify the issues that make for a well-told story: dynamic premise, clear introduction of a story's promise, engaging characters acting out of that promise, narrative tension, dramatic plot, and an understanding of how multiple characters can advance a story along a unified story and plot line.

2) It helps writers to see how a story is more than a sequential arrangement of events. It's a process whereby the story moves toward a dramatic state of resolution and fulfillment.

3) Perceiving the process of setting out the elements of a dramatic story, a storyteller can begin with a stronger foundation.

To start the outline process, write your premise across the bottom of a piece of paper, laid out horizontally.

(see diagram, page 117)

If you're having trouble creating a premise, refer to the chapter on Techniques for Creating a Story Premise.

Outline Notes

The premise for *The Lovely Bones*:

> A family's passage through deep grief leads to renewal.

What's at Stake

The next step is to identify what's at stake in your story.

Finish this sentence:

> "What's at stake in my story about love, courage, etc., is ...."

If you're still having trouble identifying what's at stake in your story, re-read the chapter about that process.

Outline Notes

> What's at stake in *The Lovely Bones* is whether a family will survive the bones of the family being broken when the youngest daughter is murdered.

Creating a Story Question

Once you are clear about what's at stake in your story, phrase that issue as a story question. This story question is then answered by the action of the story's events, characters, plot devices, arrangement of ideas, etc. For example, in *The Lovely Bones* what's at stake is whether the Salmon family will survive the murder of Susie.

The story questions that arises from what's at stake in the story are:

> Will Susie's family be able to heal from their deep grief over her murder?

You have to read to the end of the story to find the dramatic answer to that question.

Note: This is a story question. While it typically refers to the story's main character and his or her goals, in *The Lovely Bones* this question reaches out to everyone in the surviving family.

For the purpose of creating this story, its conflict is presented as a question, not a statement. The question of whether Susie's family will find healing and survive as a family is in doubt.

To set out your story question, finish this sentence:

> "The main dramatic question that arises from what's at stake in my story is ...."

Put your one sentence story question just below your premise.

Story Line

The story line for *The Lovely Bones* is represented on the diagram as a line above the premise.

Write a one paragraph story line for your story.

A story line for *The Lovely Bones* could be written as:

> *The Lovely Bones* is about the murder of Susie Salmon and how her death devastates her family. Each member of the family deals with their grief in different ways, all observed by Susie in a place called inter-heaven. With the passage of time, the broken family rebonds in a way that Susie refers to as the lovely bones, and Susie is able to move on.

The purpose of writing out the story line is for storytellers to be clear that every element of a story serves to advance it toward its resolution and fulfillment.

The beginning of this story, as identified in the story line above:

> The murder of Susie and its effect on her family, friends, and even her murderer.

The middle of the story line:

> How grief over Susie's death drives apart the members

of her family.

The end of the story line:

> How Susie's family finds healing, and Susie is able to let go of her family and move on.

Place a straight line above your story question to represent your story line.

Every element of your story should advance it along this line. Because each event advances a story around resolving and fulfilling an issue 'moving' to the audience, a story generates a quality of transporting its audience toward a desirable experience of feelings and thoughts.

In a story like *The Lovely Bones*, characters act out dramatic truths. For example, after Susie's death, her sister Lindsey practices 'hardening' herself, raising the question of whether she'll ever be able to be in an intimate relationship.

Ruth, a friend of Susie's, is made to feel ashamed of her awareness of Susie and other murdered women and girls, setting up Ruth's journey toward accepting who she is.

Susie's mother and father pull away from each other in their grief, raising a question of whether their marriage will survive.

The father tries to bury his guilt that he was not there to protect Susie, but his grief cripples him emotionally.

Susie's mother realizes she did not want Susie to be born and feels trapped in her role of mother. Like her husband, her guilt and grief cripples her.

The youngest son of the family, Buckley, takes on the role

of protecting his father and being his confidant.

Every significant character in the novel is impacted by Susie's death, and Susie's ability to observe the thoughts and feelings of everyone left behind on earth allows her to perceive each character's deepest truths.

Every significant character in a story should have something that connects them to the story's promise, story line, and plot line. For some authors, that means creating an outline before writing a story, or writing a novel, or play, or screenplay. For others, it means creating an outline after a story is written.

Plot Line

Just as a novel can have an overall story question, a novel can have an overall plot question. In *The Lovely Bones* that question is, will Susie's bones be found?

Outline Notes

A plot line for *The Lovely Bones* could read:

> When Susie Salmon is killed, her father comes to suspect a neighbor but can't convince the police to act on his suspicions. His seemingly irrational belief damages his relationship with his wife. When Susie's younger sister, Lindsey, also begins to suspects the neighbor, she breaks into his house and is almost caught, but not before she finds incriminating evidence. The break-in causes the killer to flee, but he is drawn back to this community because he blames Lindsey for his life on the run. Though he is not caught and the bones of Susie are never found, the broken bones of her family heal and the murderer meets an untimely end which is celebrated in heaven by his many female victims.

Note that this plot line identifies the obstacles that block the family from overcoming their grief, for example, the father's belief that the neighbor is a killer which wounds his wife; and that Susie's body is not found.

Write a one paragraph description of your story's plot line. Begin with the statement:

"The plot line of my story is ...."

Plot is concrete. Will Mr. Harvey be caught is concrete. Will Susie's mother return to the family is concrete.

In your plot line, identify what obstacles block the movement of your story.

To help you identify those obstacles, answer the following question:

"The obstacles that block my main character achieving his or her goals are ...."

As your main character seeks to attain goals, the story's plot should escalate the obstacles that block that character's movement. The passage of time increases the father's guilt and his wife's wound over not wanting Susie to be born.

To help you verbalize this process, finish the following sentence:

"The plot of my story escalates the obstacles my main character must overcome by ...."

Outline Notes

On the story diagram, the questions for the novel's

plot revolve, initially around whether Susie's body be found?
Will Mr. Harvey be found out?
Will Susie's mother leave her husband?
Will Mr. Harvey kill Lindsey?
Will Mr. Harvey be caught when he returns to his old neighborhood?

How To Start Your Story On Page One

What do you write to set your story into action on page one? There is probably no single question that more bedevils inexperienced writers. To discover the answer, consider these story openings:

Avatar opens by showing a young marine dreaming that he is flying over an exotic planet. He wakes to find himself in a crippled body and wonders if it would be possible to stay in the dream.

Pride and Prejudice introduces two characters who seem made for each other... except for their issues of pride and prejudice. Can they overcome those issues to be together?

The Girl with the Green Tattoo begins with an old man receiving a flower in the mail from an unknown person he believes to be the murderer of his niece.

Water for Elephants opens with a stampede of elephants in a carnival and a possible death.

By identifying what's at stake in your story and creating characters and events in need of resolution, you set your story into motion from its opening lines.

How you set out what's at stake in your story – in a manner subtle or blunt, through physical action, emotions in transition, a declaration of thoughts – is a personal preference. Only when what's at stake in your story is clearly communicated to your audience can they assign meaning to the actions of your characters.

If your audience has to wait forty pages to discover that Susie's family is being torn apart by grief, your story starts on page 41.

If Rocky's desire to prove he is somebody is withheld from the story's audience, the story only develops drama over its course and outcome when that comes out.

To guide you to answer the question of what sets your story into motion on page one, answer the following:

> "The dramatic issue at the heart of my story is ...."
>
> "..." is my main character, because his or her actions manifest the movement of my story by ...."
>
> In *The Lovely Bones*, the dramatic issue at the heart of the story is the grief that tears the family apart. The movement of the story is toward the healing of that grief.

Now, finish the following:

> "My opening scene sets my story about... (courage, renewal, rebirth, etc.) into motion on page one by ...."

Outline Notes

> In *The Lovely Bones*, Susie's death and ability to remain an observer of her family and friends creates a vehicle to explore this family's grief.

Plot Questions

Once writers can communicate a story line and plot line for their stories, they can set out the elements/events of their plots in relationship to their stories. Again, a plot should be recognized as an aspect of a story's movement.

What question, based on what's at stake in your story, do you set up in your first ten pages? In one sentence, explain how that question arises from what's at stake in your story.

> "The first obstacle that my main character must con front and overcome is ...."

To fit the story diagram onto a single page, I have limited the chapter questions to the most prominent. Every chapter of your book should generate drama over its outcome.

Outline Notes

> In *The Lovely Bones*, the first obstacle that Susie must deal with is thinking that she can change the lives of those she left behind on earth.
>
> For Susie's parents, the issue is that they are both broken at the same time and therefore can't help each other.
>
> Lindsey's identity at school comes identified with being the sister of the dead girl.
>
> Ruth's awareness of Susie after her murder is not acceptable to Ruth's mother.

Story and Characters

The story outline refers to those characters – or groups of

characters – who in the main affect the course and outcome of the story: Susie, Mr. Harvey, Lindsey, Ray, Buckley, Susie's mother and father, Len, the detective, and Ruth.

Answer the following:

> "In my story about ... my main character feels compelled to act because ...."

> "The dramatic purpose of the character who opposes my main character is ...."

Every character in a story should have a discernible dramatic purpose the storyteller can identify. For example, the characters who are Susie's friends – Ray and Ruth – are also impacted by her death.

Outline Notes

> In *The Lovely Bones*, the answers to these questions revolve around the story being about how a family deals with devastating grief, and how that death impacts others.

The characters who oppose Susie are Mr. Harvey and the grief others feel. Lindsey, for example, practicing 'hardening herself.'

Conflict

By binding together every character, a story's premise ensures that when characters act, they find themselves in conflict with other characters. Because only one person or group can shape the outcome over what's at stake in the story, this generates conflict.

It is a hallmark of a well told story that its conflict escalates the drama over its outcome.

For your outline notes, finish the following:

"The characters in my story are in conflict over what's at stake in it because ...."

"They feel compelled to resolve this issue no matter what price they must pay because ...."

"The following actions and events make visible and concrete my story's conflict ...."

"The following actions by my story's character's escalate the level of conflict in my story by ...."

Some of the most open conflict in *The Lovely Bones* is between Susie's father and Mr. Harvey, her murderer. Susie's murder also overwhelms the mother's ability to maintain a facade of being a good mother and shutting out her guilt that she didn't want Susie to be born.

Stories and Ideas

A major element of a story is the ideas and issues that arise from its premise. Most of the characters in *The Lovely Bones* could have, without Susie's death, led 'normal' lives. But the deep states of grief they go through force them to come to a deeper realization about who they are and what's important to them. Passing through this fire purifies them and gives them a deeper emotional life.

Is it better to lead a normal, peaceful life, or to be passed through this kind of fiery ordeal? In real life, many people are destroyed in these fires. In stories, they are often purified and become stronger. It's a reason some people prefer stories (even tv sitcoms) to real life.

Finish the following:

"The main idea at the heart of my story is ...."

Outline Notes

The ideas at dramatic play in *The Lovely Bones* are whether passing through grief can strengthen a family. Another significant idea is whether getting vengeance on a killer is necessary to move on.

Drama

Because the issue at stake in the story is raised as a question, the storyteller generates drama over its outcome. The more drama a story generates, the more the storyteller creates the effect of a page-turner: a novel an audience can't put down. Drama, however, is a fundamental effect of all stories. A story must develop drama to communicate that what's at stake has enough value that its characters are willing to engage in conflict to shape a story's course and outcome.

Finish this sentence:

"The drama in my story is generated by ...."

Outline Notes

Some of the drama in *The Lovely Bones* arises from the questions of whether Mr. Harvey will be caught and Susie's bones found.

Story Complications

Here is where the action of the story's plot can more clearly be seen.

In this story, Susie's mother leaves her family, forcing another major re-alignment, with Buckley becoming a confidant of his father.

Ruth comes to accept her gift of being a living chronicle of murdered women.

The purpose of putting your characters in a position where they must act with strength of emotion is so your audience experiences those states of potent action and feeling.

In your story outline, write:

> "By creating the following obstacles with my plot, my protagonist and those who aid the protagonist will be driven to stronger and stronger states of action ...."

When I speak of action, movement and determination here, I'm not speaking just of physical movement. This movement could be a movement of feeling, or a movement of thoughts, or toward illuminations of ideas.

Outline Notes

> Susie gains an understanding of what she meant to the others she left behind.

Complications

In a typical American commercial film, the story's characters reach a point where it seems courage will be defeated, that love will not prevail, that the ruthless and oppressive will overcome the noble and heroic. In his analysis of story structure, Syd Field, in his book, *Screenplay, Foundation of Screenwriting* [56], calls this plot point two, a point where all seems lost to the story's main character.

Considering plot point two from the perspective of movement, it signifies a story has moved to a place where those who have internalized the story most deeply fear it will not be fulfilled in a favorable way. The storyteller creates this effect for the very purpose of making a particular fulfillment, i.e., that courage does win the day, love does prevail, the noble person does overcome the unjust, that much more potent and dramatic.

For your outline, finish the following:

> "At this point, all seems lost to my main character because .... "

Outline Notes

> In *The Lovely Bones*, all seems lost when the mother leaves the family, it becomes clear Susie's bones will never be found and Mr. Harvey is still free to kill again.

Fulfillment

Moving past this point where all seems lost, a story can move ahead to its fulfillment. In a story about courage, this would be the time that courage would win the day. Through the actions of the story's characters, the story's premise is fulfilled.

For this part of your outline, finish the following:

> "The fulfillment of my story is ...."

> "The fullfillment of my story is made visible and concrete by the actions of the story's characters as they accomplish ...."

A distinction must be made here between the resolution of character goals and the fulfillment of a story. As a character's goals are resolved in a story's climax, the action of the story's plot is resolved. But it is by the action of the story's characters to resolve a story's promise that the story itself is fulfilled. That's why I say that the fulfillment of the story and the climax of its plot are two separate issues.

Now, at the end of this outline, look again at your story premise. Did the elements of your story serve that premise? Along the way of creating the outline, you might discover you had a different premise in mind. Resolving that kind of issue is the purpose of an outline.

Outline Notes

> The fulfillment of *The Lovely Bones* is that Susie's family heals from its grief and Susie is able to move on in the after-life.

Diagram

(This is a partial diagram designed to fit on one page; to see the full diagram go to: http://www.storyispromise.com/storydiagrams.pdf)

Story Diagram for *The Lovely Bones*

By Bill Johnson

Intro of Story   Story Movement   Story's Fulfillment

Story Line ----------> ---------------->----------> ------> X

Grief   Healing

Susie's death
  Ray suspected____
    Father beaten ____
      Mr. Harvey flees _____
        Mother leaves_____
          Susie intimate with Ray _____
            Mr. Harvey's death_____

Story Question: Will Susie's family survive their grief over her death?
Plot Question: Will Susie's bones be found?

Summary

Now that you have an outline and notes for your story, my last questions for you are:

Does your story question arise from what's at stake in your story?

Do the opening scenes of your story introduce your main character and his or her issues and goals in a way that makes clear the connection to what's at stake in your story?

Do you see how creating a series of questions around resolving issues and events draws your audience through your story to experience its resolution and fulfillment?

Do the obstacles that block the movement of your story operate to escalate the drama over your story's outcome?

Do the events mentioned in your story line and in your plot line intermesh in a way that together they operate to advance your story toward its resolution and fulfillment?

Does the action of your story resolve and fulfill your story's promise?

The purpose of this outline process is that you be able to answer these questions BEFORE you begin writing.

If it's difficult for you to work through the sequence of your story before you write it, some writers set out story, plot and character issues and ideas on 3 x 5 cards they can then easily rearrange. You can write ideas for scenes on individual cards, develop interesting character issues, think up dialog as it comes to you, without feeling like you're making a commitment to any particular idea, event or character action. For some people, this process helps free up their creative juices. Once you've collected a number of scenes, you might then use the outline process to give them a sense of dramatic order.

Some screen writing programs allow writers to create outline notes alongside a script or incorporate notes into a script. These can allow you to create story notes as you write a script.

Some writing programs ask a series of questions designed to help you better understand the elements of your story.

Or, it might work best for you to write a complete draft of your screenplay, novel or play, then use the outline process to help you with rewrites.

If your main character embodies your issues in life, are you making that character's issues and goals accessible? Or, are readers finding your main character diffuse and your minor characters more interesting?

The overall goal here is to help writers understand better how the elements of a story inter mesh to create the effect of a well-told story. Once writers learn how to outline a story, they can begin a particular story with an understanding of how best to dramatically set out its elements. The result is a story that starts from a solid foundation, instead of a story that never quite overcomes a weak beginning. Just as important, a story designed to open with a strong, clear dramatic focus communicates to its audience that this is a story world created by someone who understands the art of storytelling.

Such stories naturally draw in and sustain the attention of an audience.

The Story Director outline process is designed to guide writers to see clearly what the promise of their story is. To perceive what questions arise from a promise being acted out. To understand what sets a story into motion from its opening lines. To perceive which details most clearly and potently evoke the movement of a story. To understand how to transfer the tension over a story's course and outcome from its characters to its audience. To perceive what kind of fulfillment will offer an audience relief from the tensions generated by a well-told story.

The ability to understand what words, which images, which characters, what dialog, which events most dramatically set a story into motion around resolving its promise...

...which words, images, characters, events and dialog sustain and escalate the drama over a story's course toward its resolution...

...what events, action and dialog create a fulfilling resolution of a story's promise...

...is at the heart of the art of storytelling.

Chapter Questions

Did creating the diagram help you see how your story line and plot line work together?
Did it help you see the process of thrust/counter-thrust in your story?
Did it help you to see how your story line and plot line should intermesh?
Do you need a larger drawing surface? Some people lay out butcher paper over the top of a table or counter, or tack it up against a wall so they can see the progression of notes as they have new ideas. Use the outline system that helps you the most.

Complex Story, Simple Questions

Stories operate to transport an audience. In many stories, this process begins with a main character who engages the attention or interest of an audience around a particular goal. Once the audience wants to know what will happen, the audience is drawn into the story. Often the particular goal of a main character identifies what a story is about.

In *The Hunt for Red October*, Ramius desires his freedom from oppression. Each step he takes to gain his freedom increases the obstacles he must overcome, so the novel's plot creates escalating tension. Since he's trying to escape to America in a Soviet submarine, readers can easily track the progression of the story's plot and the fulfillment of the story's promise, that he gain his freedom.

I call this a story line and a plot line. Gain freedom from oppression, story, can he escape to America, plot. Note how each issue can be framed as a story question and a plot question. (I have a full breakdown and diagram of Hunt at

http://www.storyispromise.com/hunt.pdf)

The Lovely Bones is contemporary fiction and has a greater depth of characterization and plot.

A novel doesn't have to operate on this simple, transparent level. Anthony Doerr's novel *All the Light We Cannot See* explores an idea, how World War II affected ordinary people. The purpose of the story isn't just the outcome of a quest, the actions of the characters in total convey ideas about the nature of war and its aftermath.

This essay is about how Doerr organized the novel in both complex and simple ways to make it dramatic, thoughtful, and compelling.

In the Beginning...

The novel starts with a title, Zero, and a date, 7 August 1944. Since the story moves through time, this is a quick way to orient readers as the story progresses.

The opening, Leaflets, is two paragraphs. It's a warning that bombers are on the way and mortars with incendiary rounds are being fired.

Simple question, what is the target? One clue, that the mortars are being fired from nearby beachfront hotels.

Next is the two page chapter titled The Girl. This introduces a blind girl who can hear the sound of the planes approaching. This chapter sets up a simple question. Will the girl survive the bombing? The answer comes about half way through the book (and sets up another complication/simple question that is answered at the end of the book).

Note the reader is allowed to focus on this simple dramatic question, will the girl survive? The question is not elusive or a metaphor.

The blind girl is fingering a model of the city that is about to be bombed. These models will be a significant part of the story for several reasons that come out at different times.

The next chapter is titled The Boy, and introduces Werner, who seems (note the word seems) to be attached to a German anti-aircraft unit stationed in a hotel near the girl. This chapter ends with Werner's question, "Are they really coming?"

The reader knows more than Werner that yes, they are coming.

The next chapter is Saint-Malo. It offers details about the town (last German fortress on the Breton coast) and an overview of the war at that time.

Note the main characters are introduced first, the town and what's happening in the war, second. Struggling writers often begin with an introduction to a story's environment and history ahead of a novel's main characters.

In the chapter titled Number 4 rue Vauborel, the young girl, Marie-Laure, goes to the miniature town created by her father and retrieves a plum-sized jewel from a hidden compartment. It comes out that she lives in the house with her great uncle Etienne, with whom she has lived for four years. The chapter ends with Marie-Laure whispering, "Papa?" as she holds the jewel.

Simple questions, what is this jewel and where is her father? What does he have to do with the hidden jewel?

As with the other questions so far, the questions are clear, simple, and direct. They aren't buried in details about environments or what characters look like. Doerr chooses to highlight the important details that he wants his readers to focus on.

Next chapter, Cellar, focuses on Werner, who still seems attached to an anti-aircraft unit; he's working with a receiver that has him in contact with nearby German forces. This chapter introduces Frank Volkheimer, a giant German soldier who works with Werner, and Bernd, an engineer. Frank tells Werner they will be safe in the cellar. Werner remembers listening to a French radio broadcast when he was young. The last line,

He sees a flock of blackbirds explode out of a tree.

This foreshadows something that will be covered soon in the novel.

In this final chapter in the beginning of the novel, Bombs Away, the approach of the bombs is described in metaphors. The last line,

In the cellar beneath the Hotel of Bees, the single light bulb in the ceiling [where Werner is] winks out.

This is the last chapter to begin the novel.

The next section of the book is titled One, 1934.

The title of the first chapter is Museum National d'Hhstorie Naturelle.

Now we get more detail about Marie-Laure, that she's six and losing her eyesight, and her father works at the museum as a locksmith and that a precious gem, the Sea of Flames, is hidden away in the museum. There's a story/myth that the gem offers healing to whoever holds it.

The gem will have a significant role to play in the novel, so the long story about it is justified.

The chapter ends with the girl blind.

Note the difference if the novel had started here with Marie-Laure and the story about the gem. There would have been no questions to capture the attention of readers.

Next we meet Werner and his sister Jutta growing up in an orphanage in a poor coal-mining town in Germany. Werner is frail and has snow white hair, which makes him an oddity in the town.

Next, we discover the life that Marie-Laure's father sets up for her when she goes blind, and we learn that her mother died in child birth.

We have been drawn in to want to know more about these two characters.

The chapters continue in the past, setting out the lives of Werner and Marie-Laure. From this point on, I will talk about the novel in more general terms.

Werner finds a radio and explores how it operates. He and his sister Jutta listen to broadcasts from France. Marie-Laure's father builds models of their neighborhood in Paris to help his daughter navigate when she goes outside. First, with him, then later on her own.

Doerr develops a metaphor that coal is a form of light, since it came from light that helped plants to grow. Coal is a form of light we cannot see. The gem Sea of Flames is also a form of light, a form of light that has accumulated stories about itself.

Now rumors begin to circulate about the Germans invading France. Werner continues to develop his ability to build and work with radios. Marie is given part one of a novel in Braille, and she learns that she and her father must leave Paris, and he is taking something important from the museum.

This raises questions. Will they be able to escape Paris? Find shelter with an uncle who suffers from delusions caused by combat in WWI?

Werner fixes a radio that belongs to a local Nazi leader. What will happen to Werner when he is of an age to leave the orphanage and work in a coal mine?

These questions are clearly presented.

Section Two of the novel begins with the date, 8 August 1944, ten years after Section One.

This section takes up in Saint-Malo just after the bombs have fallen. Marie survives; is it because of the jewel she holds? Werner is alive, but he is buried in the basement of the hotel with Frank Volkheimer, and with no way out.

What will happen to Marie now, and Werner? The answers to the questions raise new questions.

This is unlike a novel like Hunt, where you have a few basic questions and have to read to the end of the novel to get answers.

Section Three moves to June 1940.

Marie and her father make their way to a sanctuary in Saint-Malo. Marie meets her uncle Etienne. Werner goes to an institute to be trained as a Nazi Youth and makes friends with Frederick, who loves birds, and is clearly at risk from the faster, stronger boys and the head of the institute.

What will happen to Frederick is a question that pulls the audience forward.

This section of the novel introduces German Sergeant von Rumpel who is given the task of tracking down the Sea of Flames, which the audience knows is in the possession of Marie. He tracks the stone to the museum in Paris. He knows four people were sent out with four stones, only one real. Readers know that Marie's father took the real stone.

Werner's technical abilities are noted and he is taken aside to train with radio equipment. Frank, the largest and most dangerous boy in Werner's group, is assigned to protect Werner. Frank is the soldier who will later be buried in the hotel basement with Werner in Saint-Malo in June 1944.

In this section we discover that Uncle Etienne transmitted the material that Werner and his sister listened to while in the orphanage.

Marie's father gets a telegram that he must return to the museum, and he prepares to go. Marie will not hear from her father again. The question over his return will consume Marie.

Frederick gets his first serious beating at the Nazi youth camp.

Section Four is titled 8 August 1944.

Note how the shifts in time raise additional questions but also deepen reader's sense of knowing the characters.

Sergeant von Rumpel is now in Saint-Malo, closing in on the Sea of Flames. He has cancer and is dying, so his desire to find the stone and use its healing powers is now clear.

He makes it to Laurie's house, and she hides. In a typical action novel, the hero or heroine has one quest. Now that Laurie has survived the bombing, she must survive being stalked by von Rumpel. The outcome for that question comes late in the novel.

Werner and Frederick realize they could die in this basement, so now the question become how or if they'll get out.

Section Five, January 1941.

This section opens with Werner and Frederick. Frederick has been beaten and Werner did not intervene, but both seem to accept that this is just the course of Frederick's life and Werner can do nothing.

Werner does join Frederick for a trip home, and Werner learns more about Frederick's love of birds.

Marie's father has been gone 20 days, and the museum says he never arrived; and occupation authorities won't tell her his whereabouts or know nothing, leaving Marie to despair.

The boys in the camp are ordered to participate in the death of prisoner, but Frederick refuses, which ends a chapter, leaving open for a moment what will happen to him.

Soon, Frederick's treatment and beatings worsen.

Marie is taken into the town by a friend of her uncle. She is introduced to other women who have shops in town, and she is asked to help the women resist the German occupation.

Von Rumpel uses his patience and cunning to use interrogations to begin gathering information about what happened to the Sea of Flames when Germany invaded France.

Marie gets a letter from her father, saying he is in Germany and well-treated.

Section Six of the book, Someone is in the House.

Although Marie is blind, she can track von Rumpel by the sounds he makes as he searches for her.

In the basement of the hotel, Brand the engineer dies and Werner works on a radio, not with hope, but to occupy himself.

Marie is terrified she'll be found when the house goes silent, but what does the silence mean?

These short chapters now end with urgent questions, drawing readers forward at a faster pace.

Section Seven returns to August 1942.

Werner is now part of a unit in the Wehrmacht. Riding on a train toward the front, Werner sees train after train loaded with the dead and prisoners going past. He's getting a different introduction to the war than he received in the Nazi youth training camp.

Marie and her uncle now use an illegal radio to pass messages to the British; Werner's job is to track down these illegal radios. This raises the question, was he in the town of Breton to find Marie and her uncle?

As Werner tracks down illegal radio transmissions, Volkheimer is the stone-faced executioner who kills the operators, but there's a suggestion that the giant Volkheimer has a gentle side underneath his warrior's exterior.

Werner comes across soldiers who have lost their eyelids to frostbite.

Doerr is giving a close up of the way various soldiers and civilians are affected by the war.

A burglar is arrested with what turns out to be a second fake Sea of Flames, which tells the increasingly ill von Rumpel he is on the right track.

As the warm looms over Breton, Marie increasingly thinks of the world in tones of gray, not the colors she knew when young.

Werner deals with diarrhea, the common killer in war.

von Rumpel discovers the third fake stone.

The resistance of the women in Breton draws more scrutiny, which readers can anticipate will bring Werner to the town.

In another town, Werner mis-identifies an antenna and a mother and small girl die. To hold onto his sanity, he remembers a line from the French radio broadcasts he listened to as a child, that *'So, really, children, mathematically all of light is invisible.'*

Her uncle gives Marie a copy of Twenty Thousand Leagues Under the Sea. She had read the first book of a two book set and had always hoped her father could give her the second book. Life goes on, even during a war.

This section ends with the request for Werner's services to track down the illegal broadcasts in Breton.

Section Eight, 9 August 1944

This section starts with an ill-aimed American shell killing some Frenchmen being held in a camp, speaking to the randomness of death in a war. Later, this raises a question of whether Marie's uncle died in the shelling.

As the city is shelled, Marie can hear von Rumpel moving around the house. She can tell he is ill. von Rumpel believes the house not being destroyed proves the power of the Sea of Flames.

Marie finds her uncle's radio and begins to tell a story that Werner listens to in the basement of the hotel. Werner prays that Marie remain safe, but the section ends with the line, 'But God is only a white cold eye, a quarter-moon poised above the smoke, blinking, blinking as the city is gradually pounded to dust.'

This suggests that not even God can protect those involved in a war.

Section Nine, May 1944

Werner and his crew reach the coast of France, and Werner is warned to avoid stepping on a mine, foreshadowing something that happens later.

We discover what led von Rumpel to Saint-Malo, and how Werner and the others set up to track down the illegal transmissions. Werner realizes the voice he intercepts is the same French voice that told the stories that enthralled him as a child. He does not report the location of the signal to Volkheimer.

Finding the uncle's house, Werner sees Marie walking down the street, and she passes by him. It's a thrilling moment that these two main characters have been brought together.

von Rumpel finds Marie in the city and tries to interrogate her, but she escapes.

All the major characters are now gathered in Saint-Malo.

Marie gets a letter from her father that she realizes is a code about where to find the Sea of Flames that he's hidden in the uncle's house. The uncle transmits a code that identifies where an anti-aircraft battery is...on the ramparts of the hotel where Werner is working in the basement.

The Americans are days away from entering the town, but a friend of the uncle warns him he could be picked up and sent to a camp outside town. And he is picked up.

This section ends with Werner seeing leaflets falling from the sky, the leaflets from the opening of the novel. Readers know what the leaflets foretell.

Section Ten, 12 August 1944

In the basement of the hotel, Werner listens to Marie plead for help from von Rumpel.

Marie's uncle watches the bombardment of the town from a nearby camp where he and other men are being held.

Marie continues to read about Captain Nemo over her uncle's radio.

von Rumpel, in a room below Marie's hiding place, is almost incapacitated by cancer.

Marie can take no more of hiding. She puts on a record to play music through the house.

Volkheimer hears the music on the dying radio in the basement hotel and it energizes him to build a crude barrier and toss a grenade at what used to be a stairwell.

Listening to the music, von Rumpel hallucinates that a daughter is singing for him.

Volkheimer and Werner escape the hotel basement, with Werner determined to rescue Marie.

von Rumpel searches again for Marie. A lit candle ignites some curtains.

Werner enters the house and comes across von Rumpel on the sixth floor of the house. von Rumpel gets the drop on Werner with a pistol and that's where a chapter ends.

Again, the endings to chapters now have an urgency that pulls readers forward.

A passage gives an overview of the war, from Saint-Malo to the last of the Nazi Youth going out to their deaths, to Marie's uncle thinking what he and Marie can do if they survive the war.

It is Werner who survives the shoot out with von Rumpel, and he rescues Marie.

Werner and Marie share a meal of canned peaches. During a cease-fire, he tells her which direction to go with a white flag. Will they ever meet again, she wonders? He doesn't know.

The Sea of Flames is possibly returned to the sea by Werner from its resting place in the replica of the house. He keeps the miniature house and a key that unlocked the hiding place of the stone.

Werner is quickly picked up by French resistance fighters. Marie re-unites with her uncle. Now eighteen, with none of the future others planned for him, Werner cannot imagine a future for himself.

Werner leaves the sick tent he has been transferred to and steps on a German mine. He dies in a flash of light.

Section Eleven, 1945

Jutta, Werner's sixteen year old sister, in January 1945 is sent to work in a factory in Berlin. In March, she is told to help clean bombed streets.

When the Russians arrive, Jutta and some other girls are raped repeatedly.

After the war, Marie lives with her uncle in Paris, aware of all the other displaced people attempting to find their lives again. She decides she will go to school.

Twelve, 1974

Volkheimer installs and repairs TV antennas. He is living the life of the almost but not quite dead yet, when he gets a package that includes Werner's pack, a notebook, and the broken miniature house. It reminds Volkheimer that he was just a giant child who killed many men in the war.

Volkheimer makes a trip to see Jutta, and to tell her what he knew about Werner. Jutta knows she left a part of her life back in the war years.

When she opens Werner's duffel, she sees the house, and letters, and a letter to Frederick. She thinks, 'What the war did to dreamers.'

Jutta takes a trip to Saint-Malo with her son, Max. She is led to the still standing house that the miniature house replicates. She finds out a blind girl lives in the house. But that is all.

Marie has returned to the house she grew up in. Her uncle has died, leaving her money to search for her father, but just finding a note in a German prison camp ledger that a prisoner with his name came down with the flu.

Jutta comes to visit with Max. She leaves the miniature house with Marie, who promises to send a record that Werner and Jutta listened to as children.

Marie wonders what Werner did with the stone when he went back to retrieve the miniature house from a grotto.

A passage called Sea of Flames conveys that the stone is still in the sea where Werner left it, 'Crawled over by snails. It stirs among the pebbles.'

Frederick's mother opens a letter from his duffel bag forwarded by Volkheimer. Frederick is still brain damaged and obvious. The envelope contains an image of birds.

An owl appears on a patio and Frederick seems to be aware of it. He speaks, "What are we doing, Mutti (mother)." Inside his damaged mind, a light has flickered.

Thirteen, 2014

Marie, now old, wonders what kind of messages travel the ether, and... 'Every hour, she thinks, someone for whom the war was memory falls out of the world'

But captured in this lovely novel by Anthony Doerr.

The novel demonstrates how simple questions can engage and hold the attention of readers in a complex novel told by a master storyteller. As questions are framed, the readers are naturally drawn forward.

Bravo!

Writing Out a Story's Spine

Writing one page that reflects the spine of a story—the central issue resolved by a main character—can greatly help in the creation of a one-page synopsis. Understanding a story's spine is also valuable when describing a story to agents, producers, and editors.

Many writers struggle with writing out a story's spine because they want to set out the actions of their characters and plot. To describe a story, however, is a separate issue from writing about a character's goals or one's plot. For example, *The Hunt for Red October* is about freedom battling oppression.

To describe *The Hunt for Red October*, then, is not the same as talking about the actions of its main character, Ramius.

> A story spine of *The Hunt for Red October* might begin*: This is the story of one man's battle to be free of the system that oppresses him.*

Note, this line identifies what's at stake in the story; namely freedom battling oppression. It's not necessarily the best first line for a synopsis, but it can serve as a guide for what follows. It does set out the spine of the story. Ramius acts out the story issue of a man who will not be denied his freedom, but the story itself is about this issue of freedom battling oppression.

To continue:

> *To gain his freedom, Ramius, the commander of the Soviet nuclear-missile submarine* Red October, *sets in*

motion a plan to escape to America.

Note that Ramius is described in relationship to what's at stake in the story, the issue of freedom.

> *Ramius has long hated his oppressors, the communist party that rules Russia and his native Lithuania, but he's been held in check while his wife was alive. With her passing, he has no restraints on his desire to be free or to punish his oppressors.*

This gives a sense of why Ramius desires to be free: it is to escape the oppression of his communist masters, whom he loathes. Even though this appears to be describing Ramius, it's describing him in a way that makes clear his relationship to the story itself.

> *To set in motion his plot to escape to America and freedom, Ramius must kill his political officer. Then he gives his crew orders that they must follow blindly, because he's the ship's captain. Ramius knows one of the crew has been trained to kill him if he acts suspiciously.*

This description continues to tie Ramius's actions into the story's underlying premise, that he can act to gain his freedom but must take risks. It is the nature of a story that the actions of a story's characters and its plot generate drama over its outcome. A synopsis should offer an idea about a story's drama. Because Ramius is part of an oppressive system, it is guaranteed that his orders will be obeyed. This description of the story ties these elements into its premise. The synopsis raises a dramatic issue that plays throughout the story. How long can Ramius hide his true purpose from his assassin?

> *Ramius must avoid detection by his fellow submariners when they are ordered to find and detain him. Later, to find and destroy him. His communist oppressors fear what a free man armed with nuclear missiles might do.*

Note the repetition of the story's main theme, freedom, and

the escalation of the drama over the story's outcome. Ramius's oppressors now actively hunt him. Note how this synopsis shows that with each step Ramius moves toward freedom, while others double their efforts to stop him. This, in brief, is the purpose of the story's plot, to increase the drama over the story's outcome.

> *Ramius's outmaneuvering of the Soviet submarine fleet alerts the Soviet surface navy to find and destroy him. The Soviet navy going on alert in the Atlantic puts the Americans on the alert. When they learn that a nuclear-armed submarine is on a course toward America, decisions must be made about the nature of the Soviet threat. If the* Red October *is a rogue submarine, the Americans will destroy it. Tensions escalate in Washington, D.C. and Moscow. CIA analyst Jack Ryan suspects Ramius's true purpose.*

Note how this introduces Jack Ryan, the other main character of the story. His actions revolve around the idea that Jack is listened to because he operates in a free system. This description of Jack ties his actions into the story's underlying premise.

Ramius and the Red October narrowly avoid being destroyed by a Soviet attack submarine. Now the American military must make a decision. Should Ramius, a rogue military commander, be destroyed? Is he a threat to America? Jack Ryan puts into action a plan to prove that Ramius is attempting to escape to America, while bringing a tremendous prize — a new type of submarine with a revolutionary propulsion system.

Again, this ties Ramius's action to what's being acted out in the story, a battle between freedom and oppression.

To conclude:

> *In a climactic confrontation, Jack Ryan boards the* Red October *and is able to kill the KGB trained assassin. Working together, Jack Ryan and Ramius stage a fake explosion and sinking of the* Red October. *Through his*

own undeniable courage and with the aid of Jack Ryan and other Americans, Ramius gains his freedom.

The spine ends with a reiteration of what was at stake in the story and its fulfillment. At each step of creating this story spine, it has been clear what's at stake in this story. To simply describe the actions of a story's characters and its plot is to leave out what actually engages the interest of an audience.

You can use a one-page story spine to write a synopsis for your script that communicates what is dynamic and engaging about your story. In working with students, I've found they often create a flat first sentence when they talk about a story and its premise in a concrete way. Often, the second sentence of their synopsis is the natural opening. For example, I recently read the first sentence of a synopsis that began:

The Price is a tale of political intrigue and one man's struggle to find redemption in a corrupt world.

The second sentence of the synopsis read, "In a world where advances in science allow a handful of people to create truth for a price, one man struggles with the worth of his soul." This second sentence is a potential opening sentence for this synopsis. It sets out the issue at the heart of this story while suggesting its plot.

Another possible opening sentence is, "Craig Bowman thought he knew the price of his soul until his was sold."

Choose the opening sentence for your synopsis that communicates the purpose of your story in the strongest, most engaging language. Show your synopsis to others with different opening sentences to find out which version creates the most interest.

A few suggestions:

> Your story synopsis should be clear and easy to read. A synopsis that is difficult to read suggests a story that will be difficult to follow. *Keep it simple.*
> In your synopsis, move from an overview of your story and plot to a strong, personal sense of the roles of your main characters in acting out your story. Use your description of your main characters and their actions to create a spine

for the body of the synopsis.

The more characters you introduce, the more you need to explain, the greater the chance your audience will feel lost. Follow the spine.

Use your synopsis to demonstrate how your plot increases the dramatic tension for your story's main characters. Express the main thrust of the story along your story line and plot line.

Suggest the fulfillment of your story as it is acted out by your plot. For example, the beginning to a synopsis of *Cold Mountain*[57], by Charles Frazier, could read:

> *A wounded Confederate soldier at the end of the Civil War believes the violence of the war has destroyed his soul, and by making his way home to Cold Mountain, an Indian ritual will heal him.*

This opening naturally suggests the role of the main character in the story, what's at stake, the time, the place, the setting, the goal of the main character, and a sense of why this story would engage the interest of an audience.

The appearance of your synopsis is important. Does your synopsis easily fit onto one page using a 12–point font, with at least one-inch margins and white space at the top and bottom of the page? Remember, a synopsis is a summary of your story, not an explanation of your plot or a history of your characters.

When you finish reading your synopsis, do you feel enthused again about your story, or are you tired of wading through details?

If you're struggling to write a one-page synopsis, try starting again. Write about one thing — how your main character feels compelled to act out the promise of your story, and what they go through to fulfill that promise. Mention only those characters who interact with your main character, and the significant events your main character deals with, and the narrative tension your character resolves.

Before you send out your synopsis, set it aside for a few days, then read the synopsis again. Does reading your synopsis make you want to read your story? If not, consider writing another synopsis.

If you are going to offer a verbal synopsis to an agent, editor, or producer, practice it out loud until you're comfortable with what you want to say and you can speak about your story with some of the passion and interest that led you to create it.

Remember, a synopsis is an overview of your story, characters, and plot, not an explanation of your story, characters and plot.

Good luck. Writing a great synopsis can be difficult. If you still need help, get Elizabeth Lyon's book *The Sell Your Novel Toolkit*[56]; it has a great section on writing a synopsis. She's helped many authors get published.

Chapter Questions

- Are you beginning your story synopsis with a dramatically interesting sentence that sets out the role of your main character in acting out your story, and a suggestion of what's at stake for that character?
- As you use the story spine to write a synopsis, are you referring the events you describe to your story's promise in a way that creates a clearly identifiable spine for your story?
- Does your synopsis read well? Is it fresh, engaging, dynamic? One page?
- Does your synopsis clearly suggest what's at stake in your story and build dramatically from beginning to end?

Using The Reviews

I review movies, books, and plays as a way to teach story structure. If you are new to this process, I suggest you read a review, then rent the movie, or view the play (both have been filmed), or read the book. The goal is that you can "see" or read the points being made in the reviews.

I've found that many struggling writers are blind imitators. They think they are doing what successful authors are doing but they are not. My goal is that writers learn to fully see what successful writers are doing and then internalize that understanding and apply it to their writing.

section four

Story reviews

section four

reviews of Popular Stories

films: *The Godfather*
         Rear Window

Plays: *Romeo and Juliet*
         'night, Mother

novels: *Wild*

         City of Glass

Using Families in Storytelling

Review of *The Godfather*

Screenplay written by Mario Puzo and Francis Ford Coppola. Directed by Francis Ford Coppola. Actors: Marlon Brando, Al Pacino, Diane Keaton, Robert Duvall. Based on the novel by Mario Puzo. Released in 1972. Available on DVD and Blu-Ray.

A difficult aspect of storytelling is introducing characters in a way that they are bound together in a way that serves the purpose of a story.

Conflict only happens when something binds characters together.

Unless something binds characters together, their actions will fail to advance a story.

This flaw most often is apparent when a novel or screenplay begins with an introduction of several characters, but each introduction stands alone. This forces readers to memorize details until some story purpose arises.

The film The Godfather is a great example of using family in telling a story.

The movie opens with an Italian father telling the Godfather how his daughter was violated and beaten by two non-Italian boys. But the father has never acknowledged the Godfather or asked his friendship, or shown him respect. It is only when the father offers his fealty to the Godfather that he agrees to avenge his daughter's injustice.

The father goes from his fealty to the American way of life to fealty to the Godfather and now being part of the Godfather's family.

We now move to a family wedding at the Godfather's mansion and the wedding of his daughter. This is a quick way to introduce the Godfather's family, but the Godfather says no family photo can be taken until Michael arrives.

Every character featured in this scene will have a role to play in the film.

A photographer does take a photo of another major gangster and his 'family' which gets his film destroyed. This frames the question, who is this other man in relation to the Godfather?

Michael now shows up in a military uniform with his non-Italian girlfriend. He introduces his girlfriend to Tom, the family lawyer who is also considered family although he is not Italian. Sonny, who is hot-tempered, is Michael's older brother.

Michael's explanation of who Tom is begins to set out the structure of the 'family' and how it operates. Michael's girlfriend not being connected to the family gives a reason for her to want to know more.

In the wedding party, the newlyweds dance the swing to American music instead of what has been the Italian songs played previously.

It's a subtle way to point out the changes happening to the family as a new generation comes forward.

Interspersed with the wedding scenes, the Godfather manages the family business as it's a tradition that others can ask him for favors on the day of a Sicilian wedding.

An Italian-American movie star and singer makes his appearance. Michael explains to his girlfriend that he's the Godson of the Godfather. The Godfather gets his Godson out of a contract with a band leader by threatening to kill the band leader. This introduces the line about 'an offer he couldn't refuse.'

Michael tells his girlfriend, "That's my family, Kay, not me."

This sets up a major issue for this film and the sequels, how Michael ultimately becomes the leader to this family and the new Godfather. Also note in this opening scene that Kay doesn't leave Michael when she finds out some of the activities of his family. It's a choice that will later haunt both her and Michael.

Michael then introduces his oldest brother Fredo to Kay. Fredo is drunk and off-putting, but the scene conveys Fredo's role in the family dynamics.

The Godson cries and asks the Godfather to get him a major part in a Hollywood movie over the obstruction of a Hollywood producer. While this is happening, Sonny is having sex with a bridesmaid.

The Godfather smacks his Godson and demands he act like a man.

The Godfather dismisses him and tells him he will make the Hollywood producer 'an offer he can't refuse.' He also says the new son-in-law will only have a minor role in the family business, which sets up another major plot complication.

This sets up an anticipation over how he means to induce this change of heart in the producer.

They can now take the family wedding photo and Michael insists Kay be part of that, suggesting his determination to make her part of his life, a major issue that will play out in the films.

The Godfather dances with his daughter, ending the wedding scene. It's twenty-seven minutes into the film.

The major characters have been introduced and the different complications that will chart the course of the story have been laid. The minor characters who work for the family have also been introduced as they participate in the wedding.

It would have been difficult to introduce this many characters without the context of the family and the family relationships.

The next scene is a plane landing in California. Tom meets the Hollywood producer, who introduces Tom to his prized horse. He also explains why he's rejecting Tom's offer.

The next morning the producer wakes up in his palatial bed with his horse's head.

An iconic moment in movie history.

The following pivotal scenes are Tom and Sonny recommending to the Godfather that he get into the drug business to protect the future of his family and to protect his family against any machinations from five other crime families.

The request is that the Godfather put up some cash and offer the protection of the politicians and police on his payroll.

At a meeting with a representative of this drug business, the Don refuses this offer. That he cannot maintain his standing in his community or maintain control over his politicians and police if he becomes involved with drugs.

This sets up the thrust of what subsequently happens, an assassination attempt on the Godfather, the death of Sonny via his brother-in-law's machinations, and soon after the Godfather's death and Michael's ascension as leader of his family.

The family he told Kay was 'not him.'

Michael lies to Kay that he ordered his brother-in-law's death.

As the film ends, Kay watches as Michael's underlings now kiss his hand and address him as Don.

Michael has become the head of the family he wanted to escape, and Kay, whether she wants it or not, is now part of that family.

A powerful tragedy told through a focus on family.

Truly revered as one of the greatest films.

Developing and Sustaining Suspense

A Review of Rear Window

Screenplay written by John Michael Hayes and Cornell Woolrich. Directed by Alfred Hitchcock. Starring: Jimmy Stewart, Grace Kelly, Raymond Burr. Available in DVD and Blu-Ray. Released in 1954.

Alfred Hitchcock is a master storyteller who has a thorough understanding of how to create and sustain suspense.

Rear Window opens by having a camera moving out a rear window over a courtyard and slowly panning across the view, then coming inside the window to reveal the sweating brow of Jeff, played by Jimmy Stewart, and a thermometer that reveals his temperature (a shot repeated during the course of the film).

The camera returns to the outer view of the courtyard denizens who can be seen from Jeff's rear window, including a beautiful young blonde dancer dressing and stretching, over to more prosaic views, then back to Jeff for a reveal that he has a large body cast on from his waist down his leg down to his foot. The camera then pans over to a busted camera and an image of a race car overturning, suggesting how he broke his leg. The camera then pans a wall of photos of disasters, suggesting Jeff's life outside the apartment as a world-traveling photographer, ending on a fashion magazine and a beautiful woman on the cover.

Jeff takes a call from his employer thinking his cast is coming off that day instead of the following week. During the call, Jeff continues to admire the semi-clothed dancer across the courtyard, notices a musician composing on a piano, and a salesmen returning home (Raymond Burr, playing Lars Thorwald). Jeff is bored and wants out of this apartment.

Lars goes out to tend to some flowers and has a nasty comment for a neighbor, setting out his angry personality.

A nurse, Stella, comes in to work on Jeff and they get into a conversation about his girlfriend, the society girl on the cover of the magazine. Jeff complains she is 'too perfect.'

Note the use of Stella to convey how Jeff feels about his girlfriend and marriage. Minor characters like Stella offer a film's main character like Jeff someone to reveal thoughts and feelings.

Jeff tells Stella that he is determined to head off his girlfriend's desire to get married.

Jeff resumes watching his neighbors, now including some newly weds who pull down a shade. Again, all the people in Jeff's gaze represent a view of humanity, marriage, and relationships. All of those characters and relationships have a subtext that speaks to what the story is about. Every detail serves a purpose.

Now night, Jeff wakes to find his girlfriend Lisa (played by Grace Kelly) closing in for kiss. She's an absolutely, stunning, radiant beauty. And she's wearing a dress that costs $1,100 that she's wearing for free as part of her fashion magazine work, but the price tag gives Jeff pause, which turns to consternation when she desires to upgrade some of his mementos.

They are clearly an odd couple with conflicting world views.

Then it turns out she's catering the evening with a meal from an expensive restaurant. She plants the idea of his opening a studio so he won't need to travel. He tells her to 'stop talking nonsense,' which also affirms what he already told Stella about not wanting domestic bliss with Lisa.

What Lisa wants and what Jeff wants as the story opens are dramatically opposite. An implied question, what could change this for Jeff? Whatever it is, it won't be easy to accomplish.

Jeff notices a neighbor preparing an intimate, candle-lit dinner for a handsome stranger ... who is imaginary. Jeff toasts her as she offers her toast ... until he realizes she can no longer sustain an imaginary gentlemen caller. Another version of an adult relationship.

Jeff and Lisa have a frank conversation about his settling down in New York ... and he's not going along with her argument. He wants his freedom.

He's so insistent on demanding his freedom, she's willing to give it to him from that night forward ... suggesting their relationship is over.

Later that night, Jeff hears a scream and Lars's character takes trips out with a suitcase multiple times in the middle of the night. He's also pulled his blinds, so Jeff can no longer see his wife in bed.

While Jeff sleeps in the morning, Lars leaves his apartment with a woman dressed in black. Now the audience knows something Jeff doesn't, but it's unclear who the woman is.

Jeff tells his suspicions about Lars to Stella.

Jeff now watches Lars with binoculars and then a long range lens and sees Lars wrapping a saw and a butcher knife into a newspaper. The suspense over what Lars is up to increases. Lars goes to sleep on a couch and you can see the question in Jeff's eyes, 'where is his wife?'

A new night scene resumes with the camera looking around the courtyard, then coming into Jeff's apartment and a cuddle and kiss with Lisa, but Jeff only wants to muse about Lars who didn't go to work this day.

Lars returns with a length of thick rope and goes into his wife's bedroom with the blinds closed, but Jeff can see his shadowy figure moving around the room.

Not being able to see clearly what Lars is doing increases the suspense. Like Jeff, the audience strains to see what is happening.

Jeff tries to convince Lisa that his suspicions are valid and not an over active imagination. The conversation conveys more information about why he suspects Lars of murdering his invalid, nagging wife.

Just like the conversations with Stella, the conversations with Lisa advance the story and plot. In a subtle way, Lars and his nagging wife and his possible solution of getting rid of her have a subtext for Jeff. What would Jeff do to ensure his freedom from Lisa? Is Lars a kind of shadow self for Jeff?

This subtext gives the film psychological depth.

As the scene with Jeff and Lisa continues, the look on Lisa's face conveys that she sees something across the courtyard. Jeff uses his lens to see that Lars has used the rope to tie up a large case, and his wife's mattress is now rolled up as well.

Now Lisa is the believer. This increases the drama of the story and raises a more urgent question, what will Jeff and Lisa do next?

Jeff calls a detective he knew in the war (WWII) to tell his story about Lars. Meanwhile, he pulls Stella into believing his obsession about Lars ... just as moving men arrive to take away the trunk.

When the detective does arrive, he doesn't buy into Jeff's suspicion, again upping the suspense over what Jeff will do now.

The detective leaves but returns with news that other tenants saw Lars and his wife leaving for the train station at 6 am, while Jeff slept. Jeff doesn't believe it. Jeff raises the issue of someone going into the apartment to find proof of a murder. The detective tells Jeff why this can't happen without a warrant, but it also plants the idea for what will happen later with Lisa.

Jeff realizes Lars is packing to leave and Jeff now feels more desperation to get some proof about the murder. Jeff observes Lars taking items from his wife's purse, including a wedding ring.

When Lisa shows up, she convinces Jeff that Lars's wife would not leave without her jewelry. Lisa also comes prepared to spend the night to help keep watch on Lars.

Note the escalation in drama over the relationship of Jeff and Lisa, a relationship that he still wants out of but he needs her help to watch Lars.

The detective returns with news that the trunk had the wife's clothes and she picked up the trunk in another city. For him, case closed.

Lisa agrees with the detective and closes Jeff's blinds. No more courtyard show that night.

Lisa reappears in a stunning nightgown, but the night is interrupted by a scream. A woman in an apartment across the courtyard sees a little dog she has lowered in a basket lying still near some flowers tended earlier by Lars.

The dog has a broken neck. Why would someone kill the dog?

All the neighbors respond, except for Lars, who sits smoking in his dark apartment.

Jeff figures the dog was killed because it was nosing around the flowers Lars had been tending. Jeff has a photograph that shows a change in a particular flower bush.

Determined to prod Lars, Jeff writes a note, 'What have you done with her?'

Lisa puts the note under Lar's door; Lars sees and just misses seeing Lisa flee the scene, twice.

The suspense becomes more intense.

Lisa and Stella discuss the wedding ring. Was that ring finger buried in the flower garden?

Jeff calls Lars to set up a meeting at a local bar to talk about his wife's estate, suggesting he knows Lars killed his wife. He does this so Lisa and Stella can check on the flower bed. Jeff says he'll use a flashbulb to tip them off if Lars returns.

They find nothing, but then Lisa climbs the fire escape to Lars's apartment while a flustered Jeff watches.

This scene is crucial, because Lisa is now proving she's the adventurous kind of woman Jeff said he wants to marry. She's taking up residence in his fantasy life, which the shot on Jeff's face reveals as it's happening. A wonderful character revelation, all conveyed with no dialogue.

The script is giving Jimmy Stewart the actor a character to play.

Lisa finds something in Lar's apartment, a necklace ... but Jeff sees Lars returning. He, and the audience, can only watch in mounting suspense. What will Lisa do?

Lars enters his apartment and finds Lisa; Jeff calls the police to report an assault in Lars's apartment to rescue her.

Lars grabs Lisa and turns off the lights. Jeff can only watch. The suspense is incredible.

The police arrive. While they question Lars and Lisa, she signals Jeff that she's wearing the wife's wedding ring. Lars notices what she is doing and now knows Jeff has been watching him.

Stella gets the lights out in Jeff's apartment and he and Stella try and figure what Lisa's bail will be. Stella leaves to bail out Lisa while Jeff gets a hold of his detective friend, unaware that Lars is leaving his apartment and looking Jeff's way.

In the dark Jeff whispers to the detective on the phone, which has the effect of drawing the audience in to Jeff and his intense state of feeling.

Jeff can't see Lars, and when his phone rings he assumes it his friend, but it's Lars.

Jeff strains to see in the dark and hears a door slam and footsteps. Is it Lars coming up to Jeff's apartment?

The suspense again increases exponentially.

Jeff in his cast and wheelchair is desperate to protect himself while he hears footsteps approaching.

A shadow passes in front of his door.

Jeff takes up his camera flash and multiple bulbs.

Jeff's door opens and we see Lars's face in a dim pool of light.

"What do you want from me?" Lars demands, now in the dark. Again the tension mounts.

Hitchcock lets the scene unfold so the audience is fully locked in the suspense. It's a masterful scene.

Jeff defends himself by blinding Lars with the flash until Lisa and the detective are at Lars's apartment. Jeff calls for help as he's throttled by Lars and then hung from his apartment window.

As police rush in to grab Lars, Jeff falls and is caught but clearly injured.

As the police and the detective gather around Jeff in the courtyard, it comes out that Lars buried his wife's head in a hat box in the flower garden, then moved the hat box when the dog wouldn't leave the flower bed alone.

Mystery solved.

Days later, the camera sweeps around the courtyard returning to domestic, if not bliss, normalcy.

Jeff, a smile on his face, now has two legs in casts and a Lisa, dressed now in casual clothes, relaxes on his bed with an adventure magazine and a fashion magazine. Clearly she's sealed the deal with Jeff and it seems he will soon have the life and wife he said he wanted.

A great film.

Hitchcock fully understood how to use Jeff's rear window as a frame to tell a story and how to build, sustain, and increase the suspense.

Hitchcock is rightly revered as a master storyteller.

Rear Window is one of the great examples of visual storytelling.

The Power and Passion of Love & Hate

A Review of *Romeo and Juliet*

> Romeo and Juliet was written by William Shakespeare. The edition of the play reviewed was published by The New Folger Library, Washington Square Press, ISBN 0671-72285-9.

This review explores how Shakespeare structured this story and brought it to life. Romeo and Juliet opens with a prologue announcing that the story's star-crossed, young lovers will die and their deaths will reconcile their warring clans. Shakespeare opens his story by boldly announcing the climax of its plot. Why does he do this? Because the better the storyteller, the stronger his understanding that a story is a journey and that every step of that journey must be made engaging and dramatic, must be more than the sum of its parts. Shakespeare does what most inexperienced writers would be loathe to do—give away his ending—because what makes his story satisfying is a separate issue from the mechanics of its plot.

Furthermore, by telling the audience the story's outcome, Shakespeare gives the story an added poignancy. Knowing the lovers will die makes their every step toward that fate more deeply felt. This knowledge that the lovers will die speaks to drama as not only the anticipation of action, but also the anticipation of feelings and thoughts that are aroused in the story's audience.

Act One

SCENE ONE

Act One opens with some of the men of the Capulet clan meeting those of the Montague clan in the street. A brawl erupts, citizens join in, and the heads of the houses of Capulet and Montague come upon the scene. The Prince of the City then arrives. He declares that if there is more fighting, those who are guilty will face a penalty of death.

The dramatic purpose of this scene is to introduce the two families who are bound together by an ancient blood feud that has grown to a lethal hatred. The scene does this through a measured introduction of characters that gives the audience time to assimilate who a particular character is, the personality of each character, and the relationships between the characters. Because this story is about a conflict between love and hate, introducing the hate that fuels the story's action also serves to set the story into motion.

In the aftermath of the brawl, a question arises as to the whereabouts of Romeo, a young Montague. It is revealed that he has been shedding tears and avoiding his kinsmen, but the reason why is unclear. It is left to Benvolio to discover the cause of Romeo's distress.

Romeo enters as the others exit. Through Benvolio's probing, the audience quickly learns that Romeo is lovesick.

"Out of her favor where I am in love," he laments. (1.1.173)

The dramatic purpose here isn't to withhold that Romeo is lovesick, but to present that he is. Struggling writers often withhold the real feelings of their characters for some later revelation. Shakespeare, on the other hand, introduces Romeo in a state of intense emotion and then finds a way to escalate the intensity of his emotions.

SCENE TWO

The Senior Capulet enters, mentioning the ban on any further fighting and that this ban should be easy to uphold. Note how Capulet's words will come back to haunt him. During this scene, Count Paris reminds Capulet of his desire to wed Juliet, a girl not quite fourteen. Capulet wishes that Juliet be older before she weds, but Paris presses his suit. Capulet invites him to a party that night, and they exit.

Our introduction to Juliet, even while she remains off stage, offers a sense of who she is. Further, we see that Juliet's life is at a moment of potential transition from young girl to wife. She too is a "ripe" character.

Enter Benvolio with Romeo, who is still caught up in being lovesick. They immediately come upon a servant sent out by Capulet to announce a party, but the servant cannot read. He asks Romeo to read the invitation list. It turns out that Rosaline, for whom Romeo pines, has been invited to this party. The servant, grateful to Romeo for reading the list, invites him to the party as long as he's not a Montague.

Benvolio suggests Romeo go, that seeing some of the town's other beauties might aid his recovery from his infatuation with Rosaline. Romeo answers, defending Rosaline, "One fairer than my love? The all-seeing sun / Ne'er saw her march since first the world begun." (1.2.99–100)

Shakespeare maintains a measured, brisk, pace throughout these opening scenes where he introduces us to the principle characters and their issues. The playwright then begins bringing them together in a way that escalates the story's dramatic tension. Romeo's going to a party at the Capulet's is inherently dangerous.

SCENE 3

This scene opens with Lady Capulet, Juliet's nurse, and Juliet, alone in Juliet's chambers. The nurse is a folksy, humorous character. She ends a long answer to a simple question with the hope she live long enough to see Juliet marry.

That becomes the opening for Lady Capulet to broach to Juliet her parents' desire she consider marrying Paris.

Juliet answers, "I'll look to like, if looking liking move. / But no more deep will I endart mine eye / Than your consent gives strength to make it fly." (1.3.103–105)

They exit to attend the party.

Again the author's measured, brisk pace of introducing characters and their issues to maintain each scene's dramatic impact.

SCENE 4

When Romeo, Mercutio, and Benvolio enter the party, they discover it is a masquerade, which means their faces are not visible. Romeo and Mercutio pause to talk about dreams, then Romeo says, "I fear too early, for my mind misgives, / Some consequence yet hanging in the stars." (1.4.113–114) Something about this moment troubles him, but he nevertheless goes to the party.

Having Romeo and company pause before entering the party allows the drama about what will happen at the party to build.

SCENE 5

Capulet welcomes Romeo and company. Romeo sees Juliet and exclaims, "O, she doth teach the torches to burn bright!" (1.5.51)

The purpose of this scene is to show Romeo falling in love with Juliet, so it is not delayed. The question now becomes, what will be the outcome of this love he feels for her?

Many writers struggle because they build up to a moment of dramatic tension and then back away. Shakespeare begins a scene with dramatic tension and quickly works to heighten that tension.

Tybalt, who crossed swords with Benvolio in scene one, recognizes Romeo's voice and sends for his sword. The elder Capulet orders Tybalt to stand aside, and even praises Romeo for being known as virtuous. Allowing Romeo to stay is an act that will come back to haunt him. Tybalt protests, but Capulet rebukes him and orders him to not upset the party. Romeo takes Juliet's hand and speaks to her, "If I profane with my unworthiest hand, / This holy shrine, the gentle sin is this: / My lips, two blushing pilgrims, ready stand /To smooth that rough touch with a tender kiss." (1.5. 104–107)

It is the purpose of the scene to show how quickly and deeply Romeo falls in love with Juliet. His falling in love is not delayed, nor does it happen off stage.

Juliet is quickly swayed by Romeo's passion. Juliet responds, "Good pilgrim, you do wrong your hands too much, / Which mannerly devotion shows in this; / For saints have hands that pilgrims' hands do touch, / And palm to palm is holy palmers' kiss. ((1.5.108–111)

Romeo kisses Juliet once, then again. Juliet's nurse calls her away, and Romeo learns from the nurse that Juliet is of the house of Capulet. Romeo exclaims, "O dear account! My life is my foe's debt." (1.5.132) Again, the playwright maintains his brisk pace of setting up and advancing the story.

Juliet, on learning Romeo's identity, says, "My only love sprung from my only hate! / Too early seen unknown, and known too late! /Prodigious birth it is to me / That I must love a loathed enemy." (1.5.151–155)

This is the end of act one. All the major elements are in place: the hatred of the Montagues and Capulets, the idea that Romeo is lovesick and in love with the idea of love, the fate that will befall the next person to disturb the peace, and finally—the fact that Romeo and Juliet are in love. The curtain closes on a note of high drama and emotion. The storyteller has brought the audience to this height of emotion because very little is withheld for some later plot effect or revelation. What is important to the setting up and advancement of the story has been presented in a clear, dramatic way.

When Shakespeare writes that one character doesn't like another, an audience can surmise the two will meet in either that scene or the next. Because of this arrangement of the story's elements, the audience develops a sense of trust that the playwright won't introduce characters for no clear dramatic purpose, or introduce information but then delay its import.

Shakespeare writes every moment of every scene to bring out its drama. If characters are angry, they speak poetically of their anger and what they intend to do to resolve it. When they are lovesick, they speak of heavy hearts; vengeful, they speak of the joys of vengeance. Each moment he creates heightens the drama of that particular moment. The struggling writer is forever doing what I call describing the furniture. He or she describes characters, events, and environments as if from rote, while the dramatic richness of what should be the heightened moments of a scene are held back for some later revelation or perceived plot effect. Shakespeare is a master of the moment, the scene, the act, and the story.

Wonderful introductions to characters who can be expected to dramatically advance the story in its second act.

Act Two

SCENE ONE

The second act opens with a Chorus that posits a problem for Romeo and Juliet, "Being held a foe, he may not have access." (11.1.9) However, the chorus also points out, "But passion lends them power, time means, to meet, / Temp'ring extremities with extreme sweet." (11.Chorus. 13–14)

Just as the opening lines of the chorus foretold the end of the story in the prologue, this chorus foretells what will soon transpire in the second act. Again, with a master storyteller, it's the journey the story creates for its audience that is moving, not a withholding of the destination for dramatic effect.
The action of the scene opens with Romeo's two lines, "Can I go forward when my heart is here? / Turn back, dull earth, and find thy center out." (11. 1 1–2)

Romeo goes over a garden wall into the Capulet estate. Romeo is a lovesick, rash, impulsive character. Shakespeare reveals that to us by having Romeo voice just two lines before going over the wall to return to Juliet. He doesn't think about it, doesn't discuss it with others, he simply acts on his feelings in a way that advances the story.

Many writers struggle because they spend a great deal of time setting up why characters will do a particular thing when they eventually meet. Shakespeare arranges for characters to meet because it is in those moments that their goals and feelings are naturally revealed.

Walking along a dark road, Benvolio and Mercutio see Romeo go over the wall into a field. Both Benvolio and Mercutio realize there's no point in trying to find Romeo, who they think has gone off to find Rosaline.

SCENE TWO

Romeo goes forward across a field and to the Capulet's estate. Standing in a garden, he sees Juliet on a balcony. He speaks of his love for her, "Oh, that I were a glove upon that hand, / That I might touch that cheek." (11.2.25– 26)

Juliet speaks from her heart, "O Romeo, Romeo, wherefore art thou Romeo?" (11.2.36) She continues, "What's in a name? That which we call a rose / By any other name would smell as sweet." (11.2.46-47) Poetic language treasured through the ages. Juliet speaks of her feelings for Romeo, "My love as deep, The more I give to thee, / The more I have, for both are infinite." (11.2.141–142) She adds, "Yet I should kill thee with much cherishing. / Good night, good night. Parting is such sweet sorrow / That I shall say "Good night" till it be morrow." (11.2.198–200)

Beautiful, beautiful language. Spoken in the moment, from Romeo's heart, offered to Juliet's heart, and passing through the hearts of the audience. With these words Shakespeare is not limiting himself to describing what Romeo and Juliet look like as they speak to each other, but bringing out the full range of emotions the characters express in a situation Shakespeare has created by design for that purpose.

SCENE THREE

Romeo meets with Friar Lawrence and asks that he perform the marriage to Juliet. Friar Lawrence chides Romeo about being so recently lovesick over Rosalind. But he agrees to the marriage because it would end the feud between the two clans. Romeo says of his marriage, "Oh, let us hence. I stand on sudden haste." (11.3.100) Friar Lawrence replies, "Wisely and slow. They stumble that run fast." (11.3.101)

The Friar's comment foreshadows what acting in haste will lead to.

Romeo meets Juliet and the Friar arranges their marriage. Again, the story is advancing.

SCENE FOUR

Mercutio and Benvolio wonder about Romeo and think he's still madly in love with Rosaline. It is revealed that Tybalt has sent some kind of challenge to Romeo's father, possibly a challenge to duel Romeo.

The nurse comes upon Mercutio and Benvolio with a message for Romeo from Juliet, but first there is a comic exchange between the nurse and Mercutio. Their exchange varies the pace of the story. Romeo asks the nurse to have Juliet meet him at the cell of Friar Lawrence to be married.

SCENE FIVE

Juliet waits impatiently for the nurse. When the nurse returns, she delays relaying Romeo's message and instead offers a list of her aches and pains. When Juliet does finally learn that all she needs to do to marry Romeo is to meet him at Friar Lawrence's cell, she is ecstatic.

SCENE SIX

Romeo and Juliet meet at the Friar's cell. They leave with the Friar to be married. The Friar encourages "Come, come with me, and we will make short work, / For, by your leaves, you shall not stay alone / Till Holy Church incorporate two in one." (11.6.35)

The preceding four scenes have all been brief and focused, and therefore have quickly advanced the story. Because the story is not about the details of how Romeo and Juliet get married, Shakespeare does not dwell on those scenes. Once a scene has fulfilled its purpose of advancing the story in a dramatic way, it is concluded.

This scene ends Act Two. The act answers the question, can Romeo and Juliet be together? It also raises the question, will they be able to be together in the third act? It's important that a storyteller be able to advance the story in the second act at a measured but brisk pace, even while leaving open a question to draw the audience back into the third act. Many writers struggle because they withhold and delay a great deal of a story to create a single, powerful revelation. Shakespeare, however, made the journey of the story itself a series of potent revelations. And each act ends of a revelation or dramatic note that maintains a hold on the attention of the audience.

Act Three

SCENE ONE

The intensity of the story is heightened in the opening scene of Act Three. Benvolio and Mercutio come upon Tybalt. The three taunt each other, and then Romeo arrives on the scene. Tybalt challenges Romeo to a duel, which Romeo refuses, hinting that he and Tybalt have no cause for quarrel now: "And so, good Capulet, which name I tender / As dearly as mine own, be satisfied." (111.1.73–74)

Romeo's words infuriate Mercutio, who draws his sword and challenges Tybalt. Tybalt mortally wounds Mercutio. Romeo responds: "…Tybalt, that an hour / Hath been my cousin! Oh, sweet Juliet, / Thy beauty hath made me effeminate /And in my temper softened valor's need." (111.3. 117–120)

Tybalt again challenges Romeo and is slain. The prince, together with the heads of the Capulet and Montague clans, is immediately upon the scene. For his part in Tybalt's death, the prince exiles Romeo from Verona.
That ends the scene.

SCENE TWO

Juliet is awaiting Romeo when the nurse enters with news of his banishment.

Juliet speaks of killing herself out of grief at the loss of Romeo, "I'll to my wedding bed / And death, not Romeo, take my maidenhead." (111.2.149–150.)

The nurse promises to find a way to bring Romeo to her.

SCENE THREE

Friar Lawrence tells Romeo he is banished, thinking it a good end to a bad situation. Romeo feels only the loss of Juliet. The nurse arrives with the news that Juliet is mourning the banishment of Romeo. Plans are made for Romeo to come to Juliet, and for the friar to arrange their departure from Verona.

SCENE FOUR

Count Paris approaches Capulet and pressures him to agree to his marriage to Juliet. Capulet gives in and agrees to a marriage that takes place within three days.

The dramatic purpose of this scene is to escalate the pressure on Juliet to forsake Romeo.

Shakespeare introduces characters when they serve a dramatic purpose. For example, he earlier introduced Count Paris asking for the hand of Juliet. That scene served the dramatic purpose of showing Juliet being considered for an arranged marriage. The count's new proposal escalates the drama around whether she can be with Romeo. Similarly, Friar Lawrence enters the story only when he has a dramatic purpose to serve, arranging the marriage of Romeo and Juliet. He's not introduced earlier as a background character because that would serve no dramatic purpose. Many writers struggle because they use the opening scenes of their plays to introduce characters whose dramatic purpose only becomes clear much later.

SCENE FIVE

As another day dawns, Romeo and Juliet prepare to separate. Juliet says,

"Then, window, let day in, and let life out." (111.5.41) Romeo responds,

"Farewell, farewell, one kiss and I'll descend." (111.5.42)

SCENE FIVE

As another day dawns, Romeo and Juliet prepare to separate. Juliet says,
"Then, window, let day in, and let life out." (111.5.41) Romeo responds,
"Farewell, farewell, one kiss and I'll descend." (111.5.42)
Juliet has a premonition of Romeo's death, which frightens her. Romeo departs, and Juliet's mother enters the room. She vows to Juliet that when Romeo is exiled, someone will be sent to kill him. When Juliet is told of the plan that she is to marry Count Paris, she counters that it is only Romeo she will wed.

Juliet's father refuses to hear why she resists marrying Count Paris. He exits the stage. Juliet's mother likewise will not listen to Juliet and also exits. Juliet sends word to her parents that she's going to see Friar Lawrence to seek absolution. Her final words are, "If all else fail, myself have power to die." (111.5.55.)

In this scene, Juliet shows herself to be a character willing to die rather than submit to her parents concerning the marriage to Count Paris. Hearing these words at the end of Act Three, the audience is made aware of to Juliet's dramatic dilemma and to one solution; it is also drawn to the next act to find the answer to what she'll do. Another powerful, well-developed act.

Act Four

SCENE ONE

Count Paris visits Friar Lawrence to arrange his marriage to Juliet. Paris explains her reluctance as arising from her grief over Tybalt's death. Juliet arrives and speaks to Paris about her love for Romeo, but in a veiled way. He, not understanding, takes his leave. Juliet pours out her anguish to the Friar, and shows him the knife she will use to take her life if something cannot be done. The Friar gives Juliet a potion that will make her appear dead, explaining that she should take it the night before her wedding to Paris. Juliet agrees to take it. Once again she acts out her determination to control her own fate. The Friar also tells Juliet that he will send a note to Romeo via a courier so that Romeo will not be alarmed at her apparent death.

Once again, Shakespeare brings together the principles whose actions advance the story. Because Romeo's thoughts about his exile to another town and his journey there, for example, serve no dramatic purpose to this story, so they are not included.

SCENE TWO

Juliet returns home and finds her father preparing for her wedding. She pretends that she will honor his request to marry Count Paris. Her father is so delighted, he says the wedding should happen the very next day.

Shakespeare deliberately heightens the dramatic pressure not only on Juliet, but on the audience as well. The storyteller is always looking for ways to increase the dramatic pressure on characters, not reduce it.

SCENE THREE

Juliet speaks to her mother, saying that all is in preparation for the next day. These are words rich in irony. Juliet explains, "No, madam, we have culled such necessaries / As are behooveful for our state tomorrow." (4..3.7–8) She takes out the vial and wonders if it is really a poison that will kill her and save the Friar the embarrassment of having married her to Romeo. Juliet drinks from the vial with these words, "Romeo, Romeo, Romeo! Here's drink. I drink to thee." (4.3.59–60)

SCENE FOUR

The elder Capulet and the nurse stay up preparing for the wedding. When they hear the approach of Count Paris, Capulet sends the nurse to awaken Juliet.

SCENE FIVE

The nurse finds Juliet seemingly dead and calls for others to come see Juliet's body. Lady Capulet is first on the scene, followed by Juliet's father. They mourn Juliet's death. Moments later, Friar Lawrence arrives with Count Paris. Friar

Lawrence instructs the parents that Juliet's body be taken to the church for her internment.

These five scenes constitute the Fourth Act. They all revolve around Juliet's determination to do whatever must be done to be with Romeo and not marry Count Paris. In these scenes, Juliet comes to life as a fully dimensional character whose actions advance the story to its final act.

Act Five

SCENE ONE

A man brings Romeo news of Juliet's death. Romeo is bereaved, but still asks if the man brings a letter from Friar Lawrence. When the answer is no, Romeo instructs the man to hire a horse to take him to Verona. As soon as the man departs, Romeo speaks of his intentions, "Well, Juliet, I will lie with thee tonight." (5.1.36) As always, Romeo speaks directly about his intentions, and by making his intentions clear, the drama of the story is heightened.

When Romeo tries to buy a poison to take his life, the apothecary hesitates because it's against the law. Even this moment in the story is presented in a way that its drama is heightened. Will the apothecary sell Romeo the potion or not? The answer isn't just given to us that he will. The audience is allowed a moment to not want the apothecary to sell Romeo the potion. In that way, the emotions and attention of the audience is held within the story.

SCENE TWO

Friar Lawrence is told the letter he sent to Romeo about Juliet's seeming death was not delivered. Friar Lawrence realizes he must immediately break in to Juliet's tomb to forestall a new tragedy.

SCENE THREE

Paris comes to see Juliet in her tomb. Soon afterwards, Romeo arrives, determined to join Juliet in death. He asks that Balthasar, his companion, take a letter to his father. Paris comes upon Romeo and blames him for Juliet's death, thinking that she killed herself over grief for Tybalt. Romeo tries to tell Paris that he's at Juliet's tomb to join her, but Paris insists on taking Romeo into custody. Romeo, not recognizing in the dark who challenges him, draws his sword and slays Paris, who asks with his dying words to join Juliet. Romeo realizes then that it is Count Paris, a kinsman of Mercutio, and this adds to his grief, that he has taken the life of someone who also loved Juliet.

Romeo opens Juliet's tomb and says, "For here lies Juliet, and her beauty makes / This vault a feasting presence full of light." (5.3.85–86)

Romeo kisses Juliet, then drinks his poison. As soon as he falls dead, Friar Lawrence comes on the scene and finds Paris and Romeo. At that moment, Juliet awakes and asks for Romeo. Friar Lawrence, hearing others approach, wants to take Juliet away to be a nun, but she refuses. Friar Lawrence leaves, and Juliet picks up Romeo's dagger, saying, "O, happy dagger, / This is thy sheath. There rust, and let me die." (5.3.175–176) She kills herself.

Others arrive and a search is mounted to find out if anyone is in the vicinity who understands what has happened. The heads of the Capulet and Montague clans are sent for, as is the Prince of Verona. Balthasar and Friar Lawrence are also found and brought to the tomb. Finally, Romeo's father arrives with news that his wife died that night.

The prince demands an explanation of the events. Friar Lawrence tells him how events transpired to lead to the deaths of Romeo, Juliet and Paris. The prince reads Romeo's suicide note, then turns to Capulet and Montague and says: "Where be these enemies?—Capulet, Montague, / See what a scourge is laid upon your hate, / That heaven finds means to kill your joys with love, / And I, for winking at your discords too, / Have lost a brace of kinsmen. All are punished." (5.3.301-305)

Capulet responds, "O brother Montague, give me thy hand. / This is my daughter's jointure, for no more / Can I demand." (5.3.306–308)

Montague replies, "But I can give thee more, / For I will ray her statue in pure gold, / That whiles Verona by that name is known, / There shall no figure at such rate be set / As that of true and faithful Juliet." (5.3.309–131)

The play ends with a summation by the Prince and the final lines of the play: "For never was a story of more woe / Than this of Juliet and her Romeo." (5.3.320–321)

As with all the other scenes of the play, these final scenes bring together characters at the height of their emotions. The plot also advances the story to its fulfillment, that the love of Romeo and Juliet is so great as to defy even death and reunite their families. The great storytelling craft of Romeo and Juliet reveals why Shakespeare is rightly renowned as one of the great artists of all time.

Chapter Questions

In what way do you give your story a sense of dramatic passion that will engage the interest of your audience?
In what ways do your characters speak with passion about their feelings?
In what way does your story create a richness of feelings similar to those expressed in this play?
When you read your stories, do you feel emotionally moved and thoughtfully engaged?
When your characters are in dramatic, desperate situations, do you feel caught up in the drama you've created?

The Art of Creating Drama

A Review of 'night, Mother

> Written by Marsha Norman. Available in paperback from Noonday Press, a division of Farrar, Straus and Giroux. 1983 ISBN: 0374521387. Can be purchased from Amazon.com or through book stores. The play won a Pulitzer Prize for Drama in 1983. It is also available as a film and on audio cassette. Page numbers used for citations are from the Noonday Press edition of the play.

'night, Mother by Marsha Norman is a brilliant play.

This story explores the life of Jessie Cates who lives with her mother, Thelma. The play opens with Jessie asking her mother where a particular gun is kept. She finds it with Thelma's help. As she cleans the gun, she quietly announces she's going to kill herself at the end of the evening. Jessie's announcement sets off a fierce struggle between mother and daughter, with Thelma using every strategy she can conceive of to talk Jessie out of her plan. Thelma becomes so desperate, she resorts to telling Jessie the truth about a number of issues that have affected her life.

The play illustrates a central facet of what creates drama in a story: the anticipation of an outcome for a dramatic issue. In this case, that means that Thelma and the story's audience learn early on of Jessie's plans, and they are therefore thrust deep into the heart of a story question: Will Jessie really kill herself, or can Thelma find a way to stop her?

What's at stake in this story is made chillingly clear.

Of all the many issues that bedevil the inexperienced writer, one of the more damaging is the myth that one creates drama by withholding information. In 'night, Mother, the more reasons Thelma offers to convince Jessie to kill herself, the more she reaffirms Jessie's belief that her life is useless, that it's simply better to end her suffering with a clear mind.

By setting up her story question so concretely, the playwright uses the situation to compel Thelma into what is for her completely unexplored territory: her own heart. What follows is a review of the play's structure and how it makes concrete Thelma's journey to a dark, bitter illumination.

'night, Mother

The play opens on what appears to be a typical Saturday night for Jessie, a woman in her late thirties to early forties, and her mother Thelma. Thelma finds the last snowball—some junk food— in the fridge. Jessie asks for some black plastic bags. It's on their schedule that Jessie give Thelma a manicure. All are the events of a routine, predictable evening between Jessie and Thelma. Then (Noonday Press edition of the play), Jessie asks, "Where's Daddy's gun?" (p. 7)

Life for Jessie and Thelma is such a dull routine, Thelma doesn't even pause to consider the request odd. She even helps Jessie figure out where the gun is kept. It's only a few minutes later that Thelma asks, "What do you want the gun for, Jess?" (p. 9) "Protection," answers Jessie.

With the introduction of Jessie's question about the location of the gun, the playwright began setting the hook for her story question.

Thelma at first considers that she and Jessie have nothing worth stealing because what was valuable was stolen by Jessie's son, Ricky. Thelma says, "I mean, I don't even want what we got, Jessie." (p. 10)

This conversation about what Jessie might be seeking protection from provides information about the other characters in her life, principally Ricky.

Jessie begins cleaning the gun. By page twelve, the stage directions state that Thelma is now concerned about the gun and asks why Jessie wants it. Jessie replies, "The gun is for me." Thelma says, "Well, you can have it if you want. When I die, you'll get it anyway." (p. 13) Jessie says, "I'm going to kill myself, Mama."

The hook of this story has just been set.

At first Thelma upbraids Jessie for her bad "joke," but Jessie patiently insists she's serious. Thelma then insists the gun won't work; the bullets are fifteen years old. Jessie tells her that Dawson, her brother, told her where to buy new bullets.

As Jessie describes Dawson's enthusiasm to tell her about bullets, the playwright has found an avenue to introduce a major, if unseen, character. Thelma threatens to call Dawson, to have him come and take the gun away. This leads Jessie to insist that if Thelma makes the call, she'll kill herself before Dawson can get there, and she and Thelma won't have their last evening alone together. Jessie says, "I'm through talking, Mama. You're it. No more." (p. 17)

Thelma responds that in all likelihood, Jessie will only shoot off her ear and turn herself into a vegetable. This is an important exchange, because it sets the story on a course of exploring the emotional terrain of both Jessie's life and her life with her mother. From the moment Jessie makes her announcement about her impending suicide, everything about that terrain stands in bold relief.

Thelma continues trying to find something that will give her leverage over Jessie. That Jessie can't use her towels when she kills herself, that she can't use the gun because Jessie's father gave it to Thelma. She then switches tactics, trying to find out why Jessie wants to kill herself. This continues the story's exploration of Jessie's life and her relationship with her mother. All of this minutia is given dramatic weight because of Jessie's promise. Finally Jessie says, "And I can't do anything better either, about my life, to change it, make it better, make me feel better about it. Like it better, make it work. But I can stop it. Shut it down, turn it off like the radio when there's nothing on I want to listen to." (p. 36)

This is delightful dialogue, spare, evocative, tightly written. It cuts to the heart of Jessie's reasons for wanting to die.

In the next series of exchanges, it is revealed why a friend of Thelma's refuses to come into her house. She's seen the death in Jessie's eyes. This revelation of Jessie's intentions is a potent way for the playwright to use what's at stake for Jessie—her life or death—to explore the reality of Jessie's life. For probably the first time ever in her relationship with her daughter, Thelma begins to speak a deeper truth to Jessie.

This new dialogue leads Jessie to ask whether her mother ever loved her father. Again, Thelma speaks a truth she's never voiced before. It leads to the revelation that Thelma suspects Jessie's father also suffered from the seizures that have plagued Jessie's life. The secrets Thelma has kept from Jessie spill out in a torrent. That Jessie's father never really went fishing. Instead, he'd just sit by a lake in his car. Until this night, Thelma had created an almost impenetrable surface of meaningless chat that only Jessie's impending death has been able to breach.

Jessie and Thelma next talk about Jessie's ex-husband who Thelma had introduced to Jessie. During the marriage, Jessie fell off a horse. The accident was thought to have led to her seizure disorder. But one of the truths that is uncovered is that Jessie began having seizures as a child, but Thelma covered it up. It was something she didn't want to think about, so she found a way to simply go on. Thelma explains, "I don't like things to think about. I like things to go on." (p. 52)

As Jessie talks about her former husband, another area of her life comes into stark relief. Again, the playwright has found a way to use Jessie's impending death to give each revelation about her life a quality of clarity.

When it is revealed that because of her medication Jessie can now think more clearly, Thelma jumps on that as a reason to live. But for Jessie, the medication had another effect. "If I'd ever had a year like this, to think straight and all, before now, I'd be gone already," she says. (p. 68)

As the time nears for the night to be over, Thelma tries in desperation to find some way to forestall Jessie. "I didn't tell you things or I married you off to the wrong man or I took you in and let your life get away from you or all of it put together." (p. 72) But as that final moment of Jessie's life draws near, Thelma becomes calm and pliant. She simply accepts that Jessie will end her life. She repeats to Jessie her suggestions about what Thelma should say to the people who come to Jessie's funeral.

Jessie goes into her room to do the deed. Thelma collapses and cries out, "Jessie! Please!" (p. 89) The gunshot answers with a sound like "no." (p. 89)

Thelma, "Jessie, Jessie, child… Forgive me. (pause) I thought you were mine." (p. 89) Thelma, following Jessie's instructions, goes to the phone and calls her son Dawson.

This is a profoundly moving play. The principle that I want to point out one last time is that it develops its drama not from hiding what's at stake— Jessie's impending death—but by setting it out in a way the storyteller develops drama around the outcome of the question: Will Jessie kill herself?

It is the nature of drama that one can only have a story if there's a cause behind what sets the story into motion. 'night, Mother is an example of where something blunt and obvious— Jessie's impending death—can give dramatic meaning to mundane events such as making cocoa and eating a caramel apple. The storyteller who fails to set up an issue that connects with an audience risks assembling words and images to no purpose. By making what's at stake in this story clear and direct, the storyteller frees herself to begin the real task that faces every storyteller: Bringing an audience fully into and involved with the world these story characters inhabit.

'night, Mother is a great example of the art of creating a potent, dramatic story by early on revealing what's at stake and steadily increasing the tension around a situation characters are driven to resolve.

Chapter Questions

> How do you introduce what's at stake in your story as a story question?
> How do you introduce this question in a way that ensures your audience will care about the outcome?
> How does your plot operate to increase the dramatic pressure on both your characters and your audience?
> How does the plot of your story force your characters into a territory of new feelings and new truths about themselves?

Story as Physical Journey

A Review of Wild

Written by Cheryl Strayed. Published by Knopf, ISBN: 978-0-307-59273-6.

Coupling a story to a physical journey is one way to create a clear quality of movement, that underlying dynamic that makes a story 'work.' The stages of the physical journey can correspond to the stages in the story.

Cheryl Strayed's memoir *Wild*[62] is a wonderful example of this kind of storytelling.

Wild starts with a prologue that takes a dramatic scene from deeper within the story, when Cheryl has lost one hiking boot and tosses another off the trail. This raises powerful questions: what brought her to this point, and could she continue the hike, or how could she continue, in this situation?

She also conveys she is alone, a stray; that with her mother's death her step-father withdrew from her life and her siblings drifted away, and she drifted into odd jobs, drugs, and casual sex.

This leads to an answer to why she is on the Pacific Crest Trail: to find herself. This raises the question, will she find herself by finishing the hike? We have to read to the end of the book to find out. Because as a reader I want to know, the prologue has done its job.

The prologue ends with the line that even bootless, Cheryl had one option, "To keep walking." This is also a powerful metaphor for how to live life.

Cheryl then goes to the beginning of the hike, the thoughts that crystallized the idea, the preparation, the packing, the real decision to begin the hike, which makes her realize the hike had another beginning, her mother's death from cancer.

The plot of the memoir - the hike along the trail - now connects to a deeper layer of emotions and understanding.

Many people think of plot as a sequence of events, but those events must be connected to something deeper to have meaning. This is true whether the story is Fellini's 8 ½ or the action film Lethal Weapon. The action of the plot events striking characters puts characters into deeper states of feeling, and the reader gets to experience those states.

But first, Cheryl sets the story and plot into motion together in the prologue. Then, when we want to know more about her, she gives us more, by returning to her life with her dying mother and the exchange:

I did not want to do this, but I did, inexplicable, as if I had a great fever that could be cooled only by those words. I went so far as to ask her directly, "Have I been the best daughter in the world?"

She said yes, I had, of course.

But this was not enough. I wanted those words to knit together in my mother's mind and for them to be delivered, fresh to me.

I was ravenous for love.

This is pure, heartfelt emotion and need.

When her mother dies, Cheryl writes...

I didn't know where I was going until I got there.

It was a place called the Bridge of the Gods.

Now that we understand something about Cheryl, now we are ready for the hike to begin, at least if Cheryl can check into a motel for a night. Because she doesn't have a home to return to or knowledge of where she'll live when the hike is over, this moment of trying to check into the cheap hotel reflects something deeper about Cheryl's situation in this world. By not having/owning/nesting some place, she's free to chart her own course.

Most worldly people surround themselves with things (job, home, spouse, child) and feel rooted to this world, or, in some cases, stuck, bound to a life half-lived out of duty and half lived out of fear.

At this moment, Cheryl thinks back to her marriage with Paul, again matching the journey to emotions.

This chapter ends with, 'I only knew that it was time to go, so I opened the door and stepped into the light.'

The use of the word light here echoes with that understanding of dying and going into the light. Cheryl is giving birth to a new life for herself. She's not withholding the purpose of the trip, she's setting it out with bold, lucid clarity, so her readers can share the moment and the journey. Struggling writers can't escape the flawed idea that storytelling is about withholding information, instead of being about revealing information that allows readers to share a story's journey.

The physical journey onto the trail in Wild is announced as Part Two of the book. It has a comical beginning, with Cheryl at first unable to get her heavily loaded backpack hefted onto her shoulders. The natural metaphor is of the heavy baggage we all carry, but in Cheryl's case, she's aware of the weight of her baggage for the first time.

When she needs to get the pack on again and a young man offers to help, she turns him down. The Cheryl before the trail probably would have been glad for the help. It's subtle, but it defines how her character is changing even in the opening moments of the journey.

Within an hour, her mind is telling her to give up, but Cheryl had made a deal with herself:

'I knew that if I allowed fear to overtake me, my journey was doomed. Fear, to a great extent, is born of a story we tell ourselves, and so I choose to tell myself a different story from the one women are told. I decided I was safe. I was strong. I was brave. Nothing could vanquish me."

A powerful realization, and because she's using it in a situation that would seem to be overwhelming, it has a powerful impact. But she still has to prove out this new identity by finishing the journey.

Getting through to her first night on the trail, Cheryl reads a poem over and over again, 'Power.'

On this second day, she comes to the realization, 'I was in entirely new terrain.'

Now she experiences the reality of a mountain and as the days mount, she comes to understand after an encounter with a bull, '...was how few choices I had and how often I had to do the thing I least wanted to do. How there was no escape or denial. No numbing it down with a martini or covering it up with a roll in the hay.'

So she walks on, choosing to go forward, not back, into this new life that will not be numbed down.

If Cheryl had taken the path of writing one chapter in the present and then one in the past, she would have needed to find another way to create the same powerful fusion of story and plot and physical journey. For some struggling writers the underlying problem is they want to use writing about the past as a way to explain or introduce their story, plot, and main character, before setting their story into motion. It risks making the beginning of a story a recitation of details of events and situations and people, without giving a reader a context or a reader to care or feel invested in what happens next. As she continues the hike, Cheryl finds herself in a now awareness. 'I saw no one, but, strange as it was, I missed no one.'

She experiencing life in her own skin, not as an on-going reaction to others that is constantly mulled over and dissected into dust, until the next anxiety train pulls into the station.

As she continues on the trail, Cheryl begins to hear about the snow in the Sierra Nevada mountains, and she meets an experienced hiker who tells her it might not be possible to get through the snow-covered trail. That gives her pause, but his belief that she's doing fine also lifts her spirits. Now she has a new mantra at night:

Who is tougher than me? No one.

The sadness for most people, they have a different answer.

As she continues, Cheryl realizes she can bear the unbearable. She continues...

'I had only just begun. I was three weeks into my hike, but everything in me felt altered. I lay in the water as long as I could without breathing, alone in a strange new land, while the actual world all around me hummed on.'

Going through a period of hot sun and lack of water, she appreciates the unending depths of pleasure in drinking a Snapple.

Facing hiking a section of the trail with now too small boots and only sandals, she must 'ride into battle like a warrior' to get through the next section of trail and the new boots waiting for her.

Here we catch up to the prologue, when losing one boot, she throws the other after it. Now she must finish this portion of the hike in sandals that are held together with duct tape.

In a clear cut forest, she sees a metaphor for the destruction of her family after her mother's death. And half way through her hike, she realizes she's had so many amazing experiences, she no longer need feel amazed that her step father abandoned her when her mother died.

'There were so many other amazing things in the world.

'They opened up inside me like a river...I laughed with the joy of it.'

'I felt fierce and humble and gathered up inside, like I was safe in this world, too.'

She is transforming, and she writes in a way that allows us to share the moment.

The memoir continues, the hike now moving into Oregon, stopping in Ashland, then back on the trail.

Now, she confronts her feelings about her mother, who kept her and her siblings isolated from others, who died before Cheryl could grow up and feel distant to her, to share her failings with friends. Until she realizes, her mother had always given her all the love she had to offer, and Cheryl begins to heal inside.

Now the story picks up pace, and she writes about hiking through Oregon, 'I skipped it, I spun it, leapt it in my imagination...'

As she nears the end of the trail for her, sleeping in a futon with three young man, she realizes, 'For once I didn't ache for companionship. For once the phrase woman with a hole in her heart didn't thunder through my brain.'

As the hike comes to an end, she is now ready to release the final weight she carries on the trail, the burden of her memory of her mother.

Now at the end of her journey, she thinks to the universe, 'Thank you,' and, 'it was enough to trust that what I'd done was true.'

Cheryl Strayed's Wild, a powerful, powerful work, deserving of its acclaim.

The Artist as Storyteller

A Review of City of Glass

> Written by Paul Auster. Published by Penguin USA (paperback). ISBN: 0140097317. Full title: City of Glass (The New York Trilogy, Vol 1). Available through Amazon.com and bookstores.

What makes a novel the work of an artist? My answer is that an artist is concerned not just with how a story's movement affects an audience—creating an action story that thrills, for example—but with why an audience desires particular experiences from stories. The artistic storyteller uses a story to illuminate some aspect of the artist's own world and explores ideas about being human.

A question I'm asked is, are the principles an artist uses to create a story the same as those that apply to more simple, popular stories? My answer is yes.

The purpose of this review is to break down, sentence by sentence, the opening page of a novella, *City of Glass*, written by an artist—Paul Auster. Following that review, I'll explore how the opening page of the novella sets up the story's issues and promise in a way that is resolved in an artistic, thoughtful manner.

City of Glass opens with: "It was a wrong number that started it, the telephone ringing three times in the dead of night, and the voice on the other end asking for someone he was not." This sentence raises a number of questions. Who is the narrator who knew it was a wrong number? What did this phone call "start?" Who is this someone "who was not?" This first sentence foretells that more information will emerge later about the nature of the phone call, this idea of chance, and the nature of reality. The audience must keep reading to find out what these revelations will be.

"In the beginning, there was simply the event and its consequences." Even though the writer slips the phrase, "In the beginning..." into this fourth sentence, we're already deep into the beginning of the story. The phrase, "there was simply the event and its consequences," speaks on one level about plot in a story—this happened, so that happened. This fourth sentence offers a kind of Newtonian world view—event and consequence—that the author will re-examine through the telling of this story.

The artist further defines the terrain this story explores when he says: "Whether it might have turned out differently, or whether it was all predetermined with the first word that came from the stranger's mouth, is not the question." He is telling the audience that this story and its outcome will not turn on a simple examination of events in a Newtonian world that operates via cause and effect. This artist intends to take his audience on a penetrating journey of exploring chance and reality. Again, Auster writes to set out his dramatic purpose, not to conceal it.

In the sixth sentence: "The question is the story itself, and whether it means something is not for the story to tell," a judgment about a story is being made by its observer as well as its artist-creator. The audience is reminded that it is a participant in the story and its meaning. This is a view that explores a reality different from a Newtonian one.

This first paragraph has done its job of drawing the reader in. It is beautifully written, and each sentence has a clear, direct dramatic purpose. Each sentence communicates that this is a story about the nature of chance and reality.

The second paragraph begins, "As for Quinn, there is little that need detail us." This is a beautiful introduction to a character, giving us a name there's no real reason to pay attention. Which guarantees, of course, that the reader pays even more attention.

Note how the narrator of the story casually slips into a confidence with the story's audience when he says, "is little that need detail *us*." (Italics added.) The audience has become a participant with the author in observing the events of the story.

In the second sentence, "Who he was, where he came from, and what he did are of no great importance," the artist cleverly plays off the common understanding of how to introduce a character in a way that leads the audience to care about the character's goals and issues. Auster confounds that expectation in a way that leads the audience to want to know more about what we're told we don't need to know. And the audience asks the deeper questions—why don't we need to know more about this character? What's the author up to? We have to keep reading to find out. The paragraph continues: "We know, for example, that he was thirty-five years old."

Who is this "we" who "knows" about Quinn? By not asking a question, the artist implicitly asks a question. Similarly, the artist coyly pulls us deeper into the story with: "We know, for example, that he had once been married, had once been a father, and that both wife and son were now dead." Auster has hooked us with the question of this being a story about chance and the nature of reality, and now he's offering us information in an off-hand way about a character we're told is not important. Personally, I have to keep reading to find out what Quinn does or doesn't have to do with this story.

When we read the next sentence, "We also know that he wrote books," it's hard to escape the "aha" factor. Is the author letting us know in a sly way that this "unimportant" Quinn is his stand-in? Again, we have to keep reading as the mystery around Quinn and who he is deepens with every sentence that assures us he's of no consequence.

In the sixth sentence, Auster writes: "To be precise, we know that he wrote mystery novels." Of course. What better setting for a story about the mystery of chance and reality than a narrator who writes mystery novels? It will be a natural meditation for him.

"Those works were written under the name of William Wilson, and he produced them at the rate of about one a year, which brought in enough money for him to live modestly in a small New York apartment." This sentence both introduces a question—why William Wilson?—while easing away from another potential area of inquiry, how does the narrator maintain his living standard. Since our narrator has no need for money, he won't be pressed by this common issue. The sentence also gives the story a place, New York.

The story continues: "Because he spent no more than five or six months on a novel, for the rest of the year he was free do as he wished." In other words, Quinn has the time to become absorbed in the story's mystery. "He read many books, he looked at paintings, he went to the movies.

"In the summer he watched baseball on television; in the winter he went to the opera." By suggesting the details of this character's life are unimportant, the author finds a clever way to give them a sheen of importance.

However, with the next sentence, "More than anything else, however, what he liked to do was walk," we feel we are being set up for another revelation. "Nearly every day, rain or shine, hot or cold, he would leave his apartment to walk through the city, never going anywhere, but simply going wherever his legs happened to take him." This concludes the "simple" introduction of Quinn, the unimportant man, and is the last sentence of the first page.

In the rest of the chapter, we're told that through walking without volition, Quinn could bring himself to a state of emptiness. In the past, Quinn had not been so empty, but he'd given up on the personality he'd been born with to let William Wilson, the writer, be his public self. "Quinn continued to exist, he no longer existed for anyone but himself." Quinn, through William Wilson, keeps the world at a distance. Quinn even stops dreaming. Then comes the night of the opening sentence, the phone call. The caller is someone looking to speak to Paul Auster, of the Auster Detective Agency.

The "hook" for this story has been set. The terrain for the story is now clear. Later, at the end of the first chapter, the unidentified caller phones again, and this time Quinn says that HE is Paul Auster, the detective, to find out more about the caller. The caller professes that someone means to kill someone, and only Paul Auster can help.

We are given almost no choice but to turn the page and start reading chapter two. The search for answers to this story's probing questions must continue.

Along with its artistic vision, this opening chapter plays to the principles of other well-told stories written in a more mundane fashion. It opens with a question that pulls us in, who is the caller? It broadens to, who is Quinn? It broadens again to, what relationship is Quinn the narrator to Auster, the fictional detective, to Auster, the novella's creator? Who is this person who will be killed without Auster's intervention?

Unlike the more mundane story that builds to one revelation, Auster creates revelations around a layered texture of drama. Drama that revolves around the story's core dramatic issue: the nature of reality as it is expressed through chance and how a fragment of the receiver's personality that must deal with a perception of an event.

Auster draws us into this world with great skill and clarity of purpose.

In chapter two, Quinn as Paul Auster meets the phone caller, the wife of a husband she fears will be murdered by his father who's being released from prison. She seeks to hire Auster/Wilson/Quinn to protect her husband. But this is merely the surface of the story. Auster sets out a deeper realm by having the son Quinn is hired to protect having been raised by his father as part of an experiment to find a way to return to a pre-tower-of-Babel world. A world where "things" have a fixed, understandable meaning that can be expressed in a pure language.

On a certain level, it's a call for a return to a world of Newton, where one can confidently speak about the world as a kind of cosmic clock.

Auster the author takes his audience into a deeper mystery that what will be the outcome of this "case." The real "mystery" of the story revolves around the author illuminating ideas about the nature of reality, personality and chance, a world that exists outside of the Newtonian framework.

In the story, the narrator becomes obsessed with the mystery of why the father wants to kill his son, and also with the old man and his ideas about the nature of reality. But the deeper the detective Auster/Quinn/Wilson becomes absorbed and obsessed with finding the "truth" about the old man's intentions, the more bereft he becomes of finding any kind of truth about what's been happening in the story. By the end of the novel, Auster the novella's creator appears as a character. Even more illuminating, the actions of Auster the author are taken to task by a character who serves as kind of an over-soul, one who sits in judgment on the activities of Auster and the characters in the world he's created.

The final frame for the novella creates a continuum that reveals a relationship between the fragment of the author (Paul Auster) who creates the fragments of characters (Quinn, the old man) who act in a way that where so many people live fragmented lives.

At each stage of the story, the audience is taken not only further toward the resolution of the story's surface mystery, but also into an examination of the role of chance upon the formation of fragments of personality. Each chapter takes us through a corresponding series of revelations that resolve the story's mystery while exploring the nature of personality.

Where a more straight forward story could be diagrammed as having an intermeshed plot line and story line, in this story the plot line also advances the reader along a story line composed of a perception of events designed to make the reader a participant in the ideas of the story. Just as Auster the "author" of the novella becomes a character in the story as a fragment of his personality.

To break down and diagram this story would be to reveal not only a series of events, but an examination of the ideas that underlie the telling of the story itself. This, again, is the prime difference between the artist as storyteller and the writer of popular fiction. The artist creates a story world that asks the audience to explore their own terrain of thoughts and perceptions as part of taking in the experience of the story. Where a mundane story would ask, who's the murderer, etc., Auster asks, what's the nature of the self that asks these questions?

That difference in focus and intent is a prime difference between art and popular entertainment.

Auster is both an artist and a storyteller, a brilliant writer who is a joy to read.

Chapter Questions

What questions about the meaning of life does your story raise?

What illuminations about life does your story offer?

How does your story take on a depth of dramatic purpose as it advances?

Do you see the characters in your stories as reflections of you? If so, how does that affect what kind of stories you write?

Do you ever want to become a character in your stories? Why, or why not?

PART TWO

Deep Characterization

(Paragraphs double-spaced in this section).

Deep Characterization

When I developed the a story is a promise concepts, I thought that if I could teach people the mechanics of telling a story, their writing would improve. Some writers improved; others didn't. As I worked with writers who had been taking writing workshops for twenty years (not just my classes and workshops) and still struggled to understand the mechanics of storytelling, I began to question why.

I saw many problems fell into particular categories. First novels were often written around main characters who are stuck, emotionally numb, unable to express intimate feelings, too conflicted or wounded to act, or diffuse.

I came to recognize writers were creating characters who are extensions of the writer's inner dramas. A storyteller who feels "stuck" in life creates a main character who mirrors that state. Emotionally numb authors create emotionally numb main characters. Writers with issues around intimacy create characters unable to express or feel love. Wounded writers create wounded characters who can only react, not act. Writers who want to appear complex create characters who are diffuse. Writers with a need to be acknowledged create story worlds where they are listened to and acknowledged.

I came to see that the promise of this kind of storytelling is internal; it is meant to transport the storyteller, not the storyteller's audience, to a place where the storyteller can process his or her feelings, or rearrange events and outcomes to meet his or her needs. The "stuck" storyteller can experience what it feels like to be free; the numb author can experience a moment of deep feeling through a character who finally achieves an ability to feel; the character unable to love can find themselves able to feel and express love.

Generally only on the last page, last paragraph of a novel. Which makes that last page, last paragraph the real beginning of a story about a dramatic character making choices versus a passive character reacting to the writer's choices.

A story meant for an audience generally needs characters who pass through a range of feelings as they confront and overcome plot obstacles that block them from getting what they want. Other characters experience powerful illuminations about life on their story journeys. Stories we tell ourselves need only help us rearrange the events of a bad day to a desired outcome. Stories we tell ourselves can have characters who are symbolic to us—father, mother, spouse, ex-girlfriend, boss, in-laws—but have no meaning to an audience. We "get even," "get justice," "get what we deserve" through these characters, experience love, experience revenge; we are champions and heroes on our inner stages. But that means nothing to an audience. They have their own inner stages on which to tell their own stories.

Stories we tell ourselves are a promise to ourselves.

To help writers learn the mechanics of telling a story meant for an audience, I realized I would need to understand how the symbolic characters who act on these inner stages become stand-ins for story characters.

In my first attempt to teach this concept, it just happened I met four young women at a writer's conference who were all in the same critique group. When I set out some of the character types I'd developed and asked each young woman to think about and then talk about what character types from their personal life informed their writing, each young woman gave an answer, and the other three all immediately responded, "no, that isn't it at all, it is really X."

When each of the young women spoke, the others all had the same response: "the issue that informs her writing isn't X, it's Y".

That's when I recognized the underlying problem some writers wrestle with is that they transport story characters from their inner stage to a public stage where these characters are supposed to be performing for an audience. But those characters often keep their backs to the audience while they perform for their creators, their real audience.

That's why I call this process of recognizing the difference between personal storytelling and characterization and telling a story to an audience deep characterization.

To help writers learn the mechanics of telling a story meant for an audience versus fulfilling an internal story promise, I realized I would need to understand how these various inner characters complicate a writer's attempts to tell a story. For example, what inner promise is fulfilled for the emotionally numb author who creates emotionally numb characters? One answer: that writing about an emotionally numb character allows an author to experience feeling through the situations a story character is placed in.

The meek will inherit the earth, in the guise of Rambo or Bambi, at least in a perfect fantasy.

As I began to talk to emotionally numb authors, I came to see that such writers created minor characters who embodied the feelings the writers were able to express. For example, the writer's anger, guilt, and judgmental feelings. The minor characters who embodied these powerful feelings were quite lively and dramatically focused; they came to life because they were driven by their singular feelings. As characters, they hit pure, powerful notes. They often dragged or bullied the emotionally numb, passive main character through a novel, screenplay, or play.

If you're doing that, you have company; I do it. Sometimes I have to write a story, see that I'm venting over an old relationship or, in the words of a friend, I'm putting things in a story that I should have left in a therapist's office. Then I start over. I'm not suggesting that writers not use their personal life and issues as fuel, just to recognize what happens when this process takes over and leaves no fuel to "move" an audience.

Yes, powerful minor characters can "move" an audience, but when the central character of a story is diffuse, powerful minor characters simply highlight the main structural flaw and weakness of a story.

My goal here is to help people who have dedicated themselves to leaning the craft of storytelling but have found themselves 'stuck' at a level that traditional classes have not helped them transcend.

I'm not exploring how these issues affect writers from a distance. I have to deal with them in my own writing.

We share this journey.

Character Types

I'm going to set out the inner character types in this chapter. You'll notice on occasion I offer the same advice. For example, I suggest people write beside each paragraph what a story character is feeling, and how his or her feelings change because of what's happening in a scene. Or, that the writer think of him or herself as an actor playing their main character.

One aspect to this problem of writers learning the craft of storytelling is the intense focus on solutions. Many new writers want quick answers to the question of how to write a good novel, play, or screenplay. They want answers on how to write good dialogue, gripping scenes, stronger characters, and build powerful plots. I came to see that as long as some writers are endlessly in a quest for solutions, it can mask the real, underlying problem, that writers are unaware of this process of overlying their needs and issues over their main characters.

Therefore, when I set out what some of the most common of these character types are, my main advice to writers will be to stop and think about what they are doing. Are you creating these characters to use as vehicles to vent? To process your feelings? Deal with your anxieties? To turn your failed dreams into fictional truths? Avenge personal defeats?

In my case, the answer is yes. Then I try and move on and write a story.

Now, the character types.

The Wounded Writer

The wounded writer creates a main character who is too wounded to act. This type of main character gets dragged through the story by minor characters. Since most stories are advanced by active characters, wounded characters kill the drama of a story. These main characters become the least interesting character, because they are the least able to act to shape a story's course and outcome.

Suggestions: Give a story's main character a positive goal, something he or she is willing to act to gain in spite of obstacles. If you can't stop yourself from creating a wounded main character, try making your wounded character a friend of the main character, a parent, a spouse, a lover. Or, if your main character is wounded, allow the audience to share his or her feelings (or ideas) as the character acts to shape the outcome of a story in spite of his or her wound.

Examples of stories with wounded main characters who act:

Prince of Tides, by Pat Conroy, is a novel about a wounded character who only finds healing when he acts to save his sister.

Tell No One, by Hank Coben, is about a man who believes something in him died when his wife and soul-mate was murdered. When he discovers she's alive, he is compelled to find out what happened.

Funerals for Horses, by Catherine Ryan Hyde, is about an emotionally scared young woman who goes in search of a missing brother.

What popular novels or movies do you recall about wounded characters? Successful stories can teach you how to make your wounded character active.

Something to consider: If you feel you've been victimized by life, are you recreating that mind-set in your main character? If you're trying to write popular fiction, readers who feel victimized by life generally prefer to identify with powerful, determined characters.

The Martyr

These storytellers have sacrificed or subsumed their desire to write to take care of the needs of others. One way martyrs deal with this disappointment is to become numb. Martyrs tend to create main characters who are also emotionally numb. Because stories are often journeys of feeling for readers, story characters who are numb aren't accessible to a story's audience. Things happen to them, but they have no visible, emotional response.

Suggestions: Accept that you've experienced creative disappointments in life and get in touch with those feelings. Then allow your main characters to have their own feelings, disappointments, hopes, and dreams.

Some writers might have a personality that is so defined by the martyr role, it's difficult for them to not express it. I suggest such writers recognize that they might need to write a story that expresses that feeling, then move on and write another story that doesn't go down this path. I find in writing short plays that I often have to write two plays; one that vents my feelings and overrides my original story idea, plot, and characters, then a second play that is a story with characters and a plot not connected to my inner drama.

Examples of stories told with active characters who martyr themselves:

Silkwood, starring Meryl Streep, is about a woman working

at a nuclear plant who sacrifices herself to save others.

Norma Rae, starring Sally Field, is about a wife and mother working in a mill in the South who makes great sacrifices to get her fellow workers the protection of a union.

The Exorcist, by William Peter Blatty, has a priest who sacrifices himself to save a young girl possessed by a demon.

Something to consider:

Think of yourself as an actor on a stage playing a character. As an actor, what would you need to do to express to the audience what your character is feeling? As an actor, what would you need to do to express what your character wants, and what they are doing to get what they want? The goal here is to make the character and his or her feelings and dramatic goals accessible to a story's audience.

The Unacknowledged Writer

These writers can shove main characters aside at key moments to expound on their beliefs or ideas. In life, these writers might not feel recognized for their ideas, so they create a world full of characters who become their audience. For these authors, a main character is often a vehicle for the authors to expound on their ideas.

Minor characters tend to be under described, because they function as an audience for the main character, while "bad" people are very detailed because they are people the author wants to get back at for not listening. Such characters are often the barbarians at the gates, very dramatic folk. Their deaths are often graphic and detailed. This organized violence can be a safety valve for unacknowledged writers who feel stuck in life.

Suggestions: To understand how to incorporate ideas into

stories, read writing books about theme and story (*The Art of Dramatic Writing*, by Lajos Egri).

Learn the difference between a story that is an explanation or exposition of your beliefs (a lecture aimed at your audience), and a story that acts out a belief (*Moby-Dick*, for example, demonstrates how a good cause becomes evil).

If you have a strong desire to express yourself, consider finding an outlet to express your ideas, a web blog or journal, for example. Or, just accept that you're creating a story world to explore ideas that interest you and have fun sharing your work with others with similar interests.

Something to consider: Exploring the downside of being *too* acknowledged. For example, Samuel Clemens was known all over the world as Mark Twain. People everywhere loved Mark Twain. Very few people cared about Samuel Clemens, or Norma Jeane Mortenson (Marilyn Monroe), or Reginald Kenneth Dwight (Elton John).

Examples of main characters who are unacknowledged:

The Ambassadors, by Henry James, features a provincial American who wants to test himself in the cultured airs of Europe. He discovers he doesn't want to return home to a more circumscribed life.

Rambo, starring Sylvestor Stallone, is about a returning Vietnam war vet who feels his sacrifices and the sacrifices of other vets have been ignored.

Main Street, by Sinclair Lewis, features an energetic, cultured young woman who moves to a small town with her new husband and finds her sense of identity worn away by small town values and norms.

Everything's Under Control

Some people internalize a need to not rock the boat. They act reflexively to make sure that in every situation, everything is under control and that no problem is too large to be fixed. When such people create main characters, they, too, tend to not make waves, or do anything to draw attention to themselves. They actively work to make sure any tension is deflated, or happens off stage and is resolved with a minimum of conflict.

I came upon this archetype when working with a writer who had a main character committing suicide, but not in a way that would discomfort anyone, draw attention to himself, or make waves.

What helped this writer was to recognize why she'd created such a character and to become consciously aware that her main character could have larger than life feelings and out-sized needs, and that was okay. She came to understand that her need in her own life to not rock the boat could give her an understanding of a character with a need to shake up his or her world.

Popular characters in stories are often people who break the rules.

Examples of main characters who break the rules:

In *The Wolf of Wall Street,* the main character lets nothing get in his way of a fabulously wealthy, hedonistic life.

In *Lethal Weapon,* Roger Murtaugh is a family man who wants to finish out his time as a detective and retire. His partner is the out-of-control, suicidal Martin Riggs.

In *Magic Spells,* by Kristy Yorke, a mother tries to protect her mute son because she blames herself for his condition.

Something to consider: We live in a world where we are conditioned to obey the rules. It's difficult for some people to even conceive of breaking rules. Some writers will need to keep a running account of how a main character is breaking rules to ensure that action ends up on the page of a story.

It's My World, Keep Out

Do you ever watch the Animal Planet channel and the programs about a Meerkat or Hyena needing to find a new clan to live with? There's tremendous life and death drama. If the animal is rejected, it will die.

Humans evolved from animals and are territorial. In modern life (no hunter gathering, no farms where people "own" a piece of land) how do people gain and maintain personal territory? Personal storytelling is one method. We can create any space and territory, create and enforce the boundaries we don't always have in life, and enforce our rules.

This kind of storytelling can fail because it is really about meeting the needs of the author. The author's focus is on setting up their boundaries and enforcing their rules, not transporting a story's audience.

Some writers do this unconsciously. A big cue to recognizing this is when a writer finds themselves going into a long lecture about the "rules" that govern their story world before allowing anyone to enter.

Suggestions: Trying to help or work with other writers who are territorial means setting up clear rules about boundaries and asking permission to enter and finding out what's off limits in their story world. If you are in a critique or support group with writers who are overly protective of their story worlds, either accept how that limits what the group can accomplish, learn to deal with angry outbursts or long defensive explanations when you cross some boundary, or move on and find another group (or Meerkat clan) to join.

Examples of characters who retire to a personal world:

In *The Station Agent*, a dwarf retires to live in an old railroad station. He finds himself unable to escape the needs of others or being the center of unwanted attention.

The Iceman Cometh, by Eugene O'Neil, features Larry, who has retired from the progressive movement to live out his life in a run-down dive, surrounded by self-deluded alcoholics. Larry tells himself he's given up on humanity, but a salesman named Hickey forces him to realize he's not a bystander to life.

Catcher in the Rye, by J.D. Salinger, features Holden Caulfield, who finds himself unable to escape from all the phonies in his life. He's also mystified about what happens to the ducks in Central Park when the pond freezes over in the winter.

The Spear Carrier

In an opera, the actors with no lines who portray crowds of people in the background are known as spear carriers. When storytellers devalue their own lives, the risk is that they create main characters who are not really main characters. The action of these characters doesn't drive the story forward; when these characters are in a scene, they are generally the weakest characters or passive about responding to events. They wait for someone else to take the lead.

Suggestions: Give a main character a goal he or she is determined to resolve and fulfill no matter the obstacles. Writers who consistently create spear carrier main characters should consider making these characters the friend or spouse, the wise friend, or mentor. Even the antagonist who blocks the main character.

Nick in *The Great Gatsby* is a minor character who observes the action. What makes Nick's observations dramatically interesting is that he doesn't always understand what he's seeing.

In the documentary *Twenty Feet from Stardom*, some back up singers truly strived and failed to become stars in their own right, while others were comfortable in the role.

Sam Gamgee in *The Lord of the Rings* is the faithful companion of Frodo. Without Sam, Frodo would not be able to fulfill his quest.

Something to consider: If you're a spear carrier in life, let yourself imagine yourself as a story character who's larger than life; a character who goes on some great quest or hero's or heroine's journey. Explore what it's like to be an ordinary person who rises to the occasion.

I, Robot

This type of main character is a recording device. He or she enters a room, looks around, and the storyteller records what the character sees. This allows the author to view and have feelings about the events of a story and its characters from a safe distance. Since the robot/character lacks feelings no matter what is happening around it, it's hard for an audience to identify with the character, or care about the outcome of its actions.

Creating a robotic main character allows the author to put that character into situations so the author can experience feelings about what's happening to the character.

In a story about ideas (alienation, for example), robotic characters can serve a purpose. But, the idea at the heart of the story needs to be dramatically acted out and accessible to the story's audience.

Suggestions: In the side margins of your story, write down what your main character feels about the environment and situation he or she is in, and how that feeling changes based on what's happening.

Examples of robotic characters:

The Terminator is about a shallow young woman who becomes a tough survivor when she must help save herself from an unfeeling robot.

In the *Sarah Connor Chronicles*, a spin-off from the Terminator movies, a female terminator has the ability to process and develop emotions to better understand humans. That raises interesting questions about how she'll respond to and act on those feelings. Will she develop empathy? An ability to love?

West World is about middle-class people who go to a western theme park to get into shoot-outs with robotic gunslingers programmed to die. When the robots come to life and start acting out their roles with lethal determination, some weak tourists must fight for real or die.

Something to consider: Many people fear "going out of control" if they experience their feelings. You can use story characters to explore your feelings, and explore allowing your story characters to have feelings different than yours.

I Am Ideas

Some people love coming up with ideas, exploring ideas, and talking about ideas. Getting living, breathing characters to bring those ideas to life can be a struggle.

As a writer, I'm often approached by idea people who think

my taking a year to turn their idea into a novel means a 50/50 split of any advances, option money, or royalties. Coming up with idea is easy; understanding how to turn ideas into stories, and doing the work involved, takes effort and determination.

An idea person can actually come up with the occasional good idea. However, in screenwriting classes, I often find that someone's great "idea" is based on a half-remembered episode of Barnaby Jones.

Being an idea person is different than being an unacknowledged writer. Unacknowledged writers often will take the years or decades required to develop their ideas into novels, screenplays, and plays. The unacknowledged writer creates a story world specifically so their ideas can be acknowledged.

Suggestions: After you've come up with a good story concept and have a sense of how to introduce your idea in a dramatic way, write an overview of the dominant feelings of your main character for the course of your story. Figure out how the ideas of your story impact that character's feelings. When you think about a scene, consider what action creates a shift in feeling for your main character. Write how you intend to make that feeling shift visible (on the body, via dialog, or action).

Then go through the same process to figure out the main feeling of the character who blocks your main character, and how you intend to make that character's feelings accessible. Consider giving your antagonist, the character who blocks your main character, ideas that are in opposition to the main character's, such as a character who idealizes the concept of honesty in conflict with a character who idealizes falsehood.

The first time you do this, it'll be work. The second time you do it, it'll be work. It might always be work. But, it needs to be done. It's also possible that once you think through the ideas of a story during an outline process, you'll be "done" with the story. Consider that you can take ideas deeper, in new directions, or that characters can embody ideas that are a threat to everything you believe. Put your ideas into conflict that isn't easy to resolve, embodied by characters who won't be denied the expression of their ideas.

Examples of characters who embody ideas:

Thomas Pynchon is a writer who explores the idea that corporations with assets in Europe and America aided the Nazis in his novel *Gravity's Rainbow*.

Gunter Grass explores post-Nazi Germany in his great novel, *The Tin Drum*. I once exchanged emails with an author who'd met Gunter Grass at a party. When asked how he wrote a novel, Gunter responded (I was told) that he focused on the story.

Woody Allen often plays a character who ponders the big questions of life.

In the film *Submarine*, a young Welsh boy with an overactive imagination falls in love for the first time while he must scheme to keep his mother from having an affair with a childhood sweetheart.

Virginia Woolf's *To The Lighthouse* explores what it means to be a woman and an artist in Victorian England. Woolf is one of the great artists for exploring ideas in stories. She can pack more ideas into a single sentence than can be found in some genre novels.

Something to consider: If you want to be considered an artist or write literary fiction, you need to explore ideas in your stories. You can write out some of your ideas before you write a story, or as you develop a story.

Most stories transport an audience as characters act to

achieve concrete goals. In a story about ideas, the audience can be transported to an illumination of ideas.

I Am Feeling

Some people are great at creating characters who are passionate and deep feeling, but coming up with an overall concept for a story eludes them.

Suggestions: Write out the core idea of your story (think of your story's promise). Then, consider how to introduce that idea through your main character in a dramatic context (in a way that suggests a need for resolution and fulfillment). When you introduce other significant characters, introduce them in ways that suggest they have something to resolve. Work out the concrete obstacles of your story, and the physical journey your characters must take (and take the audience on).

As characters pass through obstacles in a story, they should pass through a range in feeling, and, when characters are in danger, they need to react and act, and not just ponder their feelings.

Examples of main characters who are passionate in stories:

In *Mr. Jones*, Richard Gere plays a man who is manic-depressive, an example of what happens when feelings go out of control.

Martha, in Edward Albee's *Who's Afraid of Virginia Woolf*, has volcanic feelings. She acts on all her impulses, no matter the cost.

In the film *Drop Dead Fred*, a young woman going through a divorce reverts to child-like behavior when she returns home to live with her mother. Her child-like state brings back a destructive imaginary friend who acted out in ways she could not. When she gets her life back on track, she no longer needs an imaginary friend to act out her feelings.

Something to consider: Most stories are a journey of feeling for an audience. You must create characters who have feelings about the situations you put them into and the characters they meet. Those feelings make them accessible to your audience.

The Fearful Persona

Some people go to great lengths to create a public persona that is confident and successful. If what underlies a storyteller's public persona is fear, the risk is that the storyteller creates characters who are an extension of the writer's fears. Such main characters might be afraid to act, or afraid to act in a way that reveals too much about the storyteller's underlying fears. Or, the characters blocking the main character might be too fearsome for the main character to overcome, so confrontations happen off-stage.

If a writer is fearful about self-revelation or afraid of intimacy, a story character might be unintentionally emotionally crippled. There's an artificial surface to the character, but no sense of what lies beneath.

Suggestions: Accept that to be human is to have issues around fear; allow your characters to have their own personas and fears. I've passed through deep states of terror in my life, and these experiences influence my writing (I have a large shadow self). That means I have to let go of stories that indulge or become enmeshed in my fears.

Accept that writing to process your feelings is okay. I do it all the time. I expect I'll be doing it until the end of my life.

Examples of stories with fearful characters are:

In Khaled Hosseini's *The Kite Runner*, the main character's failure to intervene to save another boy from being raped leaves him emotionally "stuck" in life.

Good Night, and Good Luck is a film about the McCarthy era and the fear of being branded a subversive by a demagogue.

In the film *A Room With a View*, a young woman in Victorian England finds herself forced to choose between a very circumscribed, proper life or getting in touch with her sensual feelings and acting on them.

Something to consider: If your fear is debilitating, or maintaining a courageous public persona becomes too draining, I suggest getting professional help.

I Am Objective

We live in a culture that praises being objective and denigrates being subjective (it's only feelings, stay with the facts). Writing is often taught as an objective process (the who, what, when, why, where journalistic-style of writing; or essay writing that explores an idea or concept in a tightly ordered fashion).

Story audiences generally perceive stories in a subjective way. A good story induces feelings, creates epiphanies about life, brings a world alive to the senses, and creates characters who ring true.

Unlike the I, Robot character type which limits what is seen to a main character, objective writing can be used in every facet of a story: describing an environment, establishing minor characters, relating details.

Suggestions: If being objective is how you write a first draft, do that. Then go back and objectively write beside each from sharing an experience, and writing to simply relive or keep alive an experience that has become part of the writer's internal "story." People who have been through powerful experiences can have a tremendous need to write about it. This said, advising someone about how to turn a personal story into a memoir that speaks to a larger audience can be difficult, because advice can appear to be "not listening" or "understanding" or appearing to diminish the truth of an experience.

Suggestions: To make a memoir accessible to an audience can require using storytelling techniques like setting out a story's promise, understanding a character's dramatic truth, setting out what blocks characters from achieving their goals. To simply relate, "This happened, then that happened," etc. might be enough for family members, but not a larger audience.

Examples of stories about personal issues:

In the film *When a Man Loves a Woman,* a man marries a woman he finds to be quixotic and adventurous, only to discover her antics are fueled by ever-increasing amounts of alcohol. When she stops drinking, they are forced to redefine the roles in their marriage.

Betty Henshaw's *Children of the Dust* is a memoir about a share-cropping family forced by the dust bowl to leave Oklahoma and journey down Route 66 to California. She captures what it's like to grow up in absolute material poverty but with great family love.

Angela's Ashes, by Frank McCourt, is an example of how a memoir can take a young boy being raised in a dysfunctional, poor, Irish family and turn it into powerful storytelling. A side note, Frank McCourt's mother has followed him to readings and exclaimed from the audience that there was a high level of "story" in his memoir.

The Frustrated Writer

I come across screenwriters who create main characters who find the key to success is to have beautiful, sexy girlfriends sleep with producers, sell their boyfriend's scripts, then die. This speaks to the writer's frustration of selling a script. I've also read manuscripts where a main character is seething with anger over the author's divorce, loss of a job, etc.

Suggestion: Read stories by authors who channeled their anger into good storytelling. Dickens is probably one of the most popular storytellers of all time, and his stories seethe with an undercurrent of anger. I believe that great storytellers accept their personal feelings and issues, and accept that their characters have their own issues and concerns.

You can be angry about the injustices of life and use that as a fuel to tell powerful stories. Just be aware of the difference between telling a story and stepping onto a soap box to lecture your audience.

Examples of stories by writers with something to say about society:

John Steinbeck's *The Grapes of Wrath* gave voice to the Oakies, families forced out of Oklahoma and abused as farm laborers in California during the great depression in the early 30s.

Joseph Heller's *Catch-22* is about the amoral use of power. Set in the Mediterranean during WWII, a bombardier named Yosarian tries to survive being killed by the Germans and his American commanders.

In Charles Dicken's *Oliver Twist*, Dickens gets across his disgust with the Poor Laws that condemned so many children to a life of servitude and hunger.

I Am Great Depths

This writer wants to be considered complex, so he or she creates obscure stories and characters that no one can figure out. I think fear underlies this archetype, and a need to be acknowledged and appreciated.

Suggestions: Read Virginia Woolf's *To The Lighthouse*. It's a story of great depth and an exploration of a culture and the ideas that support that culture.

Accept that a writer and person of great depths may have a limited audience. Accept that even if you aren't a writer of great depths, you can still tell powerful stories with characters who ring true and speak to audiences. For example, that Harry Potter wants to fit in, Rocky wants to be somebody, and Dorothy wants to find her way home. Not everyone is going to be Proust or James Joyce or Henry James.

I've worked with writers who found their voice when they switched from writing literary fiction to writing young adult novels. Some writers become trapped in a need 'to be' a particular kind of writer, no matter the cost to themselves.

Examples of writers of great depth:

The Tin Drum, by Gunter Grass, is a mythic novel about a young boy who decides to stop growing when the Nazis come to power, his life during the war, and his life in the war's aftermath.

Toto le Hero is a film about a man who believes his life was stolen from him by another boy. He has lived his life trapped in his thoughts, unable to act and gain what he wants until the end of his life.

In the film *8 1/2*, Frederico Fellini explores the life of a director who needs to finish a film but he can't make a decision; any decision. He finally must integrate all his internal narratives before he is free to act again. A lovely, graceful film.

One path to great depths is isolation and deep thought. I speak about meditation practices in later in the book; that's another path to getting to a quieter, more thoughtful place to explore ideas.

The Artiste

Similar to writers who desire to be considered a deep thinker, the writer who wants to be an artiste creates main characters who are obscure. Sentences have nouns but no verbs or verbs but no nouns.

The writer may harbor some real issues of fear: fear of failure, fear of a failure to impress, and a fear of a lack of depth.

Suggestions: being an artist means having the courage to expose oneself, and to examine life with an unflinching gaze. In this culture, being recognized as an artist often means having a degree in art, having the right pedigree, sleeping with a true artist, or imitating an artist.

Being an artist is a way of life, not an artificial persona.

There's an issue here of showing your stories to your intended audience and seeing if your ideas about the human condition are coming across in a meaningful way. Some writers retreat into "not being understood" as a way to sustain a viable fantasy of being an artist.

Examples of great artists:

James Joyce is a great artist for the ages. His short story, *The Dead*, operates on many levels to speak about the world and how people intellectualize their feelings in place of experiencing them.

Henry Fool by Hal Hartley tells the story of a garbage man who meets an 'artiste', who flaunts that he is a great literary artist and observer of the human condition. The garbage man goes on to win a Nobel Prize in Literature, while the fake artiste is exposed as a literary fraud.

Frida, a film by Julie Taymor, is about the Mexican painter Frida Kahlo and her tumultuous, eventful life. The film captures her tremendous drive to be a painter in spite of a broken body.

Something to consider:

Great artists generally create powerful characters who are accessible to readers in terms of what they want, hope for, or, in some cases, characters who are not capable of understanding themselves. But, great art is often about a purity of expression, a potent setting out of a truth about a character or a character's world, not about obscurity as a camouflage for a lack of ideas or the fear to express them.

My Characters, My Pets

Some storytellers want to keep control over their characters. The further the writer gets away from these main characters, generally the more unleashed and active the characters become. Characters who function as pets generally passively wait for instructions, sulk in silent rebellion, or become passive/aggressive.

Suggestions: Accept that you like having control, and accept that your characters probably like having control, too.

In *The Royal Tenenbaums,* directed by Wes Anderson, Gene Hackman is a family patriarch who has manipulated his children to get what he wanted.

In Bertrand Tavernier's film *Clean Slate*, a French police officer in a small African town is looked upon as the local fool. When he starts eliminating his tormentors, no one can even imagine he's the killer, even when he's found over a recently deceased victim with a smoking gun.

In Arthur Miller's play *Death of a Salesman*, Happy is the son who is his father's pet, the one who will carry on Willy Loman's deluded dreams when Willy dies.

Something to consider:

If you're suffering from writer's block, consider that your characters are refusing to act because they don't want to follow your orders.

I'm Okay, You're Not

This describes a male writer who doesn't like women, or a woman writer who doesn't like men. When writers with these kind of issues write romantic comedies, or any kind of drama that requires an intimate, loving relationship between a man and woman, what comes off the page is a lifeless relationship.

Suggestions: Write a journal entry about the kind of men or women you loathe, or make a list of what you don't like about the other sex. Or, write that scene that sets out what you really think about the opposite sex. Then let your characters have their own feelings. If you project your anger or guilt over who or what you are onto your characters, they'll come across as beasts of burden loaded down with all the feelings you can't express or try to disguise.

Examples of main characters who love, not loathe:

Tom Hanks in *Sleepless in Seattle* plays a husband who has lost his beloved wife to cancer. She's only in a few scenes, but those scenes convey his great loss over her death.

In the film *You Can Count on Me*, two teens lose their parents in a traffic accident. She grows up to be prim and proper; her brother grows up to be a wastrel who drifts from job to job, but she's the one who has lessons to learn about how to live from him.

In *Nights of Cabiria* by Fellini, a prostitute meets a nice man who wants to marry her. He turns out to be a con artist, but her love of life shines through even when her dream of a better life is destroyed.

Something to consider: Fellini had a great love of people and it comes out in his films. He isn't sitting in judgment of his characters or using their feelings or situations in life to get a laugh.

All the Pretty Walls

We live in a culture that rewards conformity and being 'normal', but we have a mental landscape that embodies a wide variety of needs and feelings. When our culture tells us that our thoughts or feelings are wrong, we sometimes expend energy to wall off that part of ourselves. Then we create characters who reflect what ideas and feelings we consider it permissible or acceptable to express.

Suggestions: Don't take the walls down, just consider what your characters have walled off and why, and give a suggestion of what that is. Also, don't put all your characters behind your walls.

Examples of stories with characters who lived outside of conventional boundaries:

On the Road by Jack Kerouvac is about a young man who hitch-hikes across America and has many adventures. I use this book as an example because Kerouvac's personal life was more conventional than suggested by this book. He used his life as fuel to write a novel that has spoken to generations of readers.

The Lives of Others is a film about an East German Stasi officer who spies on others. When he spies on a playwright, he comes to understand something about the life he has denied himself.

In *Fifty Shades of Grey*, a young woman who is a virgin explores the world of being a submissive to a dominant in a relationship, a novel which also will take many readers into an unfamiliar world and sexual practices.

Something to consider: A story world can be a place where you explore characters who exist outside of your comfort range. I believe that great artists allow their characters to have their own issues and concerns, their own demons and angels.

Rescue Me

Some writers have experienced being abandoned. A ramification of that can be a fantasy of either being rescued or being the rescuer. The downfall to projecting this fantasy over a story character is that the character has no feelings about their situation, since they were created so the storyteller could experience great feelings around the character either being rescued or being the rescuer.

The cue to recognizing this is that the character being rescued expresses no feelings about his or her situation. Since a story's audience often accesses a story's characters through their feelings, emotionless story characters are a blank wall. The author, however, sees wonderful characters experiencing powerful emotions being displayed.

Examples of stories about characters who want to be rescued:

In Funerals for Horses by Catherine Ryan Hyde, a young woman has been protected all her life by an older brother. When he disappears, she gathers the strength to go in search of him.

In the film *The Darjeeling Limited*, an adult son who has recently tried to commit suicide convinces his brothers to go to India in search of a mother who abandoned them.

In *A Confederacy of Dunces*, a slovenly young man evicted from his mother's house by her new husband finds himself selling hot dogs on the streets of New Orleans until a college friend stages a rescue.

I Can Explain

This is a variant to being objective. Such a writer often expends significant energy explaining how people get to and from cars, how they get in and out of them, how to turn the ignition of a car on (or get in and out of a house, elevator, plane, train, bathroom). When this kind of information is tacked to the beginning or end of dramatic sentences or scenes, the drama of a scene becomes muffled.

Some people have a personality that is defined by their role of being "the explainer." I've been told by a number of women how irritating it is when a man feels a need to explain the obvious to them, as if they are children. A story's audience can experience the same irritation.

Some writers have grown up with a need to justify themselves, which can lead to explanations of explanations in stories.

I once worked with a writer who had a wife represented by a highly regarded literary agent. I offered to read his novel, but he felt he didn't need my advice with his wife and her agent in his pocket. Unfortunately, his novel was rejected because it was overwritten with detailed explanations of the most obvious events. In every sentence of ten words, three of his words functioned to explain the other seven. Very tedious to wade through.

People enjoy stories precisely because they don't feel a good story is lecturing them; it provides a journey that transports them.

Suggestions: Learn to let go, to let a scene or action begin as late as possible and end when it is dramatically over. Give your audience a reason to want an explanation before you offer one. If your life is defined by being a teacher, you might need to make an extra effort to be aware when you're using a character to expound on lessons you want your readers to understand.

Examples of stories that weave in detailed explanations:

Frank Herbert's *Dune* gets across the ecology of a planet and how that ecology affects people. The short version of the movie *Dune*, by David Lynch, fails in part because the opening scenes are a detailed explanation of who the characters are instead of the beginning of a story.

In *The Hunt for Red October*, Tom Clancy demonstrates his knowledge of military hardware, but he explains that technology as it impacts the quest of a man to be free of oppression.

Tristam Shandy by Laurence Stern is about life as a muddle. As Tristam explains his life, his stories go in lazy circles and never quite seem to get anywhere, but the trip to nowhere is quite a pleasure.

The novel was turned into a movie, and the director understood he needed to convey the life-is-a-muddle conceit and not just re-create what happened in the book. The movie has a cheeky-charm all its own.

Something to consider:

Set a story into motion first. Create a compelling, sympathetic main character (or create something interesting if you are using unsympathetic characters). Once a story is in motion, your audience will want explanations.

The Supplicant

The supplicant wants to be anointed as a writer or storyteller by a piece of paper (for example, a degree), by some authority figure (such as a popular, published author), or by sleeping with an artist. As a teacher I come across supplicants who think my blessing will improve their writing.

Examples of supplicants:

Starting Out in the Evening is a movie about an aging, once-famous novelist trying to finish his last work. He's approached by a graduate student who wants to write her thesis about him, but also so she can share in his reflected glory. She sleeps with him to get the kind of private reflections that will help her gain credence in the world of writing.

In the film *I'm Not There*, each persona that Bob Dylan adopts draws in different types of people who have their own goals and ambitions in being connected to him.

In the film *All About Eve*, what appears to be an innocent young actress insinuates herself into the life and career of a famous if fading actress as a vehicle to jump start her career.

Listening To Your Characters

There are probably as many styles of creating stories as there are writers. One general path is for writers to consider what they want to say and how they want to say it.

- Some writers do this consciously, thinking about story ideas, creating character profiles, bouncing ideas off friends, joining writer's support groups.
- Some do it intuitively-they start with a character or event and ideas come as they write.
- Some do it unconsciously-they sit down and write and try not to think too much about what they are doing. They just try and get into a flow.

You might have a process unique to you.

As I covered in Deep Characterization, some writers are writing to meet personal needs. By doing this, they limit both their character development and their ability to connect with an audience. I've recently begun teaching writers who fall into this trap how to get in touch with their story characters and their audience.

The goal with these techniques is to guide writers away from "watching" a movie in their mind's eye and writing down the details, to creating a story journey that transports an audience.

First, I suggest you find a quiet place to sit. Practice some kind of meditation technique, such as mentally counting one when you inhale, for the whole breath - oooonnnneeee, tttttw-wwwoooo when you exhale, three when you inhale, four when you exhale, then start over. Do this until your mind quiets.

Another technique to quiet the mind is called watching the breath. To do this, focus gently on the point between the eye-brows, aware only of your breath coming in and out through your nostrils until your mind quiets and you have a sensation of watching yourself breath. When it happens, you'll know.

You can find additional meditation techniques on line or at a library.

When your mind is quiet, visualize your story's main character sitting alone in a room. Enter the room. Let this character tell you what he or she is trying to achieve or gain and how he or she feels about it. Let your character speak while you listen. Ask questions if you like, but mainly listen.

When you've heard this person out, respectfully thank him or her character for sharing with you, then get up and leave the room.

Next, take the issue your character spoke about and write an explicit sentence about it. It could be about overcoming grief, feeling isolated, or a need to gain control over some circumstance. It should be something that drives this character, something he or she feels so strongly about that it compels this character to act no matter the obstacles.

Write that issue as a sentence that speaks directly to who your character is and what's most important to him or her.

I call this a character's dramatic truth.

For example, for a character scarred by early poverty, your sentence could be something like this:

"She vowed when she grew up she would no longer wear hand-me-down clothes; she would have only have the best of everything."

Your sentence for a character scarred by childhood trauma might read:

"He decided when he grew up he would never again let anyone get close enough to hurt him."

Both of these sentences suggest these characters are dramatically ripe, that if put into a particular situation they will be compelled to respond.

Write this kind of sentence based on what your main character expressed to you.

The goal of this process is to learn something true and deep about your character's inner life and to then turn it into a dramatic, potent sentence that could be used when you introduce that character.

If you need a refresher on what a dramatic truth is and how to express it, go back to the chapter titled Suggesting a Dramatic Truth.

Now, again quiet the mind. This time visualize yourself meeting with the character who opposes your main character.

Allow this character to tell you why he or she acts with such force and determination.

Just listen.

When the character is done, thank them respectfully and leave.

Now encapsulate what was said into one sentence.

It's often easier to write about this kind of character, because such characters often act with great force and determination. He or she will often stop at nothing to get what he or she wants. Since characters define themselves by what they want, these characters are often fully defined dramatically.

The goal here is that the character acts from his or her own motivation and not as a plot device for your personal storytelling.

To continue, again quiet the mind. Let yourself visit the main environment of your story. What do you feel in this environment (not what you see)? What is it about this environment that most strongly impacts your senses?

Come back and take what you experienced and write a sentence that evokes the truth about that environment. Be descriptive. Rather than write, 'She found the house scary,' write, 'She felt the house would devour her family.'

Convey the emotion the environment triggered.

An environment that is alive—that interacts with a character—is an active participant in a story. Your environments should act on your characters; it should evoke feelings in them, and through them, your readers.

When an environment is described with passive details, it's like describing bland walls. Use description to make the world of your story vivid and palpable.

To continue, again quiet your mind. This time visualize yourself meeting with someone you consider to represent the audience for your story. Let this person tell you how your story speaks to him or her.

Again, listen. Let your reader tell you what about your story generates an emotional response for him or her.

When you feel the session is over, thank this person and now leave.

Take what your reader has expressed to you and turn it into a sentence.

If you can't do this, if you can only come back and write down what YOU think about YOUR story and what it leads YOU to feel, the risk is that you are the audience for your story—the sole audience.

Can you write a story that meets your needs and speaks to others?

Yes, but consider watching a friend's video of a trip to a beach in Hawaii. As you watch the video, do you have the same feelings and responses as your friend? Likely not. Watching the video triggers personal feelings for him or her of the experience. A good story creates that journey of feeling for an audience, but that requires that a story speak to an audience, that the story operate to transport an audience.

When I've led writers to use this technique in workshops, those writers who could listen to their story's characters and audience were able to use what they learned to write potent, dramatic sentences. Writers who could only tell me about how their ideas expressed their feelings and needs often could not write those potent sentences.

Some writers appeared unable to understand what I was asking; they could only relate to their ideas about their characters and not access their characters inner lives.

The risk with this kind of writing is that these characters function as an extension of the authors or function to act out some internal drama of the authors.

In a novel, allow your characters to have their own inner lives and dreams.

In a memoir, allow your real-life characters to have inner lives that are potent and deeply felt.

If needed, focus on writing one sentence for each significant story character and environment until you're writing powerful, potent sentences.

Any time you introduce a significant story character or environment, you need a sentence that comes off the page to engage the attention of your audience.

If you can do that, you're on the road to telling a good story. If you can't, understanding the bigger issues of storytelling— plot, characterization, dialog, pacing—might fail to create the effect you desire.

Understanding your characters and bringing them to life for your audience are the basic building blocks of telling a good story.

Once you internalize these techniques, you could find yourself returning to being an intuitive or an unconscious writer, but you'll be working from a bedrock of understanding.

Good luck.

Writing Fear

For many people, one of the key issues in life is security and control. One can gain a sense of security by having authority over one's personal space.

To maintain their security, such people can live vicariously through attachments to sports team. They aren't being pummeled or concussed on that field, their *team* is. They get to experience the winning and losing and bruising from safe seats. They are winning or they are losing, and something is happening that defines and adds to their persona. And when it's time to move on, they can do it with the push of a button.

Melodramatic TV series and popular novels also offer a safe way to experience danger and emotional catharsis, all with no risk.

The problem for some who want to write is that they approach storytelling from the perspective of maintaining their safety. They are like someone who observes life from a distance. They write down the details they observe, but those safely observed details don't create the same cathartic effect for their readers.

For the observers of the world, there is no risk of exposure. There is no messy, real life relationship that risks rejection, no failure that risks a persona being undermined.

The reality is their readers aren't with them behind the curtain on that high balcony observing through a distant window two strangers, say, having sex. The observer gets off, but the risk is that the person they relate the details of what they have observed generally do not. The problem is when people try and write from this perspective, they write down the details they have recorded from their experience behind the curtain, while their readers, behind their own curtains, want the experience of watching, and, in a safe way, sharing and engaging and experiencing that sexual act vicariously.

That makes porn popular but telling a story that engages and rewards the attention of an audience can't just rely on painting a graphic picture.

There are a couple of paths people with lives revolving around being safe and secure can go down if they want to be successful as writers.

They can read Part One and Two of this book and learn the mechanics of how to tell a story that transports an audience. Those mechanics allows an audience to experience an emotional catharsis and release.

This kind of writing can be found in successful authors who have found a formula for storytelling that satisfies an audience.

It's difficult for many people to learn the mechanics of storytelling because most have been trained to function as distant observers recording details. It's a journalistic, who, when, what, why, where style of writing. This happened, that happened, this happened, that happened, etc.

Another path involves taking some risks. These authors can ask themselves these questions:

How much risk am I willing to take as a writer?

How willing am I to risk writing something where I have no idea of what the outcome will be and no ambition that what I'm doing will lead to me feeling good about myself?

To start this process, look at a scene and ask yourself, what is this character putting at risk in this scene that threatens their desire for security for themselves? What has forced them in to this situation? If the character has nothing at risk, where does the drama, tension, or conflict arise from?

Looking at this scene, ask yourself, what does the risks you ask your characters to experience say about what you fear in life? What threatens your security, and what feelings would you have in a similar situation?

Get to an emotional, subjective feeling here, not an objective recording of action.

In another place in this work I note that Edgar Allen Poe isn't just relating the experience of his fears, he's exploring them. He's vividly evoking his fear of madness, not just telling us 'it was a dark and stormy night.' He takes us into the heart of a dark and stormy night.

When I read the manuscripts of struggling writers, often their best writing is when they are describing the punishments of story characters who are clearly standing in for real life counterparts who threaten the safety and security of the author. If the author can't deal with them in real life, they can deal with them in stories.

There are some great examples from popular stories of characters responding to threats to their safety and security.

In *The Accidental Tourist*, the set up for the novel is that a man who teaches travelers to go around the world in a cocoon has had his personal cocoon torn open by the senseless death of his son. The author forces this man to deal with the issues that led him to create that cocoon that gave him an artificial and unsustainable sense of security and safety in an unsafe world.

In the Harry Potter novels, the Dursley's sense of personal security is bound up in their desire to project normal personas, which is threatened to its core by Harry Potter. The conflict in Harry Potter is driven by a battle between those who think the magical world can only be a safe and secure if its members are of pure blood.

While the Dursley's are presented as comic characters, there is no mistaking what Mr. Dursley will do to maintain the security of his persona.

Politics is often a form of storytelling that revolves around getting a population to believe X is a threat to a group's safety and security, therefore Y needs to be done.

The famous quote of Goering about leading a peaceful nation to war, "All you have to do is tell them they are being attacked, and denounce the peacemakers for lack of patriotism and exposing the country to danger. It works the same in any country."

If you want to write something that generates feelings in your audience, be willing to explore your own feelings. Explore and release your own fears.

Understanding Emotional Triggers

Readers most often access characters through their feelings. Intense states of feeling are often the result of some kind of trigger, such as a person, an image, an idea, a time or place.

To understand the truth of a character is to understand what triggers these intense states of emotion for him or her.

The deeper issue is that struggling writers need to become consciously aware of their triggers and the triggers of their characters.

Why this is so was suggested in a book called Drawing on the Right Side of the Brain. The author suggests that when most people are asked to draw a face, they draw a symbol for a face—a circle, with lines for eyes, a nose, and a mouth.

That's not a face; it's a symbol of a face.

When an author creates a symbol for a face that has meaning to him or her, that symbol can be an emotional trigger.

For example, someone can have an intense feeling about his or her mother, or father, or spouse, or child. The feeling could be anger, guilt, jealousy, or some other heartache.

A symbol of that mother could be a bare description of a woman with short dark hair and glasses.

That would be an emotional trigger for a deep state of emotion for that author.

For everyone else, it's the descriptive, symbolic equivalent of the face on the previous page that conveys no emotion.

In screen writing, the equivalent is 30, blond, tall; or 40, stocky, dark-haired, the ubiquitous descriptive tags that evoke nothing about a character's dramatic truth.

This kind of descriptive language could be compared to fast food value meals. You get a stripped down burger, fries and small soda for three dollars. Think of a reader for an agency picking up a manuscript and finding this kind of threadbare, descriptive, symbolic language that evokes all the pleasure of eating value meal hamburgers. Not just one, but dozens.

You will generally get a thread-bare, 'value' rejection letter in return.

What makes this issue complex is that the emotional reaction of an author to a symbolic trigger can be unconscious.

If you are consistently told by perceptive readers that your main characters are diffuse, you need to do the work of creating characters with accessible, palpable dramatic truths. You need your readers to have the same kind of intense emotional feelings you have for your main characters and their story journeys.

If readers find your main character uninteresting or diffuse, you need to recognize what your descriptions convey.

What Lies Beneath

On the surface, it might seem odd to write about why people lie in a section of this book titled the spirit of storytelling, but to understand the situations and circumstances a character will lie is to gain an insight into that character's internal life.

If what a story character will lie about is different from what the author will lie about, that will help give the author another perspective into a character's inner life.

In life, there are many different kinds of lying. Lying by omission, malicious lying, lying to gain some advantage, to avoid unpleasant scenes with others, lies that are part of a system of self-delusion, lies to protect a loved one or one's position in life, etc.

Since the goal of drama is to create an anticipation of an outcome for a scene or situation, a revelation that a character is lying is dramatic.

An example of this comes from Carolyn Hax, who writes an advice column for the Washington Post. A mother had written to say that her adult daughter had shown up at a family event six months pregnant. After the initial thrill, the mother felt sad her daughter had never mentioned being pregnant in spite of the fact that the mother spoke to her daughter on the phone several times a week. She felt she and the daughter weren't as close as she thought.

This led to Carolyn's observations: did the mother initiate all these calls? Did the daughter feel a need for space from a controlling mother?

Carolyn didn't have the answer to the why, but note how this lie of omission raised questions about the real nature of the mother/daughter relationship. In a story, this would have raised a dramatic question about this relationship that would have drawn readers forward to get an answer.

Another example, on the television series House, a man comes in to the hospital with a medical problem that leaves him absolutely unable to say anything but what he really thinks, and he didn't think much about his wife and her aspirations. In life, this character censored or moderated what he said.

In a story, this man's revelations would raise questions. Why was he in this relationship? Did he settle for being married to someone he considered beneath him? Did he stay in the relationship because he secretly enjoyed feeling superior to his wife? And, could this relationship survive after his medical problem was resolved but his marriage was now on life-support?

Returning to real life, many people censor or moderate or doctor what they say to others. Many people feel this is necessary to get along in life; some people create a public persona that is entirely at odds with their real feelings and thoughts.

I suspect that people who censor or doctor what they say to get through life transfer that mindset to their writing. They end up with main characters who censor what they say so their actions won't upset others.

Which creates a bland, passive main character.

Now consider the person who has created a persona that they are an honest person. That author may unconsciously shy away from creating dishonest characters. Or, they might move this trait solely to minor characters. But this, in turn, becomes part of the process of making a story's minor, deceptive characters more interesting than main characters. The minor characters will say or do anything to get what they want, while the main character has boundaries set by the author's internal sense of what is acceptable to say or do.

A variation on this is to ask the question, under what circumstances would an honest person lie? To protect a family member? To get a coveted job? To save a marriage?

Lying does not have to be openly malicious or serve some external agenda. Another type of lying is the lies we tell ourselves. What lies might your main characters be telling themselves to help them get through another day?

What lies do you tell yourself to get through another day? Again, if you want your story characters to have their own internal lives, let them have delusions that are different than yours.

To get to the answer to some of these questions, practice a technique to quiet your mind.

Now, visualize yourself entering a room where your main character sits in a chair. Sit in a chair facing him or her. But, instead of your story character speaking, I suggest that you reveal to this person under what circumstances you would consider lying, to who, and for what reason, and at what cost to yourself.

This should be a lie that you would not ordinarily speak, a lie that violates your sense of who you are, but under some circumstance in your life you would feel compelled to speak.

If you are resolutely honest, than tell your story character what circumstance could lead you to lie. What person would you lie to protect?

After you've spoken, let your story character relate to you what lie they've spoken, or considered speaking, that violated their deepest sense of who they are.

If it's the same lie you've spoken of, consider that a cue that this character might be an extension of your inner life.

If that happens, you need to be take extra care to ensure your character's actions drive the story in a way accessible to your audience.

You can use your life as fuel to tell a story, but that fuel needs to advance a story that is accessible to your audience.

As always, the goal is a deeper understanding of a character as you begin a story or begin a revision. Some writers will need to complete a story to get to a place where they can have this conversation with a character. Or themselves.

Finally, quiet your mind and imagine going into that room to sit with your main character. This time, consider your most enjoyable fantasy in life. Perhaps being rich, or famous, or intimate with the famous and beautiful, or in charge of a country, or saving others in a heroic fashion, or getting revenge on someone who has wronged you. That fantasy that has become part of the bedrock of who you are.

Now tell that fantasy to your main character, and, in turn, ask your main character to tell you their bedrock fantasy.

If you want, write about your fantasy.

These fantasies can speak to a deeper truth about who you are and who your characters are.

Starting a Novel With A Stuck Main Character

One of the character types I come across in novel manuscripts is the 'stuck' main character. Typically, a stuck main character is dragged through a novel by minor characters. The minor characters act with great determination to accomplish X, some clearly defined goal, while the main character is too stuck to act.

This review of *The Kite Runner* will show how a well-told, popular novel about a stuck main character can be dramatically defined and interesting.

The opening line of the novel: 'I became what I am today at the age of twelve, on a frigid overcast day in the winter of 1975.'

Here, the author, Khaled Hosseini, informs his readers that his main character is stuck. This opening raises the question, can the main character of *The Kite Runner* become unstuck? Getting to the answer to this question will take the entire novel.

The author continues:

'I remember the precise moment, crouching behind a crumbling mud wall, peeking into the alley near the frozen creek.'

It will take the author several chapters to get to an answer to the question, what happened in the alley? Why did it have such a powerful impact on the narrator? Readers are being drawn forward to the answers.

'Looking back now, I realize I have been peeking into that deserted alley for the last twenty-six years.'

When an old family character calls in the present, the narrator relates, 'I knew it wasn't just Rahim Khan on the line. It was my past of unatoned sin.' The narrator also relates something that Rahim said during the call, 'There is a way to be good again.'

What this suggests is that there will be a way for the stuck main character to gain his freedom. In a novel with structural problems, this sense of purpose and direction would be lacking. We'd be shown a stuck character, but the character's journey would not be framed as a story question, nor would there be a clear sense of purpose that the character could move to become unstuck.

These opening two pages also mention 'Hassan the hare-lipped kite runner.' This suggests but isn't explicit that Hassan has something to do with the narrator's unatoned sin.

This one page chapter powerfully sets this story into motion toward the fulfillment of its promise.

Chapter Two introduces the narrator and Hassan as children. The narrator relates how deadly Hassan was with a slingshot, which foreshadows something that happens later in the novel. It also comes out that Hassan always took the blame for what the narrator did when some mischief was found out.

The narrator also relates how Hassan's mother, Sanaubar, led many men into sin, another issue that plays out in a powerful way later in the novel.

Hassan and his father are Hazara, and Shi'a, while the narrator and his father are Sunnis. In America, the status of Hassan and his father would be comparable to being black and Native American in the deep South in the 1920's.

Sanaubar disappears five days after Hassan's birth, for reasons that are only introduced toward the end of the novel but which, in hindsight, explain much. The deeper meaning of what happens is in the subtext.

'Hassan and I fed from the same breasts. We took our first steps on the same lawn in the same yard. And, under the same roof, we spoke our first words.

Mine was Baba.

His was Amir. My name.

Looking back on it now, I think the foundation for what happened in the winter of 1975—and all that followed—was already laid in those words.'

To find out what that means, the reader has to turn the page and keep reading.

What the author has done is set out his story promise, story question, plot question before introducing his main characters. The introduction of the characters in the second chapter begins to offer the background of the story's main characters. Struggling writers often begin with this introduction to characters ahead of a dramatic introduction to a story's promise that would give character details a context.

While Hosseini writes a novel about a main character who is emotionally stuck, the underlying story mechanics are all in place and operate to transport the audience from the first page.

The Kite Runner is a powerful, haunting novel.

Writing About a Character with a Wounded Psyche

Creating a story about a character with a wounded psyche requires that what a story is about be made accessible to an audience. When an author has a deeply wounded psyche, the risk is that he or she will create a main character who is so wounded, they cannot act. Authors might do this out of a need to process their feelings about their wound, to relive it, or to experience feelings of anger around it, but it creates a story with an inert main character who acts for an audience of one, the author.

Inception is an example of a film with a main character who has a deeply wounded psyche. The breakdown of this film will demonstrate how this story operates to transport an audience.

The film opens with violent waves and a man, Cobb, semi-conscious on a beach. What he sees is a young boy and girl building a sand castle. This raises immediate questions, who is the man? Who are the children?

A second man in a uniform prods the semi-conscious man with a rifle. The guard uses his rifle to raise the semi-conscious man's shirt, revealing a gun.

This suggests the man is on a dangerous mission. The stakes have just been raised significantly.

In the next scene, an old man inside a pagoda-like house on the beach is informed about the man found by the guards; the old man is shown a small top and a gun.

When the other man is dragged into the room, the old man asks, 'Are you here to kill me?' The old man relates that he saw something like the top when he met another man years earlier.

End of scene.

We go to another scene, in a glossy office with three well-dressed men. The young man from the beach is explaining to a powerful man, Saito, that he is an extractor, able to retrieve information from another person's mind through their subconscious, and he can train this man to protect himself. This is Cobb, the young man from the beach. To do this, Cobb says he needs complete access to Saito's secrets.

Saito offers to consider the proposal and leaves. The room starts to shake, and Cobb's compatriot, Arthur, says, 'He knows.'

Raising the question, knows what? Arthur asks, 'What's going on up there?'

Cut to next scene, rioting in a street and an explosion.

It's revealed that Cobb and Arthur are dreaming, and that they have taken hostage Saito, and are trying to probe his secrets through this dream they control.

We return to the dream world. Arthur notices someone and asks Cobb, "What's she doing here?"

Cobb goes to a woman, who asks if she jumps over a railing, will she survive?

This foreshadows a revelation about who this character is that comes out later in the film. An important seed has been planted, who is she?

She asks if Cobb still misses her, and he responds that he can't trust her any more. Again, another question: why can't he trust her?

Next, they are in a room together and he asks her to take a seat. She asks, "Do the children miss me?"

The assumption would be the children from the opening scene on the beach, and she is their mother, and perhaps he is the father.

He intends to use the chair she sits in as an anchor so he can repel down the exterior face of the building, but she leaves, and he falls and has to catch himself.

Cobb goes in through a window and kills two guards with a silenced gun. He opens a safe and is going to replace one envelope with another, but he's surprised by his victim and the woman who now has a gun trained on him. His compatriot is brought in under guard.

Cobb surrenders his gun, and Saito announces he knows he's asleep and in a dream world.

Saito wants to know who hired Cobb or Arthur will be killed. Cobb replies there's no use making such a threat in a dream, but Mal replies, 'That depends on what you're threatening," again suggesting her history with Cobb.

She shoots Arthur in the foot and says, "Pain is in the mind." This foreshadows a major revelation in the story.

Cobb shoots Arthur, who wakes in the real world as the dream world begins to implode. Cobb now tries to finish his mission, fighting his way out of the imploding dream world while reading a document marked confidential.

He's acting out here how dogged and determined he is to fulfill a job. He's not weak.

In the 'real' world, Arthur decides the time has come to awaken Saito and Cobb, who refuses to wake so he can finish reading the document. Arthur says 'dunk him,' and Cobb's pushed into a tub of water to force him awake, which to Cobb looks like the dream world being flooded with water.

Meanwhile, Saito pulls out a gun but is disarmed by Cobb.

It comes out that Saito considers what has happened an audition and that Cobb has failed.

But then it comes out that this scene, too, is a dream, a dream within a dream, and the men controlling the dream are sleeping on a train with Saito.

When Cobb wakes on the train, Arthur demands to know why Mal showed up. Cobb claims he has the situation 'under control.'

The men who set up the dream scenario flee the train car. Saito wakes and smiles. This raises the question, what is he smiling about?

This is the opening sequence for the film, Part One, so to speak, fifteen minutes and forty two second in.

A number of questions have been raised, some answered, but there is a clarity to the action even while much is mysterious.

Cobb now sits in a high rise with the top that he spins. We'll find out much later why he spins the top. He stares at it while it spins and holds his gun next to his head until the top ceases to spin.

He gets a call from one of his children, and we see an image of two children playing.

His children ask when he's coming home and he responds that he can't.

One child says he's never coming back. This raises the question, why?

A child asks if he's with mommy, and we see an image of Mal. That answers the questions of who she is and if she's the mother of these children.

I call this process question, answer, question. We get an answer about Mal, but this sets up another question, why can't Cobb return to his children?

These questions and answers are easy to track. If all we had were questions and no answers, at some point the story would be a chore to watch because the audience would be required to remember every detail.

What we know is that Cobb extracts information from people's subconscious, but Mal is interfering for reasons that will soon be made clear; and that Cobb wants to see his children again. We aren't just told he has a wound psyche, we see it by Mal showing up even in his dream world.

Although there are many dream landscapes in Inception, the questions raised on any one track of the film are clear and accessible. We understand the inner journey for Cobb (resolving his guilt over his wife's death) and his external goal, wanting to be with his children.

While this isn't fully conveyed in these opening scenes, we've been told enough to get us invested in Cobb's journey.

If all we knew about Cobb was that he extracted information from people's dreams but we only found out at the end of the film his real needs and goals, all of the spectacle to that point would not satisfy a large audience.

Inception is a fine example of a puzzle piece story constructed around the wounded psyche of a main character.

Storytelling, the Unconscious, and the Subconscious Minds

The unconscious is where we store memories. To help compact this storage of a huge volume of memories, feelings are shorn from each memory. Scientists have discovered that when people retrieve memories, they can be guided to attach different feelings to them than those that were originally experienced.

The unconscious is also where fixed ideas about who we are and what we think about our place and role in the world are embedded. Think of ideas buried there broadcasting a message, like a radio transmitter. 24/7. You might think of yourself worthy, but buried in your unconscious could be the message that you are not. Or any powerful message that drives your conscious feelings and awareness.

The conscious mind is, in most people, consumed by measuring and weighing things. Our relationships, our standing compared to others, how we judge and measure ourselves compared to others. In most people, a significant part of the conscious mind is engrossed in these issues.

Narrative tension in a story is the tension a character feels about something they seek to gain, achiever, or, in some cases, avenge. It can be the tension a character experiences from a change in circumstance that changes their standing and relationships or a change in a character's internal sense of who they are.

In life, we experience narrative tension about the 'story' of our life, and whether what we seek is within our grasp. Our narrative tension can also revolve around our desire to escape something we feel is imposed on us, whether by fate or our choices.

We also experience narrative tension when our conscious story of who we are is in conflict with an unconscious story of who we are.

An example, a nun told a story about two women. When they were young, the mother constantly referred to one daughter as the 'pretty one' and the other daughter as the 'smart one.' The 'pretty one' grew up to be a lawyer who worked at the United Nations. No matter what she accomplished, inwardly she felt stupid.

The 'smart one' grew up to be an attractive young woman who, no matter what compliments she received about her looks, felt ugly inside.

In each case, they experienced narrative tension over the internalized story idea of who they were opposed to external validation.

I heard one aware person refer to these kind of people as hungry ghosts.

When I read novel manuscripts written by struggling writers, I can tell with a certainty what they are ashamed of, who they blame for their situation in life, and what fuels the rage that burns within them. What the main character in their novel wants, that I have to guess.

Bringing this back to writing, struggling writers who unintentionally go into their unconscious to write (watch the movie created from memories, write down the details) tend to write visual information shorn of emotional content. It moves the writer because he or she attaches emotion to the events or people described, but the writing doesn't generate that effect for a reader.

Writers who have internalized an understanding of storytelling can use their subconscious to develop insight into the narrative tension of their characters. Think of the subconscious as like the engine room in a 40's film. The captain gives an order, which someone relays to the engine room, and power is made available to turn the ship in a specific direction or speed up or slow down. But the Captain never has to go down to the engine room to get that result.

One accepted idea about storytelling is that many successful writers are intuitive about creating stories. Brain scans have shown that what people often consider to be intuitive thoughts are just as often the subconscious floating ideas up into the conscious mind.

That requires that a writer have internalized an understanding of storytelling the subconscious can work with. That's the problem for most struggling writers. I often find that new writers are blind imitators. They can quote people like Stephen King's book On Writing, but their own writing is lacking.

A solution to this is for the struggling writer to gain and internalize an understanding of storytelling. This means being consciously aware of the mechanics of how to tell a story, the techniques that I cover in A Story is a Promise (and that others have covered in their own way).

The reason even this pathway will fail for many struggling writers is they have no real interest in telling a story to an audience; they are really telling a story to themselves to deal with their internal narrative tension. When the fuel for that burns out, they move on to doing something else that helps them balance their narrative tension.

Instead of learning the craft of storytelling, some writers blame their lack of intuitive storytelling ability or credit the success of other writers to their intuitive sense.

When a writer confuses their narrative tension with the narrative tension of a novel's main character, they can fail to recognize why a story character isn't coming to life and what to do about it.

I've written in another essay about how getting to the subconscious can be a pathway to the superconscious, and a deeper ability to understand a story character's narrative tension. I believe that when writers are in what is called a creative flow, their subconscious is actively generating new ideas and insights into their story, characters and plot, this rises to conscious thought, which sparks new ideas that in turn generates a strong flow of subconscious and conscious ideas for a story.

One of the pleasures of deep meditation is a sense that different aspects of the brain (left hemisphere, conscious, subconscious, unconscious) experience a clarity and unity. All the doors in the house open, so to speak.

That makes creating a story a pleasure to experience.

TRANSFORMATION

When I work with writers, my goal is that their writing transforms, becoming powerful, potent, and satisfying to their audience. For some writers, the validation of transformation comes when people who once had to be asked to read a manuscript now call and demand to read more. Or, literary agents or film producers now take the writer seriously.

In the following anecdotes, I'll write about a few people who did or didn't transform.

J's Transformation

J had taken one of my A Story is a Promise on-line workshops. Her writing was solid but lacking deeper feeling. She emailed me a short story about two young girls playing a board game. The set up for the story was that recently the mother and father of the girls had been playing a board game with relatives, a fight had erupted, and the father had left the family.

The lesson the oldest daughter took from this was that when she played a board game with her younger sister, she needed to make sure nothing got out of hand. In this version of the story, the oldest daughter was asleep when her parents argued. During the course of the story the youngest daughter cheats at a board game and the game spins out of control. End of story.

There was a lack of expression of feeling during the story, and the background details didn't express a dramatic truth.

My main cue to what had gone wrong was that the main character had been asleep during her parent's argument. That should have been a moment of powerful feeling, but the writer made sure the main character was off stage. This is a problem I often see in flawed stories; dramatic situations, but the story characters often mention in passing what happened, and the authors often either offer nothing about what characters felt or label the feelings. For example, to tell me someone is angry doesn't evoke the feeling of anger.

Of course, the author is not unconscious about what the characters were feeling, which makes the author the intended audience, not readers.

In this situation, I asked the author to write beside each paragraph what the main character was feeling and how her feelings changed based on what happened during the paragraph. If a character's feelings aren't impacted by what's happening in a scene, why should I, the reader, care?

I also asked her to write out a dramatic truth for the garden where the story happens, and how the truth impacts the characters. Often, when people write weak description, they have been advised by others to write less description, which leads to a problem of the reader being unable to 'see' what's happening.

When the author explored her character's feelings and the truth of the time and place of the story, her writing transformed. The story became powerful and fulfilling. She evoked the main character's fear and sense of loss.

The revised short story was accepted for publication.

The Three Sisters

With another writer, transformation happened, then stopped.

In this situation, a writer had taken my on-line class twice and we'd exchanged emails and phone calls, and I'd read the opening chapters to her novel several times. The writing in her novel about three sisters was fine, but I could never get a sure fix on the promise of the story, nor a dramatic truth for the main character. The one character who came fully to life was a minor character, an authority figure. He was a short man with a chip on his shoulder who overcompensated for his lack of height by walking with an exaggerated swagger.

This dramatic definition of a minor character while a story's main character remained diffuse is the hallmark of inner characterization. Clearly, this story's main character spoke to the author from that inner stage.

After many readings, classes, emails, and phone calls, the author mentioned she thought her main character was afraid of emotional intimacy.

At that moment I finally understood all that dry description of her main character, her sisters, and their environment. I now had a context for what all the conversations and events meant.

When the author worked from that understanding of her main character, her writing transformed. It became lively, passionate, vivid, and dramatic. Then it became wildly vivid and suggestive, in a few places too much so. Every detail was a revelation. She mentioned that members of her critique group preferred the early version of the story; they found her new writing too wild.

What I wanted to do was work with her to dial in her writing from being wildly suggestive to suggestive, but I never heard from her again.

TE's Process

When a middle-aged writer took my screenwriting class, he clearly relished it. He asked more questions than anyone else, and if he didn't understand a point, he asked for clarifications and embellishments.

He often took my instruction literally. When I mentioned that in a Series of Shots for an action scene in a screenplay, locations could be labeled A), B), C), D), he wrote ordinary scenes with action lines labeled A) through M).

But, he kept at it, and between classes we exchanged emails and I continued to read his work.

He decided to turn from writing a screenplay to a novel. I have mixed feelings about writers who haven't mastered one genre starting over in another, but I encouraged him to continue.

He then sent me his novel, with the first line, `Anonymity served him well.' I immediately emailed him and told him he now understood what I'd been trying to teach him and that his writing had transformed. In that one sentence he suggested his character's dramatic truth.

The character's dilemma was that he was a marine in special forces who did undercover assignments, but he was married to a well-known politician. That first sentence captured the main character's narrative tension, could he serve both his country anonymously and preserve his marriage?

Because my student's writing transformed, a successful Hollywood producer tried to find a name screenwriter to turn the novel into a screenplay, but she could not. That she tried affirmed to my student that others now took him seriously as a writer.

The novel is The President's Marine by Roland Evans Jr. The wife in this story is the President of the United States, and, more importantly, the commander-in-chief. As President, she can order her marine husband's career as a spy to be over, but as a wife she knows it would end her marriage. She, too, carries a burden in this novel.

Wonderful storytelling. I had to stay up until 2 am to finish the book. I couldn't stop. That's when I know a story is compelling, I can't stop until I'm done.

Conference Anecdotes

I've taught several workshops at Michael Steven Gregory's Southern California Writing Conferences. Michael's conferences have a lively interaction between workshop leaders and attendees.

At a conference in Los Angeles I met a writer who had written a novel about a bi-sexual policeman in a small town. The novel opened with a dramatic situation, the policeman needing to break up a brawl. The main character had no emotional reaction to this situation; everything was related in an objective, emotionally flat tone. He saw a fight, he broke up a fight.

The minor characters in the novel, however, were quite angry and vengeful, and they were going to do something about it. Their feelings were apparent and accessible to readers.

Minor character who are more dramatic and interesting than a novel's main character are one of the main tip-offs that an author is overlaying his or her feelings and needs onto a main character. That character speaks to the author in some deep, clear way, but not to the story's audience.

I met another writer who was writing a memoir. In the chapter she showed me, an adult daughter was waiting in a restaurant to meet her father. It was a dysfunctional relationship, and the daughter expected her abusive father to ask for money, which she dreaded.

The father arrived at the restaurant and was a glad-handler. Even though he was suicidal in private, in the restaurant he went to every table and happily greeted everyone. Through the point of view of the adult daughter, readers objectively observed the father approaching the daughter's table. He goes to table X and greets Y; he goes to table W and greets V. Slowly he nears the daughter's table.

There was not one expression of feeling for the daughter during this entire scene, although she had to be going through a series of conflicted, deeply felt feelings.

Readers often access a character through their feelings. In this case, no feelings, no way to access what this situation felt like for this character.

My advice, that the writer express her feelings in that situation.

For a writer to be intimate with an audience, the writer needs an ability to be intimate or familiar or emotionally accessible to themselves and to their characters. This means the writer needs to reflect on what they are trying to cast off and integrate it, so they can make it accessible to their audience.

Edgar Allen Poe did not thoughtlessly cast off his inner demons; he explored them in a way the audience could share the exploration. He seduced his audience to share that exploration no matter what type of madness or pain he explored.

Objective writing can be entertaining. Some events are so tragic, titillating, or humorous they generate within readers a subjective response.

More often, though, unemotional, vague characters are really designed to help authors experience or process their subjective feelings.

The well-respected literary agent Donald Maass has observed that some authors write as if they are afraid of offending their mothers. It's hard to tell a compelling story when an author is conflicted about expressing his or her feelings.

In his writing workbook, *Writing the Break Out Novel*, Donald speaks about what he calls Scene and Sequel. Scene is action. It's action that sets a story in motion and raises questions. Sequel is the aftermath of the action, when characters can ponder what happened. Struggling writers often begin stories with a sequel, a main character pondering some action that has happened off-stage.

This can reflect that many authors are thoughtful, but unless done correctly, starting a story with a sequel can be a terrible mistake.

When every chapter starts with a sequel, the pacing of a novel can be skewed and slow.

Science and Characterization

I've come across three articles that speak to the issue of characterization and storytelling. One, an article in Science News, (Past Impressions 9 June 2007), is about the concept of projection; the second, in Scientific American, is about the nature of creativity (The Expert Mind, 14 July 2006); the third, about the conscious and subconscious minds, is in NewScientist (New Scientist, 1 December 2007).

Projection arose as a concept in psychoanalysis when therapists realized that their patients were ascribing the personalities and qualities of others— mentor, friend, savior, mother, father— onto a therapist. The therapist could just sit in his or her chair and takes notes and be alternatingly placed on a pedestal and knocked off it.

In the article in Science News, a study showed that people often use projection when they meet strangers; that within each of us we have stored a series of character types and, whether it's appropriate or not, when we meet new people, we quickly project one of these character types onto them.

The goal of the new study was to discover if people could be led to project specific character types onto strangers. This was done by informing a subject that a person they would meet had the qualities they ascribed to a particular person, a mentor, for example.

When the subject met a person it had been suggested could be a mentor, they projected onto them the feelings they had for a mentor.

Some writers project their feelings about significant characters in their lives onto their story characters, and then do not understand why their description of these characters do not evoke the same reaction from readers. The characters only resonate to the person doing the projecting, because that character type is symbolic to them.

A goal of good storytelling is to create a subjective experience of a fictional world for a story's audience. This issue of projection shows how a writer can project their feelings onto story characters and not recognize why this projection evokes no feeling response in their readers. It's internal storytelling; we're reacting to the actors on our internal stage.

The second article, in Scientific American, explored the difference in the thinking styles of a chess grandmaster and an amateur player. Each can think about five things at the same time, but for the amateur this meant thinking sequentially, "If I move this pawn forward two places... or if I move this knight..." etc.

A grandmaster thinks about five things at the same time, but these five things are five openings and the various responses to moves for the five different openings. The grandmaster has a storage chest with many drawers, and each drawer can have mini-drawers. For each move, the grandmaster is connecting his or her short term memory—what to do on one particular move—with his or her long-term memory—everything the grandmaster has learned and internalized about chess openings.

In writing, the beginner often focuses on which of five verbs to use to describe someone walking across a room; the master storyteller has a wonderful treasure chest of understanding and information about story openings and how to set out a character's dramatic truth.

Studies have also demonstrated that grandmasters play the game of chess differently than amateurs. When a blindfolded grandmaster played twenty-five amateurs at the same time, the grandmaster wasn't memorizing the positions of pieces on the boards so much as memorizing the relationships of the pieces.

When I teach the a story is a promise concepts, one purpose is to show what connects characters in a story, what is the tension in these relationships? What has happened to change the relationships? A new job? A birth? A death? A move to a new community? Certain situations lend themselves to creating drama.

Some people are seemingly born with an intuitive understanding of the craft of storytelling, just as others are born with an innate ability to play chess or play games with balls or look good on TV. Others, however, have to build that chest of understanding that they can then access when they create the opening to a novel, or write dialog, or try to build tension in a scene.

An issue that arises in teaching the craft of storytelling is the place of teaching techniques, like outlining a novel before writing it, creating character sketches, or talking about a story idea with others, versus writing intuitively, starting with an idea or character or situation and just start writing and seeing what happens next. In an article by Kate Douglas (New Scientist, 1 December 2007, p 45-46), she writes about how the conscious and subconscious work together, referring to the work of Nathaniel Daw and Yael Niv.

In their research, Daw and Niv explored the idea that instead of having a strictly defined conscious and subconscious, that the conscious mind has a kind of auto-pilot 'to perform routine and instinctive behaviors such as fleeing from danger.' When information is scarce, however—in unfamiliar situations or the very early stages of learning [think new story here]—another system, the episodic controller, takes charge. Instead of making complex calculations, it simply recommends adopting behaviors that have proved successful in similar situations in the past. Both rely heavily on conscious reasoning, and require you to focus on the problem at hand.

'Once you have achieved expertise in a skill such as driving [or writing a story], typing or playing golf, a fourth system, the habitual controller, comes into its own.'

That, 'By asking subjects to explain their reasoning as they go, he has found that verbalizing what they are doing has no effect on people's ability to solve analytical, mathematical or logic problems but actually hinders performance on insight problems...those for which the solution seems to pop out of the blue in an aha! moment...that our subconscious thinking is the source of our inspiration—it is central to creativity.'

For some writers, thinking too much about a story blocks their subconscious from creating an intuitive flow. But, to avoid over thinking, writers need to have internalized an understanding of storytelling. Whether they got that from studying good novels, movies, and plays, or studying the craft of storytelling, or some other method, will probably be idiosyncratic to each writer.

This goes back to the chest of knowledge. If all your brain power goes into deciding whether someone is walking, sidling, gliding or moon-walking across a room, you're blocking your subconscious from helping generate ideas.

Douglas's article continues, 'A classic study into the neural basis of creativity suggests that it depends on an ability to shift gear between subconscious and conscious processing. Three decades ago, Colin Martindale of the University of Maine in Orono charted what is happening in the creative mind using EEG.... During the initial "inspiration" stage, their brains were remarkably quiet. Any activity was dominated by alpha waves, which indicates very low cortical arousal as though the conscious mind was quiescent while the subconscious worked behind the scenes. Intriguingly, you find a similar pattern during dream sleep and relaxation, two mental states associated with high creativity. This `inspiration" stage was followed by a second stage, "elaboration", characterized by far more activity, especially in the cortex, and probably associated with the conscious analysis and evaluation of ideas.

People with the greatest difference in brain activity between these two states were the most creative. More recently, Jordan Peterson at the University of Toronto, Canada, has argued in highly creative people subconscious information is more likely to spill into consciousness, giving them richer mental resources from which to make creative connections (New Scientist, 29 October 2005, p 39).'

The underlying point I see here is that someone who has internalized the craft of telling a story might need to quiet the analytical, conscious brain so they can write intuitively; while another writer might need to think through the elements of a story and have inspiration happening in the background.

I started out as an intuitive writer (I once wrote nine plays in one year), but my stories lacked structure. I now understand structure, but at a certain point in my writing I also need to get to a place of meditation and quiet my mind so the creative, intuitive inspiration can happen.

In the end, writers have to figure out what style of writing works best for them. Writing can happen on a continuum from complete planning to only intuitive writing. I use both intuition and structure. If I don't, I often end up doing personal storytelling that is fulfilling to me but symbolic and uninteresting to others.

I've found that successful writers figure out what works best for them, while struggling writers often remain stuck in a loop of unrecognized personal storytelling. I suspect others spend so much time thinking through story ideas, they block their intuitive creativity from supplying them with ideas. Others want to remain so immersed in the creative flow, they don't want to step out of it to learn how to analyze their writing.

There is no easy answer or one size fits all answer to how to understand storytelling.

PART THREE

The Spirit of Storytelling

The Spirit of Storytelling

When I started down this road of understanding the craft of storytelling that led to the concepts in A Story is a Promise, my idea was that if I taught writers (and myself), the techniques of creating a story that transported an audience, writers would write more powerful stories. Some did. Most did not.

That led me to the path of what I call Deep Characterization, the idea that there is a fundamental difference between personal storytelling (the self speaking to the self) and telling a story to an audience (the storyteller speaking to an audience).

What I discovered is authors who are stuck, emotionally numb, in need of validation, wounded, or any number of issues.

Personal storytelling is about meeting those needs.

A writer who feels unacknowledged in life can create a fantasy world where he or she is acknowledged. No plot required.

Writers who feel unacknowledged often have great skill at describing the torture and murder of characters who are symbolic of the barbarians torturing the author in real life.

No plot required.

The Spirit of Storytelling is about techniques writers can use to create characters who have their own internal lives. Characters who have their own dreams and goals that are independent of the author's dreams and goals (or nightmares and wounds).

I believe this is where great authors and storytellers such as Dickens and Virginia Woolf and Jane Austen wrote from.

I'm starting this journey with just a few techniques to offer.

My goal is to reach that place and share it with others.

Storytelling and the Superconscious Mind

In broad terms, yoga separates the mind into three aspects: the conscious, the subconscious, and the superconscious.

- The conscious mind is concerned with the senses and evaluating relationships.
- The subconscious mind stores memories and issues about the self.
- The superconscious mind, above the other two, offers a dispassionate awareness concerned with understanding.

Before I tell you how those concepts work in writing, let me give you some background.

When I first started developing the concepts of telling a story, I worked through how the mechanics of storytelling and how a story 'moves' or transports an audience. I used the basic principals I came up with to write A Story is a Promise. This book was intended to guide the reader to fulfill readers expectations when they open the cover of the book.

But there is more to a fulfilling book than a story well told. It also must resonate emotionally with its audience or offer an illumination of ideas. Characters must be more than two-dimensional; they must invite the reader to experience them as real people. Most writers know this, and they draw upon their own experiences to deepen their characters. I wrote about this in my second book, Deep Characterization, an exploration of what happens when someone creates stories to process personal feelings or issues.

While drawing on one's own experience to deepen characters is a beginning, it is just that—a beginning. The Spirit of Storytelling addresses how a writer can allow story characters to have internal lives that do not revolve around the author's issues or relationships.

So how does this relate to the three minds found in yoga? Let's take a look.

Because the conscious mind is concerned with a person's standing in life, stories exploring or illuminating relationships draw readers in. This is one reason why so many stories revolve around births, deaths, marriages, leaving home; they are a time of change for relationships. Such stories offer readers a deeper insight and connection to relationships and a resolution of issues they might not experience in life.

A recent theory in science suggests that primates developed bigger brains because as social groups became larger, we needed more processing power to track our ever-changing social status. Our lives depended on that ability. If we were low in the chain, we needed to be humble. Bold behavior could threaten the leader who held the power. Thus threatened, the leader might have us punished, even killed, to assert his authority. On the other hand, if we were in a position of power, we needed to dominate lest we be seen as weak and overthrown by another in the group.

Writing a story that draws on this part of our mind readily draws in readers, but there is a downside. If the author is fully concerned with his/her own issues and relationships, the author is likely to create stories with main characters symbolic of the author's issues. These story characters act to transport the author, not readers (or viewers), unless the reader has similar issues. This can be limiting. unless the author has created a village where the characters have the standing (or the rejection or revenge they desire, if that's the need) the reader craves.

The subconscious stores memories. Because the subconscious is a storehouse of information about life, it's easy for some writers to "watch the mental story movie" and write down the details. The downside to this writing process is that long term memories are compacted and the feelings associated with them minimized. When some writers draw upon this memory/dreamland storehouse, they write down details shorn of feeling in the writing/storytelling. This can lead to main characters who lack feeling and fail to generate a journey of feeling for the audience.

The superconscious mind is above the subconscious. It is about understanding, about expanding conscious awareness, about understanding the daily self as a way to evolve to higher states of understanding. It's not about getting even, it's about becoming aware.

Getting to the superconscious mind means a storyteller is getting to a place where characters are not tethered to the authors needs and issues, whether conscious (based on the relationships from our daily lives) or subconscious (symbolic characters and core issues from our buried mental landscape).

I believe the great storytellers of the world—Shakespeare, Virginia Woolf, Leo Tolstoy, and Jane Austin, to name a few—get to a place where their characters have fully realized, internal lives, and they are able to bring that deep understanding of their characters' inner lives to their storytelling.

For example, in Romeo and Juliet, all the major and minor characters have dramatic issues, accessible to an audience, that define who they are.

I can see all of this and know nothing of Shakespeare's internal life.

In Norman Mailer's World War II novel *The Naked and the Dead*, there are two kind of men. Men who are certain their wives and girlfriends at home are having sex with every available partner, and men too naive to realize their wives and girlfriends back home are having sex with every available partner.

In every other way, the men in the novel have their own voices, except in this circumstance, they are a projection of the womanizing Norman Mailer. This doesn't mean *The Naked and the Dead* isn't a powerful novel, with a powerful authorial voice, but it isn't a great novel. Mailer used a large, ego-centric brain to write about the varied relationships among men at war as he understood them, but he doesn't go beyond his understanding.

Pride and Prejudice is another example of a novel that gives the major and minor characters distinct, inner lives. We know about the inner lives of the parents and their daughters, and their daughter's friends based on their speech and actions. We are allowed to access these characters and their inner lives.

Based on the actions of the characters in *Fifty Shades of Grey*, we can understand something about what the audience brought with them to the novel, but we don't transcend its world via the storytelling.

This isn't to say that a popular, contemporary novel doesn't have lively characters, just that the character's connection to a particular author offers as much information about the author as it does the characters. And for some authors, it generates the different published novel, same story/plot.

Reaching the superconscious state, one feels a deeper connection to the world and a deeper recognition and appreciation and a dispassionate understanding of one's self, but this is neither an affirmation nor a judgment of the ego-centric self.

Since two of the major issues people have in life are not feeling connected or the need to be acknowledged, subconscious dreams or conscious fantasies can operate to meet those needs, but the superconscious awareness buried beneath the conscious and subconscious is what generates a craving for those experiences. It is because some of our fantasies operate as pseudo spiritual experiences that stories based on those needs are often at the heart of hugely successful stories. People crave a deeper connection to others because as spiritual beings living ego-centric lives, we are still tethered, no matter how remotely, to that awareness.

A desire to get to this superconscious state is often the first step on that journey.

Meditation, deeply focused thought, is one way to get to this state. Some triggers can also bring about this state. For me, focusing closely on specific things in my childhood can put me into a state of rapture.

You can even ask your subconscious to mull it over and offer up some suggestions. A recent scientific study found that people sometimes ascribe answers bubbling up from the subconscious to intuition, so don't hesitate to ask your subconscious to provide answers to questions; just be specific about what you're asking for.

If you are successful writing contemporary or genre fiction using the fuel from your life and relationships, or some subconscious motor, you don't need to concern yourself with a connection to the superconscious mind.

But if your storytelling is lifeless and your characters fail to compel, and you don't know why, then I encourage you to go deeply into yourself and find a route to your superconscious.

Sometimes, what you find is daunting, is more about choosing where to focus your attention. Trust yourself that you are equal to the task.

Forestalling the Conceptual Mind

The power of a story is in the intensity of its scenes. Each scene should be a complete experience unto itself, something readers can immerse themselves into.

In a powerful scene, readers can surrender themselves to the story. They can let the situation take care of them. But this requires not a dry description of events, but an unexpected revelation of feelings and illuminations of ideas and understanding.

To write an intense scene, write it as an evocation of what an environment feels like to character, what a character feels in reaction to events.

To do this, feel your way into a story, into a scene, into a moment in a scene.

Many writers enter a scene from their head, a conceptualizing of details, what's going to happen next.

It's a map of a journey, an outline, if you will, but not the journey itself.

For many, once they start down this path of understanding their story by conceptualizing where it's going next, they can't stop drawing that map.

To live in and experience a situation is different from outlining a situation with details.

Let your reader live in the unexpected moments of a scene.

Write a scene from a character's point of view as if it will be the last of their life.

Immerse your reader in that moment.

If you want to see an example of a story that heightens the effect of its moments and scenes, watch Alphaville, by Jean-Luc Godard.

Watching the film, we can never know what's going to happen next, just as the main character doesn't know what's going to happen next. Out attention is pulled into the film and becomes immersed in the main character's journey. It's a journey that is constructed one moment at a time; we're never playing through a scene just to get to the next one.

If you can't forestall your conceptual mind from taking over as you write, consider writing scenes around feelings as a separate step in your process. Focus on each scene separately, focus on each moment. Don't plan on getting to the next scene, let yourself immerse yourself in the moments.

I've found that children can do this easily, but most adults have been trained by the school system into essay-style writing. Create a thesis statement, then write to expand on that statement. It's a Who, What, When, Where, Why style of writing. It's a map for writing an essay, not telling a story.

Don't confuse the map/outline for the journey.

Take your readers on the journey and let them explore it with you.

Meditation and Creativity

When I want to get to a deeper understanding of a story, plot and character, I meditate. When I get to a place of deep meditation—a focused quiet where there are no unbidden thoughts— story ideas come to me. There is no one way, right way, best way to get to this place. I use meditation. Others might go for long walks or write in a coffee shop or write silently in a group.

This essay offers some pointers for quieting the mind. In this day and age, many techniques can be found online and in books.

I'm beginning this section of my book about writing with a technique for meditation since I suggest some meditation practices to help writers discover the deeper, inner lives of their characters.

To help writers get to a meditative state, I'll start with a simple meditation technique called 'watching the breath'.

Count a long one mentally when you breathe in and a long two when you breathe out. Count three when you breathe in, four when you breathe out. Then repeat. As you continue, let your breathing happen naturally, with no attempt to control it. You might reach a point where you feel you are 'watching yourself breathe.' That's good; allow yourself to experience this. If you back to practicing the technique, unless you've reached a place where story and character ideas are flowing. If so, stay there.

If not, practice the technique until your mind has quieted and become clear, and you can think about story ideas clearly and potently. Be careful to state exactly what you want to explore or ask for in this state. Getting what you ask for can be a terrible ordeal. I once asked to be in the middle of a literary scene. My health broke down and I ended up sleeping in a restaurant that did poetry and theater events. When the restaurant closed for the night, I'd make popcorn and people would hang out to chat about the scene in Portland.

I got what I asked for.

Another meditation technique I used came out of attending

12 step Al-anon meetings. 12 step groups have a general format of an introduction, then people sharing their experiences either around a suggested topic or speaking about something they are going through. There can be long or short periods of silence. What I did during these periods of silence was to visualize a current of energy running from the center of my forehead, just above the eyebrows (in yoga this is the spiritual eye, the seat of will) back to the medulla oblongata at the base of the skull. (To find the medulla, use your fingers to find an indentation at the base of your skull.) When I breathed in, I visualized a current of energy running in a thin line from the center of my forehead to the medulla. Think of this line as running in the shape of a banana. When I breathed out, I would visualize a current of energy running from the medulla to the spiritual eye.

During a typical 90 minute meeting, I would spend 30 to 60 minutes practicing this technique.

After a time, I could feel the current.

The technique is a powerful way to develop concentration.

The next meditative process I've used I call dreaming. I would do this while working at a job that didn't require my full conscious awareness. In dreaming, I quiet my mind, then put characters into a scene and watch what happens. I'd start with an understanding of the characters, but not what was going to happen. Often, I'd be surprised by what the characters did and said.

Another version of dreaming is speaking to my characters. Often they offer realizations about who they are and why they do what they do that confounded me. But, I got to a much deeper place of understanding. Ibsen, the great playwright, would put his story characters on a train and then travel with them, listening to their conversations.

I would also tell my subconscious to develop an idea, then make it available to my conscious mind.

The conscious mind is often concerned with relationships. What is my relationship to the person next to me, to a co-worker, to a spouse or kin? Some theories suggest our brains grew in size and processing ability as we lived in larger groups and needed more brain power to track our social relationships.

Beneath the conscious mind is the subconscious. It records details; it is objective.

I believe when people write in a purely objective way, they have contacted the subconscious. In a sense, they watch an interior movie and describe the details. It's been discovered that when memories go into storage in the mind, they are shorn of emotions to compact them for storage.

Watching and describing that interior movie can be a path to flat, unemotional writing.

I believe the really great writers write from a place of spirit, where they are free from writing about objective details or anxieties about current relationships. In such a place a writer can access deep truths about a story and its characters, without a need to use the characters to assuage the writer's anxieties or needs.

Meditation and quieting the mind can help a writer get to that place of spiritual awareness.

Intuitive Storytelling

When I started on the path of understanding storytelling, my first foundation was the concept that a story creates movement and the movement transports the audience.

All the mechanics of a story is a promise arise from and can be understood from that foundation.

This is understanding story as judgment. Beginning, middle, and end. Beginning of what? A character arc, or a plot incident, or a stranger arriving in town, or something that affects relationships. For example, a marriage, a birth, a death, a new job, a depression, a war.

Stories can explore how these affect and change relationships and events. We can assign meaning to changes and outcomes and create an anticipation for an outcome.

We can judge, then, whether a story 'works' or not based on our understanding of the mechanics of storytelling.

This doesn't mean every story will resonate with every audience. In science fiction, for example, a story might explore how a new technology affects the social construct or the basis of a society. A story about magic can explore what happens when a society operates under different rules or rules that change or that are under the control of a select few. And those stories could be well told and constructed and yet not 'work' for a particular audience.

Intuitive Storytelling speaks to a different way of understanding storytelling.

In the spirit of storytelling, a storyteller allows characters to have their own, internal lives not connected or controlled by the author's internal life and needs. This is the opposite of personal storytelling, where characters operate to meet the needs of the author.

Stories can reflect the author and the author's issues (Faulkner and his southern stories), but they can also go beyond the author.

The author becomes a witness to a story unfolding.

You don't have an agenda, a purpose, a need, a goal, you just witness.

When you surrender to the flow of life, life responds to you.

There is a current belief in science that our brains evolved and became larger as we formed larger social groups. We had more relationships to track and judge. What group do I belong to? What group excludes me? What group is friendly? A threat? Can I leave my group and join another?

Intuition that goes deep enough can also connect to a firmament of the universe, where ideas are not just on a mental landscape, but exist in the universe itself.

One way to understand this is to think of the mind as a cloud shot through with stars, some in constellations. Stars are strong collections of thoughts. They are the ways we identify who we are and what we believe. The stronger we believe something, the stronger that star will radiate particular thoughts in our mental landscape.

Constellations of thoughts can be powerful ideas grouped together.

Again, the more power and belief we have around certain ideas and concepts, the more embedded they become in a our mental landscape.

But there is a wider universe outside of ourselves.

Each individual has their own mental landscape powered by their beliefs and thoughts patterns (for good or ill).

Deep intuition means an idea on our mental landscape can call to us ideas from the bedrock of the universe. In that state, we are drawing in ideas from a universal font of creativity and not just from within.

Societies have found ways to 'name' this process. In the Bible, it's referred to as the Holy Ghost, that brings understanding. In yoga, it's referred to as Spirit, an underlying medium that connects everything in the universe.

Deep focus on a story idea is one way to access that process. Another is meditation to quiet the mind. Another is to find a way to generate a creative flow that opens one's mental landscape to outside ideas. Another is to ask the subconscious to make that connection.

I suspect that great authors who have taken their lives (Woolf, Hemingway) found themselves in a place where they could no longer connect to that flow of intuitive storytelling and found life barren without it.

To get there means to not block the path with limiting self-judgment.

When you surrender to the flow of life, life responds to you.

You become a witness to creation.

You don't have an agenda, a purpose, a need, a goal, you just witness.

That is intuitive storytelling, another aspect of the spirit of storytelling.

The Musicality of Writing Fiction

Songs are typically written in a specific key. For example, Pachelbel Canon, familiar to many as the Christmas Canon, is written in the key of D. That means there are notes that are correct and work for that song, and notes that would be discordant and "out of tune" or wrong.

(A quick side note, I'm aware that some music, singing or collections of sounds are meant to be discordant.)

On a much simpler level, the song Louie Louie, as recorded by The Kingsmen, is in the key of A Major.

Someone could change the key Louie Louie is played in, but that means it is played with different notes to a different effect and sound.

Modern jazz tunes can be played in a particular key and also improvised in many different ways. A jazz musician could play Louie Louie or Pachelbel Canon in D to an entirely different purpose and sound than what people usually associate with these pieces.

The point is, the key a musical piece is originally written in doesn't limit the choices of the way in which it can be played, but there's a difference between someone new to music hitting wrong notes and an accomplished musician improvising with the intent of creating a variation.

I'm not a classically trained musician, but I can tell the difference between a wrong note being played and a thoughtful, musical variation or interpretation.

Now lets bring that back to writing. Harry Potter is a novel about fitting in. All the choices in this novel revolve around, let's say, playing a simple rock and roll song in the key of A Major.

Because author J. K. Rowling understands the song/story she is playing, she hits the right notes. Harry Potter wants to fit in. The Dursleys want to fit in. The conflict in the world of magic is over pure blood (pure notes) and mixed blood (improvised notes, so to speak). Rowling sticks to her themes, weaving her story and characters seamlessly into her central idea. She knows the world in which her story takes place, much like a composer knows the key of his or her composition, and everything falls within those boundaries. If anything lands outside of it, it doesn't ring true, just as a musical piece that hits a wrong note will not work in a musical composition.

Now, a new, struggling writer could set out to write a Harry Potter-type fantasy. But this writer starts out with an idea for a character or a plot event, or some other starting point. To someone reading this manuscript, because the writer hasn't settled on a key to set the story, notes are discordant. Maybe the writer doesn't know the world in which the story has taken place. Maybe the writer hasn't settled on a central theme or conflict. Perhaps the characters are not well developed. These are all critical elements to creating a story that harmonizes, that brings a sense of accord and beauty to the reader.

The writer makes choices about how to describe characters, but someone the description is flat or fails to advance the story.

The words/notes aren't set/being played in the correct key of the story.

Reading manuscripts by new or struggling authors, I've found I have to get to the end of the novel to find out what the story is about, or, in this context, in what key it should be played.

That requires the author to go back to the beginning of the story and find a way to convey, what Harry Potter-like fantasy the "key" the book belongs in.

The writer chooses what type of story/song they are playing.

The foundation for my a story is a promise concept is to understand a story and to make choices based on that understanding.

Looking at stories from this frame of reference, The Dead by James Joyce, and The Hunt for Red October by Tom Clancy, are the Pachelbel Canon and the Louie Louie of stories, but each hits note correct for each song.

Criticism of a story 'not working' are an observation that the story notes don't create the effect of a pleasing song for a particular audience, with the understanding that different music appeals to different audiences.

In the movie Francis Florence Jenkins, the main character sang opera horribly off key, but an album she recorded was so odd, people bought it to hear badly sung opera or to discover what the fuss was about. This is not the audience most writers want for their novels, so it is imperative to know what "key" you are creating in, and then to use notes that are in harmony with that key.

I've come across people who had a good ear for music/language and were willing to learn how to compose a story/song that played in particular key and pleased an audience. They had an ear for the tones created by words and they could create an enjoyable story melody. Such a composition may not have obeyed all the rules of grammar, but the story and its notes worked. An example is The Davinci Code. Not great writing, but mostly in tune in a way that allowed its audience to enjoy the story, in spite of the people who pointed out its faults.

And, just like in popular music, there are those one-hit wonders who write a song/novel that sells millions of copies but mystifies people who enjoy well-played music.

If you were one of those people who were born with an ear for language and telling a story, I greatly envy you. Much of my success as a writer has been as a playwright because of my imagination and an ear for dialogue. How to create a plot, that I had to learn.

(Nancy Hill, author The Ghost Doctor and other stories available on Amazon, provided editorial feedback on a first draft of this essay.)

Writing as Exploration

Virginia Woolf is a great writer, and she felt her novel To The Lighthouse to be one of her best works.

High praise indeed.

The novel is a great example of how telling a story can be a process of exploration and not a descriptive process.

The opening lines of To The Lighthouse are a statement.

"Yes, of course, if it's fine tomorrow," said Mrs. Ramsay. "But you'll have to be up with the lark," she added.

Now begins the exploration of the character of the son.

'To her son these words conveyed an extraordinary joy, as if it were settled, the expedition were bound to take place, and the wonder to which he had looked forward, for years and years it seemed, was, after a night's darkness and a day's sail, within touch.'

This sentence conveys what he is feeling and thinking at this moment. We experience the enlivening of his feelings based on what his mother says and his thoughts about the potential of the upcoming trip.

Continuing...

'Since he belonged, even at the age of six, to that great clan that cannot keep this feeling separate from that, but must let future prospects, with their joys and sorrows, cloud what is actually at hand, since to such people even in earliest childhood any turn in the wheel of sensation has the power to crystalize and transfix, the moment upon which its gloom or radiance rests, James Ramsay, sitting on the floor and cutting out pictures from the illustrated catalogue of the Army and Navy Stores, endowed the picture of a refrigerator, as his mother spoke, with heavenly bliss.'

With Virginia Woolf's writing, this moment is like a diamond with facets and she is exploring each one. She's not writing this sentence on her way to somewhere else. The sentence conveys a complete feeling for James Ramsay.

'It was fringed with joy. The wheelbarrow, the lawnmower, the sound of poplar trees, leaves whitening before rain, rooks cawing, brooms knocking, dresses rustling--all these were so coloured and distinguished in his mind that he had already his private code, his secret language, though he appeared the image of stark and uncompromising severity, with his high forehead and bright blue eyes, impeccably candid and pure, frowning slightly at the sight of human frailty, so that his mother, watching him guide his scissors neatly around the refrigerator, imagined him all red and ermine on the Bench or directing a stern and momentous enterprise in some crisis of public affairs.'

Woolf shifts the POV here from James to his mother, quite an accomplishment to do correctly in a single sentence.

"But," said his father, stopping in front of the drawing-room window, "it won't be fine."

Another statement that sets up an emotional response.

'Had there been an axe handy, or a poker, any weapon that would have gnashed a hole in his father's breast and killed him, there and then, James would have seized it. Such were the extremes of emotion that Mr. Ramsey excited in his children's breasts from his mere presence; standing, as now, lean as a knife, narrow as the blade of one, grinning sarcastically, not only with the pleasure of disillusioning his son and causing ridicule upon his wife, who was ten thousand times better in every way than he was (James thought), but also with some secret conceit at his own accuracy of judgment. What he said was true. It was always true. He was incapable of untruth; never altered a fact; never uttered a disagreeable to suit the pleasure or convenience of any mortal being, least of all including his children, who, sprung from his own loins, should be aware from childhood that life is difficult; facts uncompromising; and the passage to that fabled land where our brightest hopes are extinguished, our frail barks founder in darkness (here Mr. Ramsey would straighten his back and narrow his blue eyes upon the horizon), one that needs, above all, courage, truth, and the power to endure.'

These sentences explore the inner lives of James, his father, and James' feelings about his mother.

Again, in each of these sentences, Woolf explores her characters, not merely describing them.

In another place, I've talked about how for a new writer, writing can be a search for a verb or some descriptive detail. Consider this as a narrow focus on a writing tool box without much inside.

The goal of writing as exploration is to lift the focus to the wider world, to consider looking outward for a detail.

In a sense, this is to ask the universe to assist in the journey.

Virginia Woolf goes on this exploration, but in a sense, so does Lee Child's in his Jack Reacher novel, The Midnight Line. When Reacher meets an unpleasant person and says he only wants an answer to a single question, and that person refuses, Child is exploring how that situation is going to play out in the same sense Woolf is exploring the inner life of her characters.

They are writing for different readers, but the underlying process and intent is the same.

For each that exploration is an open-ended process that doesn't need to start with the search for a single, particular word.

Both Virginia Woolf and Lee Child are examples of writing as exploration.

Writing in the Spirit of Storytelling

Italo Calvino's novel *If on a winter's night a traveler* is a great example of a novel written in the spirit of storytelling.

In his essay Lightness, Calvino writes, 'my working method has more often than not involved the subtraction of weight. I have tried to remove weight, sometimes from people, sometimes from heavenly bodies, sometimes from cities; above all I have tried to remove weight from the structure of stories and from language.'

In this talk I shall try to explain-both to myself and to you-why I have come to consider lightness a value rather than a defect; to indicate the works of the past in which I recognize my ideal of lightness; and to show where I situate this value in the present and how I project it into the future.'

And, 'At certain moments I felt that the entire world was turning into stone...'

Calvino openly writes in a way that removes that weight.

Traveler opens with a friendly tone about a potential reader of the novel.

'You are about to begin reading Italo Calvino's new novel, If on a winter's night a traveler. Relax. Concentrate. Dispel every other thought. Let the world around you fade. Best to close the door; the TV is always on in the next room. Tell the others rights away, "No, I don't want to watch TV!" Raise your voice-they won't hear you otherwise-"I'm reading! I don't want to be disturbed!" Maybe they haven't heard you, with all that racket; speak louder, yell: "I'm beginning a read Italo Calvino's new novel!" Or if you prefer, don't say anything. Just hope they'll leave you alone.'

Calvino continues in this way for several pages.

Italo here goes directly to telling a story to an audience. He wants his audience to know of his awareness of their part in the story.

One of the things I teach in A Story is a Promise & The Spirit of Storytelling is the difference between telling a story to an audience and telling a story to one's self. Calvino is utterly aware he has an audience and his purpose of creating a story with all the heaviness of the world removed.

At the end of his introduction in chapter one, Italo concludes...

'So here you are now, ready to attack the first lines of the first page. You prepare to recognize the unmistakable tone of the author. No. You don't recognize it at all. But now that you think about it, who ever said this author has an unmistakable tone? On the contrary, he is known as an author who changes greatly from one book to the next.'

Ending with...

'...it's the book itself that arouses your curiosity; in fact, on sober reflection, you prefer it this way, confronting something and not quite knowing what it is.'

Now, Calvino begins what at first appears to be a more traditional novel opening line but that tradition dissipates in the middle of the sentence.

'The novel begins in a railway station, a locomotive huffs, steam from a piston covers the opening of the chapter, a cloud of smoke hides part of the first paragraph.'

This kind of writing is also called Metafiction, where a storyteller who understands the conventions of storyteller chooses to ignore those conventions for a greater purpose.

Calvino is a master of this type of storytelling.

Continuing...

'In the odor of the station there is a passing whiff of station cafe odor.'

Note that Calvino does offer a simple detail to help place the reader in the scene.

Continuing...

'There is someone looking through the befogged glass, he opens the glass door of the bar, everything is misty, inside, too, as if seen by nearsighted eyes, or eyes irritated by coal dust.'

Again those specific details that allow readers to feel within the scene.

Continuing...

'The pages of the book are clouded like the windows of an old train, the cloud of smoke rests on the sentences.'

Just as soon as Calvino places us in the scene, he just as deftly reminds us he is telling us a story.

Continuing...

'It is a rainy evening; the man enters the bar; he unbuttons his damp overcoat; a cloud of steam enfolds him; a whistle dies away along tracks that are glistening with rain, as far as the eye can see.'

Again, lovely details that set us in this story world.

Next paragraph, continuing...

'A whistling sound, like a locomotive's, and a cloud of steam rise from the coffee machine that the old counterman puts under pressure, as if he were sending up a signal, or at least it seems so it seems from the series of sentences in the second paragraph, in which the players at the table close the fans of cards against their chests and turn toward the newcomer with a triple twist of their neck, shoulders, and chairs, while the customers at the counter raise their little cups and blow on the surface of the coffee, lips and eyes half shut, or suck the head of their mugs of beer, taking exaggerated care not to spill.'

Here Calvino both offers lyrical details to bring this story world to life, reminds us it is a story, then continues with those lovely details.

Like Virginia Woolf, this long sentence offers an exploration of the setting of the story and the characters there, in no haste to reach a conclusion.

This is not the kind of novel for those infected or influence by the weight of the world, but it is a blissful example of writing that is full of light.

Bravo! to the master.

May my life end in this wonderful train station.

Telling a Story in the Spirit of Storytelling

So, does any of this spirit of storytelling really matter?

In a world of self-publishing and movies shot on budgets under $5,000, trying to make an impression becomes more and more difficult.

Good storytelling stands out.

It is a pleasure to read, for both the author and an audience, or to view in a film or watch on a stage.

For those sincere about understanding the craft of storytelling, the ability to create powerful, evocative stories alone is a great reward.

Which raises the question, where am I in this understanding the spirit of storytelling?

I now understand structure and can write both simple and complex (and often, darkly humorous, esoteric, and uncommercial) stories. But they move well.

I can also recognize when I write a story that doesn't move and fix it.

I can recognize when I write a story that is personal and aimed at an audience of one, me. That allows me to start over with another story idea.

The spirit of storytelling? I'm new to the concept and am still trying to integrate it into my writing and to fulfill my deepest desire, to write a great play that will be remembered for generations.

I'm entering that part of the journey that has no map and no fixed destination.

I look forward to meeting others on the same journey. Namaste.

A Letter to My Readers

I am deeply grateful that you have bought and read my work. If you have questions, you can contact me at billjohnson at storyispromise dot com.

If you would like to continue to receive updates about this writing process I explore, please consider joining my email list at MailChimp, http://bit.ly/2uau0gz.

Thank you for your time.

Bill Johnson

Appendix

Resources

BOOKS ON FICTION

Lajos Egri's *The Art of Dramatic Writing!* How to choose and create a pivotal character. Provides an understanding of the unity of opposites as a way of perceiving characters who will feel compelled to act in a dynamic way. Explores the role of crisis, conflict, and resolution in a story.

The Elements of Style, by William Stunk and E. B. White. Great introduction to the art of writing in a clear, concise, and active voice.

If You Want to Write: A Book About Art, Independence and Spirit, by Brenda Ueland. (Also available on audio tape). Ueland writes with a rare, forceful spirit about writing with passion and feeling. A revelation about what it is to write stories.

The Novelist's Tool Kit, by Elizabeth Lyon. Elizabeth's book is clear, direct, and laid out in an easy to follow manner. Her *Manuscript Makeover: Revision Techniques No Fiction Writer Can Afford to Ignore* is also a valuable resource.

RESOURCE BOOKS:

Insider's Guide to Book Editors, Publishers and Literary Agents, by Jeff Herman. An informative book that offers detailed information about editors and agents. Find out what agents and editors like to read to have a better guide for submitting manuscripts.

Books by Writer's Digest: *Guide to Literary Agents*. This book is a good resource for leaning what agents are looking for.

The Guide to Formatting offers useful tips on preparing query letters, novel manuscripts, proposals, screenplays, and other formats for writing. Writer's Market. A resource directory updated every year, with information about publishers, magazines, screenwriting, playwriting, general information on writing, etc.

Literary Market Place, R.W. Bowker, is the industry guide to the writing industry. Published yearly, it offers information about publishers, agents, and others involved in the world of books and publishing.

The Stage Writers Handbook, by Dana Singer. This book is aimed at the world of theatre, but the issues covered— copyright, contract, public domain, etc.— offer useful information to all writers.

BOOKS ON SCREENWRITING

Writing Your Screenplay and *Selling Your Screenplay*, by Cynthia Whitcomb. Two books on screenwriting by a screenwriter who has sold 70 scripts, had 30 produced, and taught screenwriting at UCLA. A great introduction to screenwriting.

Reel Therapy, by Dr. Gary Solomon, reviews over 200 movies that cover such topics as alcoholism, abuse, mental illness, recovery, obsession, etc. This book serves as a well-written reference to movies about dealing with difficult life issues.

WEB SITES ON WRITING

Internet Movie Data Base, www.imdb, offers a wealth of in- formation about writers, casts, directors, and producers. The Publishing Law Center, has articles on legal issues of concern to publishers, editors, and authors.

End Notes

[1] I was introduced to the concept of mattering as a story issue by story analyst David Morgan.

[2] This chapter was written and edited in part with the assistance of Lawrence Booth, Founder/Director of the internationally known Film School of Half Moon Bay.

[3] Rocky. Written by Sylvester Stallone. Directed by John G. Avildsen.

[4] The Wizard of Oz, by L. Frank Baum. William Morrow and Company. ISBN 0688069444.

[5] The Lovely Bones, Alice Sebold. ASIN B000JPIB8Y

[6] I learned to make this distinction in a class taught by David Morgan.

[7] The Usual Suspects. Written by Christopher McQuarrie. Directed by Bryan Singer.

[8] The Bourne Identity, Tony Gilroy and W Blake Heron, screenplay. Directed by Doug Liman.

[9] The Glass Castle: A Memoir, by Jeannette Walls. Scribner. ISBN 074324754X.

[10] Good Grief, by Lolly Winston. Warner. ISBN0446694843

[11] The Girl with the Green Tattoo, Steigg Larrson.

[12] The Hunt for Red October, by Tom Clancy. Berkley. ISNB 0425133516.

[13] Moby-Dick, by Herman Melville. Bantam Classic and Loveswept. ISBN 0553213113.

[14] Prince of Tides, by Pat Conroy. Bantam Books. ISBN

055326888

[15] Funerals for Horses, by Catherine Ryan Hyde. Russian Hill Press. ISBN 0-9653524-3-9.

[16] A Confederacy of Dunces, by John Kennedy O'Toole. WinBooks. ISBN 0-517-12270-7.

[17] Secret Lives of the Sushi Club, by Kristy Yorke, ISBN 0425202755

[18] The Art of Dramatic Writing, by Lajos Egri. Simon and Schuster. ISBN 0671213326.

[19] The Accidental Tourist, by Anne Tyler, ISBN 0345452003.

[21] Raiders of the Lost Ark. Conceived by Steven Spielberg and George Lucas, with Andy Kaufman; scripted by Lawrence Kasdan.

[22] L.A. Confidential. Based on a novel by James Ellroy; screen credit, Brian Helgeland. Directed by Curtis Hanson.

[23] The Sixth Sense. Written and directed by M. Night Shyamalan.

[24] Twilight. Novel by Stephanie Meyer. Movie director, Catherine Hardwicke. Screenplay, Melissa Rosenberg and Stephanie Meyer.

[25] Speed. Written by Graham Yost. Directed by Jan de Bont.

[26] The Limey. Written by Lem Dobbs. Directed by Steven Soderberg.

[27] Dallas Buyers Club. Written by Craig Borten & Melisa Wallack. Directed by Jean-Marc Vallee.

[28] Avatar. Written and directed by James Cameron.

[29] Inception. Written and directed by Christopher Nolan.

[30] The Hunger Games. Novel by Suzanne Collins, movie directed by Gary Ross. Screenplay by Collins and Ross.

[31] Event Horizon. Directed by Paul W.S. Anderson. Script by Philip Eisner.

[32] The Winslow Boy. Play written by Terence Rattigan. Adapted and directed for film by David Mamet.

[33] Eternal Sunshine of the Spotless Mind. Script by Charlie Kaufman and Michael Gondry. Directed by Michael Gondry.

[34] Star Wars. Conceived and directed by George Lucas.

[35] Die Hard. Novel by Roderick Thorp, script by Jeb Stuart. Directed by John McTiernan.

[36] The Spiderwick Chronicles. Screenplay by Karey Kirkpatrick, David Berenbaum, and John Sayles; directed by Mark Waters.

[37] Batman Forever. Directed by Joel Schumacher. Written by Bob Kane (characters) and Lee Batchler (story).

[38] The Accidental Tourist. Written by Anne Tyler. Ballachine.
ISBN 978-0345452009

[39] Lethal Weapon. Directed by Richard Donner, written by Shane Black.

[40] The Lord of the Rings by J. R. R. Tolkien. Ballantine.

[41] Blade Runner. Novel by Philip K Dick; directed by Ridley Scott; screenplay by Philip K Dick and Hampton Fancher.

[42] The Kite Runner. Khaled Hosseini. Penguin. ISBN 1594480001.

[43] The Plague, by Albert Camus. Vintage. ISBN 0679720219

[44] The Stranger, by Albert Camus. Vintage. ISBN 0521539773.

[45] Animal Farm: A Fairy Story, by George Orwell. New American Library (paperback). ISBN 0451526341.

[46] The Exorcist, by William Peter Blatty. Last reprinted by Harper Mass Market Paperbacks. ISBN 0553270109.
[47] The Bad Beginning, by Lemony Snicket. Harper. ISBN 0064407667.
[48] Harry Potter and the Sorcerer's Stone by J. K. Rowling. ISBN 0439554934.
[49] Reservoir Dogs. Written by Quentin Tarantino and Roger Avary. Directed by Quentin Tarantino.
[50] Last Action Hero. Writing credits, Zak Penn, story, Adam Leff. Directed by Richard Donner.
[51] The History Boys, by Alan Bennett. Directed by Nicholas Hytner.
[52] Silence of the Lambs. Novel by Thomas Harris, screenplay by Ted Tally. Directed by Jonathan Demme.
[53] Betrayal. Play by Harold Pinter.
[54] Lars and the Real Girl. Script by Nancy Oliver, directed by Craig Gillespie.
[55] Pride and Prejudice, by Jane Austen. Wordsworth Classics.
[56] Screenplay: Foundation of Screenwriting, by Syd Field. Paperback. Fine Communications. ISBN 156731239X.
[57] Cold Mountain, by Charles Frazier. Vintage Books. ISBN 0375700757.
[58] The Sell Your Novel Toolkit, by Elizabeth Lyon. Penguin. ISBN 0936085401.
[59] The Full Monty. Written by Simon Beaufoy. Directed by Peter Cattaneo.
[60] 8 1/2. Directed by Frederico Fellini. Story by Fellini and Ennio Flaiano.
[61] Aphaville, Written and directed by Jean-Luc Goddard.
[62] Wild by Cheryl Strayed. Published by Knopf, ISBN: 978-0-307-59273-6.

Index

A
A Room With a View, 212
Accidental Tourist, 43, 65, 83, 86, 223
All About Eve, 215
Ambassadors, The, 194
Alphaville, 266
Angela's Ashes, 205
Animal Farm, 79
Appendix, 289
Aristotle, 54
Arrival, 57
Art of Dramatic Writing, 42, 283
Auster, Paul, 178
Avatar, 13, 51, 70,

B
Bad Beginning, 83
Baggage Handler, 90
Barnes, Steve, 79
Batman Forever, 64-65
Betrayal, 90
Blade Runner, 70
Bond, James, 51, 100
Booth, Lawrence, foreword
Bourne Identity, 13

C
Catcher in the Rye, 197
Catch-22, 206
Children of the Dust, 213
City of Glass, 178-185
Characters, 8–12, 95
   Characters and premise, 46-50
      Characters and promise, 5–6
Listening,, 216-221
characters and naming, 10
what's at stake, 56
Character Types, 190-215
Christmas Carol, A, 44, 57, 83, 128
City of Glass, 178-185
Complications, 98
Conceptual Mind, 265-267
Conflict, 68-70
Conflict, escalating, 72-75
Confederacy of Dunces, 31, 213
Cold Mountain, 132
Conflict, 61-63
   characters and conflict, 61-63
   escalation, 72-75,
   what is, 68-70

D
Dallas Buyers Club, 51
Darjeeling Limited, 213
Deep Characterization, 186-189
 Character types, 190–211
 All the Pretty Walls, 211
 Artiste, 208
 Everything's Under Control, 195
 Fearful Persona, 211
 Frustrated Writer, 206
 I Can Explain, 213
 I Am Feeling, 202
 I Am Great Depths, 207
 I Am Ideas, 199
 I Am Objective, 212
 I'm Okay, You're Not, 210
 I, Robot, 198
 It's My life, 200
 It's My World, 186
 Martyr, 200
      My Characters, My Pets, 209

Rescue Me, 212
Spear Carrier, 197
Supplicant, 213
Unacknowledged Writer, 193
Wounded Writer, 199

Dialogue, 86–92
Die Hard, 63
Drama, 72
Dramatic Moments, 23-26
Drama, Suggestive, 11, 113
Dramatic Truth, 27-31
Drop Dead Fred, 202
Dune, 214

E
Egri, Lajos, 42
Emotional Triggers, 281-283
End Notes, 286-289
Eskens, Allen, 70
Eternal Sunshine of the Spotless Mind, 56, 87
Everything's Under Control, 203
Exorcist, 83, 193

F
Fearful Persona, 203
Fellini, 25, 173
Field, Syd, 108
Fiction, Rings True, 112
Forestalling the Conceptual Mind, 262-263
Frida, 209
Funeral for Horses, 83, 191, 213
Fulfillment, 4–5, 11–14, 30–34, 39–41,

G
Girl With the Green Tattoo, 18, 79
Gibson, William, 80
Glass Castle, 18, 75
Godfather, 137-140
Good Grief, 18, 65
Good Night, and Good Luck, 204
Grapes of Wrath, 206
Great Gatsby, 198
Gravity's Rainbow, 201

H
Harry Potter, 5, 70, 74, 84
Henry Fool, 209
Her, 84
History Boys, 88-89
Hunger Games, 52
Human Need for Stories, 2–4
Hunt for Red October, The, 21, 214
  plot, 58-60
  plot line, 91–92
  plot questions, 94
  premise, 89
  outlining, 88–102
  story diagram, 117
  spine, 128

I
I Am Objective, 204
Iceman Cometh, 197
Inception, 18, 52, 234-238
Ideas, 76-85, 97, 112, 126, 207
I'm Not There, 215
Index, 290
Indiana Jones, 51
Intuitive Storytelling, 267-269
Ironman, 74

J
James Joyce, 207, 208
Joker, 52

K
Kite Runner, The 74, 204, 231-233

291

L
L.A. Confidential, 51
Lars and the Real Girl, 100
Last Action Hero, 88
Lethal Weapon, 65, 73, 195
The Life We Bury, 70
Limey, The, 57
Life-like characters, 5-6
Lion's Blood, 79
Lord of the Rings, 66, 187
Lovely Bones, The, 5, 95-114

M
Magic Spells, 195
Main Street, 194
Meditation and Creativity, 264-266
Moby-Dick, 28–29, 202
Morgan, David, 2
Movement, 16, 37–39, 84
Musicality of Writing Fiction, 270-272

N
Narrative tension, 38, 54
'night, Mother, 166-171
Norma Rae, 193

O
Oliver Twist, 206
On the Road, 211
Outlining, 95-114
Outline diagram, 111

P
Peanut Butter Falcon, 52
Plague, The, 78
Plot, 54-57, 74-78, 85, 89-90
complications, 89
creating, 58-61
Poetics, 54

Point of View, 134
Premise, 36–44, 45-49, 89
characters and premise, 50-53
creating, 45-49
definition, 36
examples, 47–49
Pride and Prejudice, 102
Prince of Tides, 13, 29-30, 191
Promise, 2-4, 5-12, 36
down payment, 20-24
human need, 2–4
naming, 8–12
sustaining, 14–19

R
Raiders of the Lost Ark, 51
Rear Window, 141-147
Reservoir Dogs, 87
Resources, 283
Rocky, 5, 8, 10, 15, 20, 46, 194
Romeo and Juliet, 5, 15, 20, 39, 47, 50, 72-73, 95-98, 132, 148-165
conflict, 64
ideas, 76-8
Royal Tenenbaums, 209
Rosenblum, Mary, 80

S
Safety Not Guaranteed, 84
Science and Characterization, 249-251
Secret Lives of the Sushi Club, 31–32, 84
September Issue, 66
Silence of the Lambs, 89
Silkwood, 192
Sixth Sense, The, 5

Snow Falling on Cedars, 66
Spear Carrier, 205
Speed, 51
Spirit of Storytelling, 280-282, 276-277
Spiderwick Chronicles, 64
Star Wars, 79
Starting Out in the Evening, 215
Station Agent, 195
Story,
    active voice, 93
    characters, 111
    complications, 98
    common mistakes, 127-137
    drama, 13
    dramatic truth, 25–31
    fulfillment, 67
    human need for, 2–4
    ideas, 68–70
    naming, 8–12
    premise, 33–40
    spine, 121-126
story question, 90, 103
truth, 5
Story diagram, 111
Story line, 95-114
Story Director, 101-114
Subconscious, 260-264
Submarine, 201
Superconscious, 255
synopsis, 121-126

T
Take Shelter, 57
Tell No One, 191
Terminator, 199
Tin Drum, 201
Toto le Hero, 18, 207
Thrust/counter-thrust, 82-85

To the Lighthouse, 201
Transformation, 243-248
Tristam Shandy, 214
Twenty Feet from Stardom, 197
Twilight, 51

U
Unacknowledged Writer, 201
Unconscious, 260-264
Using Reviews, 138
Usual Suspects, The, 9, 20, 23-26

V
Virginia Woolf, 209, 273-275

W
Water for Elephants, 102
West World, 199
What Lies Beneath, 227-230
What's at Stake, 62–64, 110
When a Man Loves a Woman, 205
Who's Afraid of Virginia Woolf, 202
Wild, 172-177
Winslow Boy, The, 56
Wizard of Oz, The, 5, 21, 23, 69, 74,
Wolf of Wall Street, 195
Wounded Writer, 234
Word choice, 25
Writing Fear, 221-224

Y
You Can Count on Me, 211

Contact Information

Essays, movie reviews, and information about on-line classes by Bill Johnson are available at http://www.storyispromise.com

Author videos created by Bill Johnson are available for viewing at http://www.youtube.com/oregonwritersspeak

Bill is available to teach writing workshops and presentations on writing.

Story analysis, editorial consultations and personal consultations are available by writing, calling, or emailing:

    Bill Johnson Script Consulting
    BillJohnson@storyispromise.com

www.ingramcontent.com/pod-product-compliance
Lightning Source LLC
Chambersburg PA
CBHW061632040426
42446CB00010B/1376